WILD FLOWERS OF AUSTRALIA

WILD FLOWERS
OF AUSTRALIA

By
THISTLE Y. HARRIS

Illustrated by
ADAM FORSTER

ANGUS
& ROBERTSON
PUBLISHERS

ANGUS & ROBERTSON PUBLISHERS

Unit 4, Eden Park, 31 Waterloo Road,
North Ryde, NSW, Australia 2113, and
16 Golden Square, London W1R 4BN,
United Kingdom

First published in Australia
by Angus & Robertson Publishers in 1938
Second edition, revised and enlarged 1947
Reprinted 1948, 1949, 1951
Third edition, revised 1952
Reprinted 1954
Fourth edition, revised 1956
Reprinted 1958
Fifth edition, revised 1962
Reprinted 1964
Sixth edition, revised 1966
Reprinted 1967
Seventh edition, revised 1971
Reprinted 1973
Eighth edition (Australian Natural Science Library), revised 1979
Reprinted 1980, 1986

© Thistle Y. Harris

National Library of Australia
Cataloguing-in-publication data.
Harris, Thistle Yolette, 1902-
   Wild flowers of Australia.
   Index.
   ISBN 0 207 13644 0.
   1. Wildflowers — Australia. I. Forster, Adam, illus. II. Title.
582.13'0994

Printed in Shenzhen, China

FOREWORD

OVER the past years there has been a growing interest in Australian wild flowers which are rapidly vanishing from their natural habitats. This book is a modest attempt to introduce people to a very small number of the wild flowers found in the many varied habitats of this large continent. While not pretending in any way to be a complete guide to a flora as diverse as it is interesting and beautiful, it is hoped that it may serve those nature lovers who are just embarking on a study of field botany. If, besides serving as an introduction to the study, it gives some pleasure and satisfaction, the work will have achieved its main objective; to stir the people of Australia to an appreciation and love of their wonderful plant life, and stimulate them to assist in its preservation.

The book is divided into two parts: Part I, containing the coloured plates, is a non-technical description of each plant. This is for quick and easy reference. Part II contains more precise and technical descriptions with botanical keys. The field botanist is advised to use these keys for purposes of identification, and to verify the identification by reference to the coloured figure and the more general description in Part I.

The key to the plant families is based on that adopted by Ferdinand von Mueller in his *Census of Australian Plants*, with some simplifications rendered possible by the restricted number of families dealt with here. By following this system, rather than the generally recognized more natural one of Engler and Prantl, which most botanists follow, it has been possible within the scope of this work to devise a key in which macroscopic characters could be used almost wholly for identification.

Once the plant family has been determined the student should turn to the key to the genera under the family, which again has been so arranged that in the majority of cases macroscopic features are the determining points.

Where more than one species of a genus is described, a key is provided, on the same system, for the separation of the species.

If, after faithfully using the keys, the plant is still unidentified, the fault probably lies with the limitation of the book and the student must consult a more exhaustive flora. (A list is given elsewhere.)

Wherever possible, common names have been used for the plants. In many cases, however, this has not been possible, since so many of our plants are not generally recognized by a well-known popular name. In such cases the botanical name only has been used. The derivation of the name is given in each case at the bottom of the description in Part II.

Where rainfall is not the determining factor in the flowering period—as it is in many of the plants of the arid inland—the season of flowering has been given with a fair degree of accuracy. The reader must remember that among the dwellers of the more barren regions the flowering time is far more dependent upon rainfall than upon the time of the year; therefore the time given here must be regarded as liable to variation.

Locality and distribution have been given in all cases. As far as possible, too, the distribution of the genus throughout Australia has been given, but the numbers, subject as they are to constant revision, can only be taken as approximate.

An endeavour has been made to bring the nomenclature up-to-date, and the superseded names are shown as well as the new names. A glossary of botanical terms will be found at the end of the book.

The plants depicted have been selected to include, as far as possible, the commonest of the wild flowers of all the States, with the exception of *Eucalyptus* and the grasses so characteristic of many Australian habitats. These large and important groups of plants have been omitted because it would have been possible to deal with so few species that their significance as a distinctive feature of the Australian vegetation would have been lost. The deficiency in numbers of the described species is due, in large measure, to the cost of production.

For purposes of practical reproduction a botanical sequence has not been followed in the arrangement of the plates. Strict botanical sequence (with a reference to the plate on which the species is figured) has been adopted in the second part of the work. The student, therefore, should have little difficulty in using the plates for verification of identifications made by use of the keys in Part II.

My sincere thanks are due to Dr L.A.S. Johnson, Director,

National Herbarium, Sydney, and to his staff, for a careful checking of the text and the technical names of the plants described; to the late Mr M. H. R. Rupp for valuable help in the classification and description of the orchids; and to many other kind friends who have rendered cheerful help along the way.

THISTLE Y. HARRIS

PROTECTION OF WILD FLOWERS

MANY wild flowers on Crown lands are protected under State laws. On private property protected wild flowers may be picked only with the written permission of the owner. All plants within National Parks and Reserves are completely protected.

The list of plants to which these laws apply is amended from time to time, and anyone wishing to make a scientific collection should have an up-to-date knowledge of the schedules to the Acts in which the lists appear. The restriction includes all parts of any protected plant.

All responsible people will appreciate the desirability of preserving the unique and beautiful flora of this country, and will not only refrain from destroying any part of it themselves, but will do their utmost to prevent destruction by others.

T.Y.H.

THE ARTIST

AN APPRECIATION

As I see the completion of this book, I am stirred with a feeling of deep regret that the artist, Adam Forster, did not live to see this fruition of his labour. To him the joy of painting was, itself, an abiding compensation, but to have brought others to an enjoyment and an understanding of those things in nature which were so dear to him would have been a crowning satisfaction. For Adam Forster was not only an artist, he was a naturalist whose dearest aim was to learn more of the wonders of an Australia which he loved so much. To this end his brush was a mighty weapon. In a period of less than twenty years in the later part of his long and useful career (he died at the age of seventy-eight) he painted nearly one thousand large water-colours, and, especially for use in this book, the small water-colours here reproduced, of Australian wild flowers.

In his enthusiasm he took infinite pains to make his collection as wide as possible, and to this end made many a long and arduous bush trek. I remember him, in his later years, as virile and active as a schoolboy, scrambling over rocky precipices, pushing his way through dense scrub, walking miles without apparent fatigue. And how great was his joy when some new or long-sought plant was finally discovered! With infinite care the treasure would be stowed for gentle transport; or, if it were too fragile, down he would sit, with little regard for his personal comfort, and make the painting on the spot, filled with the joy of bringing the plant to blossom again on his paper.

So great was his enthusiasm that many who knew him were stimulated to greater achievements. Just as he rejoiced when he saw his fellows learning more and more to appreciate and to love the wonderful Australian bushland, so, I feel sure, he would have wished for nothing more than to see that work carried on through the medium of this slight volume.

The author deems it a great privilege to be able in this book to assist in bringing the work and the personality of her old friend, Adam Forster, before readers and students in Australia and elsewhere.

T.Y.H.

INTRODUCTION

NATURE-LOVERS from all parts of the world speak with enthusiasm and frequently with awe of the wonderful and extraordinary plants of the Australian "bush". The multiplicity of species, their diversity of form, the richness of their colour, and their exquisite grace and beauty, are unrivalled. In addition, they constitute a flora entirely different from that of any other part of the globe. The reason for this is to be found in the early history of the development of the continent. In past geological times Australia appears to have been connected with northern lands through several continents. In early times the land was almost certainly occupied by great ferns, fern-like plants, club-mosses, cycads (like the present-day Burrawang), and other forms of plant life, but none of them with "flowers" as we know them today. It must have been a strange Australia, much more tropical than that of the present time, with vast areas of land covered with thick jungle growth, with labyrinthodonts and other primitive reptiles roaming through the moist land, and with no flowers, no birds, and practically no insects! In some parts of Australia fossil records of these primitive forms of life have been discovered.

As changes occurred in the climate and soil—resulting, generally, in the production of less favourable conditions for growth and in greater aridity—changes in the plants were then evolved to suit the new conditions. While changes also occurred in the northern lands, with consequent modifications of life to fit in with them, these changes were not similar to those occurring in our own continent. Early, therefore, in the development of plant life, lines of modification occurred, very different from those appearing elsewhere.

Further, the relatively arid conditions prevailing over our continent (and in certain parts of South Africa where a somewhat similar development may be traced) made the struggle for existence more intense. This meant a slower development in some respects, so that the many orders or groups of plants now characteristic of the less favourable parts of Australia are rather different from those in more favourable lands.

To the naturalist embarking on a career of field botany, the diversity of form among the plants he meets is somewhat bewildering. There is no royal road to identification; yet, it is very rarely in my experience that a student abandons this fascinating study because of difficulties encountered on the way. The mechanical labour of searching through books to classify specimens, of depicting them with pencil or brush or of preserving and mounting them, loses its tediousness in the joy of discovery and the wonderful revelations of nature. Indeed, the delight of bush rambles and the subsequent study become most fascinating and exciting. "The true mystery of the world is the visible, not the invisible."

As I have indicated, the identification of Australian plants is not a matter that can be easily and quickly accomplished. To know one's plants one must study them, their habits and their habitats, until one is able to interpret to some extent their remarkable adaptations. This is only learned by intimate contact with them in the field: all that books can do is to help in "tagging" the plants for easy reference.

While diversity is the keynote to our flora, we can roughly divide these plants into two groups—the "brush" plants and the plants of the more arid areas.

The "brush" or "jungle" plants are those found in selected spots along the eastern coast from Cape York to Cape Otway, never extending for more than a hundred and fifty kilometres inland, mainly in Queensland and north New South Wales, but also in a few isolated spots farther south. These plants usually occur on a rich soil, with a relatively high rainfall and humidity. Some are relics of the first flowering plants which superseded the ferns and cycads in the days when conditions were more tropical. And so they have survived only where these conditions still prevail to some degree, nearest to the equator, in sheltered, moist gullies, in damp mountain gorges and plateaux with high rainfall.

Among the brush plants one finds mainly straight-limbed tall trees and creepers; tall or climbing because the presence of a high temperature and moisture content makes growth rapid, with a consequent shutting out of light from lower vegetation. The leaves are usually large, dark-green and very rarely covered with any protective substances such as hairs or wax. The flowers are mostly small and inconspicuous, the flowering period often infrequent since conditions are at all times reasonably favourable, and the fruits or seeds rarely wind-carried, because currents of high velocity cannot penetrate the dense growth.

To give a list even of the commonest of these brush plants would not be possible. Here, however, are a few: Coachwood (*Ceratopetalum apetalum*), Sassafras (*Doryphora sassafras*), Figs (*Ficus* spp.), Brush Box (*Tristania conferta*), Red Cedar (*Toona australis*), Illawarra Flame-tree (*Brachychiton acerifolium*), Rosewood (*Dysoxylon* spp.), Silky Oak (*Grevillea robusta*), Firewheel-tree (*Stenocarpus sinuatus*), Lilly-pillies (*Acmena, Syzygium* spp.), Hoop Pine (*Araucaria cunninghamii*) and, following the streams, Black Bean or Bean-tree (*Castanospermum australe*). Among these are many of our valuable softwood timbers.

Among the second group of plants—which constitute by far the major portion of our flora—are those which have accustomed themselves to harsher conditions, particularly in respect of available water-supply. Such conditions prevail over a great part of Australia. Scarcity of water to plants may be due to a variety of causes; it may be due to low rainfall, a condition true of much of the inland area of Australia and to some parts of the western side of the continent near the coast; it may be due to soil conditions where, though rainfall is good or fairly good, the soil is so porous that it can retain the moisture only for a very brief period, as on many stretches of coastal land where the soil is sandy and coarse. Again it may be due to high concentration of dissolved substances so that the plant is not able to take in very much. This is true of swampy land where there is plenty of water but where it has dissolved so much substance from the soil that the plant can obtain very little. These three main types of habitat have been conquered by our plants in a variety of ways. One general result is obvious, the rich, luxuriant growth of the jungle is replaced by a more open forest growth or a growth of low, shrubby nature. The trees of these open forest areas consist largely of Eucalypts, many supplying valuable hardwoods.

Moisture is a food material of plants. It enters the plants through the roots, passes up the stem, and a considerable amount of it leaves the plant through tiny openings on the leaves. Through these openings air, both for breathing and for food-making, also enters. In places where the available moisture supply is low, it is usual to find that some modification of these openings takes place. The plant cannot reduce them to a very great extent, since in doing so it would shut off its air-supply. Neither can it reduce the leaf surface markedly, because here the green colouring matter, necessary for the absorption of light, is contained. In many cases, however, a very happy compromise has been reached by means of which the leaf still functions efficiently as an organ of light absorption and for interchange of gases, but at the same time the water lost by evaporation, when drought conditions prevail, is often small.

One group of the Wattles, or Acacias, has overcome the difficulty in a remarkable way. These plants have abandoned altogether the true leaf and replaced it by a flattened leaf-stalk, or phyllode, in which the number of openings over a given surface is less than the number on a true leaf, while there is just as large a surface exposed to the sun as in the feathery-, or true-leaved types. These phyllodinous or "long-leaved" Wattles are almost entirely confined to Australia. There are a few phyllodinous types indigenous to some of the islands in the Pacific, the Malay Archipelago, Madagascar and the Mascarine Islands. The feathery-leaved types are found also in Africa, Egypt, Arabia, tropical America including the West Indies, sub-tropical North America and temperate South America.

Another common device probably adopted to prevent too great a loss of water as well as reducing heat input, is by having the leaves covered with hairs, wax, or cuticle which protects them to some extent without cutting off the air-supply altogether. These coverings often result in a masking of the vivid green colour of the foliage; hence the greyish-green characteristic of so much of our bushland. Very thick coverings are usually confined to the lower surface where most of the openings will be found.

The aromatic odour emanating from the Boronias, the Gums, and many other bush plants is mainly due to the oil evaporated from the leaves. This evaporated oil may serve as a barrier to the entrance of the dry air outside, so preventing loss of water. The fine, stiff leaves of so many of our Pea Flowers, Tea-trees and others, and the stiff, rigid leaves of the Banksias, Waratah, Woody Pear and so on, also prevent this to some extent.

In areas where the rainfall is intermittent rather than low or the soil is excessively open so that the water remains close to the roots for only a brief period, a method of storing the water when it is abundant is commonly adopted. So we find, among our inland plants and among those which inhabit the sand dunes of the coast, many types with thick, fleshy leaves or stems in which considerable stores of water are to be found. The wonderful little Parakeelia of inland Australia, which will exist for months without water, the Scaevolas of our sand dunes and the Bottle-tree of inland Queensland with its swollen, water-containing stem, are familiar examples.

The families represented in the above group are indeed numerous, but the commonest among them are: Proteaceae (*Telopea, Grevillea, Hakea, Banksia*, etc.); Myrtaceae (*Eucalyptus, Angophora*, Tea-trees, Bottlebrush, etc.); Fabaceae (the many Pea Flowers); Mimosaceae (the Wattles); Epacridaceae (the Heaths); Rutaceae (*Boronia, Eriostemon*, etc.).

Throughout the year some of these will be found in flower.

But in springtime the bush reaches the height of its glory. Then it is a riot of brilliant colour. Early in the spring come the Wattles with their golden glory. So rich are they in full bloom and so bountiful their production of flowers that Lowell might well have been referring to them rather than to the dandelion when he said:

> How like a prodigal doth Nature seem,
> When thou, for all thy gold, so common art.

Then come the earlier of the Pea Flowers, so many of them golden also; and the early Boronias, the deep-pink species (*Boronia ledifolia*) in the eastern States and the brown (*Boronia megastigma*) in the west; the early flowering Spider Flowers and a host of others. Later, as the spring is well advanced, come the other Boronias, the Waratahs, many of the beautiful Tea-trees, Verticordias, the Dampieras and Leschenaultias. As summer comes it brings more of the Grevilleas, the Christmas Bells and Bush of the eastern States; many of the Bottlebrushes, the Flannel Flowers of east and west. Throughout winter some of the sturdier plants continue to blossom. One can always find some blooms on the Grey Spider Flower, on many of the Banksias, some of the lovely Everlastings, and several of the Pea Flowers. It is an interesting study to make a calendar of the flowering periods of many of these.

Between these two extremes of vegetation there are certain restricted areas where intermediate types exist. Thus, on the borders of the brush forests in which Eucalypts are rarely found, where conditions are not quite good enough for true brush types to grow luxuriantly, a mixture of some of the hardier brush types such as the Myrtles, the Brush Box, and some of the Lilly-pillies, will be found growing in association with those of the Eucalypts which prefer the richer areas—Blue Gum (*Eucalyptus saligna*), Messmate (*E. obliqua*), Tallow Wood (*E. microcorys*), Lemon-scented Gum (*E. citriodora*) and others.

To the student of nature there is a wide field for study in all zones. But it is the unusual element of the Australian bush that so astonishes and delights the visitor to our great continent, so different is it from that to which he has accustomed himself in northern lands. Its quaintness captures his imagination, its vivid colouring and great floriferousness delight him, while its vigour of growth under such exigencies of soil and climate make him understand something of nature's prodigality in this land of "antipodal remoteness".

CONTENTS

PART I

POPULAR DESCRIPTIONS WITH PLATES

PLATE 1

BLACK APPLE OR NATIVE PLUM
Planchonella australis

BRUSH CHERRY
Syzygium paniculatum

NATIVE ROSE
Boronia serrulata

NATIVE FUCHSIA OR FUCHSIA HEATH
Epacris longiflora

PLATE 1

BLACK APPLE OR NATIVE PLUM
Planchonella australis

In many places on the edge of the brush forests of coastal New South Wales and Queensland, the Black Apple, a rough-barked tree of 5–30 m, with thick rounded leaves 8–12 cm long, is fairly common. The fruit is ovoid, dark purple to black, 2–4 cm long, with one to five seeds. It flowers in spring but fruits may be found on or below the tree at all seasons.

BRUSH CHERRY
Syzygium paniculatum

The Brush Cherry is one of the Lilly-pilly group. In full fruit the tree has rich reddish-purple berries like the cherries on a tree very heavy in bearing. Though usually only 3–4.5 m high, it may reach 15 m in jungle. It is handsome, with opposite broad glossy leaves and pink young foliage. The flowers are white and the petals conspicuous. It occurs on the Queensland and New South Wales coast. It flowers in spring.

NATIVE ROSE
Boronia serrulata

The Boronias are well-known small shrubby plants found in all the States of Australia in great abundance. The leaves contain a highly aromatic oil which contributes largely to the "bushy" smell that the bushman loves. Each flower has four free petals, pink in most species, and eight stamens, four long alternating with four short.

The Native Rose is one of the most popular of all our bush flowers. The strangely rhomboid leaves with their saw-like edges make it easy to recognize the plant even when it is not in bloom. It is a New South Wales shrub of the coast and Dividing Range and produces its deep-pink flowers in late spring.

NATIVE FUCHSIA OR FUCHSIA HEATH
Epacris longiflora

Many of the Epacrids inhabit the barren hilltops of the coastal districts. Native Fuchsia varies from a straggling shrub to a tall, erect plant up to 1.5 m high. In the axils of the rigid, heart-shaped, sessile leaves are the long tubular flowers, red tipped with white. This beautiful shrub of the sandstone ledges of the coast and Dividing Range of New South Wales flowers in winter, early spring, and some blossoms are found throughout the year.

1

PLATE 2

CLUSTERED EVERLASTING
Helichrysum semipapposum

In the genus *Helichrysum* the bracts ("petals") are white, yellow, brown, or pink. They form great carpets of rich colour where they abound—in Western Australia and, in the eastern States, mainly on the western plains. The Clustered Everlasting is a small perennial 30–90 cm high, with narrow woolly leaves and a large number of small yellow flower-heads on a single stem. It is found in the eastern States and in Tasmania on rich sandy loams, usually at elevations. It flowers in late spring.

GOLDEN EVERLASTING
Helichrysum bracteatum

This plant attains a height of 30–60 cm. It has broad, smooth leaves and large yellow flower-heads with stiff papery bracts ("petals") 3–5 cm across. Widely cultivated in gardens, it is available in many brilliant colours. It occurs in Queensland, New South Wales, Victoria, and South Australia: common in grasslands. It flowers in late spring and early summer.

SAW GROUNDSEL
Senecio vagus

Senecio is a very large genus of more than 1000 species, found all over the world, mostly with conspicuous yellow heads of flowers. The Groundsel of Europe is one. *S. vagus* is a smooth plant 60–90 cm high, with stalked broad leaves 12–15 cm long and deeply divided. The heads are yellow, several on a stem, fairly large. It is found in New South Wales and Victoria in the rich coastal gullies. It flowers in September and October.

MISTLETOE
Amyema congener

The Mistletoes are semi-parasitic plants which tap the food-supply from other plants and have no root system of their own. The seeds are produced in berries, with a sticky substance, and are most attractive to fruit-eating birds. *A. congener* is a semi-parasitic plant with opposite, obtuse, fairly broad, sickle-shaped leaves. The flowers are long and tubular, very handsome, with carmine-coloured petals and filaments, and long yellow protruding anthers. The succulent fruit is greenish and sticky, and is spread by birds. It occurs on the coastal plants of Queensland and New South Wales and flowers in summer.

2

PLATE 2

CLUSTERED EVERLASTING
Helichrysum semipapposum

GOLDEN EVERLASTING DAISY
Helichrysum bracteatum

SAW GROUNDSEL
Senecio vagus

MISTLETOE
Amyema congener

PLATE 3

TOOTH NIGHTSHADE
Solanum prinophyllum

NARROW-LEAF DAISY
Brachycome angustifolia

CREEPING MONKEY FLOWER
Mimulus repens

DIGGERS' SPEEDWELL
Parahebe perfoliata

PLATE 3

TOOTH NIGHTSHADE

Solanum prinophyllum syn. *S. xanthocarpum*

In the forest lands of the coast of Queensland, New South Wales, and Victoria, this Nightshade is fairly common. It is a small spreading shrub 60–100 cm high, with reddish-yellow prickles. The leaf lobes are broad and pointed, 2–10 cm long. The flowers are violet, few together or solitary, about 2 cm across. The five petals are united and the deep-yellow stamens, also united, make an attractive centre against the violet background. The berry is round, about 1 cm diameter, mottled green and white. It flowers in summer.

NARROW-LEAF DAISY

Brachycome angustifolia

The Brachycomes are considered to be confined to Australia and New Zealand. The leaves are basal and usually entire. The ray florets ("petals") are in one row—white, blue, or purple.

B. angustifolia has light-green, narrow, entire leaves on short stalks. The flower-heads are about 2 cm across, with white or pale-blue ray florets. It is found in the grasslands of the coastal districts and tablelands of New South Wales, flowering in spring and summer.

CREEPING MONKEY FLOWER

Mimulus repens

This creeping or prostrate plant is a swamp-lover, found throughout Australia, except in the extreme north. It has small, entire, rounded, opposite leaves and solitary or small groups of yellow-throated blue or violet flowers on fairly short stalks coming from the leaf axils. The flower is about 2 cm long, tubular, with five petals and is slightly two-lipped. It flowers from spring to late summer.

DIGGERS' SPEEDWELL

Parahebe perfoliata syn. *Veronia perfoliata*

This Speedwell has flowers of a rich, clear, almost unbelievable blue, with streaks of purple on the petals. It is a rather slender herb, 30–100 cm high, with opposite, broad, stem-clasping leaves 2–8 cm long. There are four petals, widely spreading at the mouth, with the two stamens protruding. It mostly inhabits rather moist rocky sites of the coastal district, tableland and sub-alpine areas of New South Wales and Victoria. It flowers in spring.

PLATE 4

BORONIA FRASERI

This is a Boronia most commonly found in the moist sheltered gullies of the coast. It has smooth dark-green feathery leaves and deep-pink flowers. The aromatic odour of the plant is very strong. It occurs in New South Wales, and flowers during September and October.

LACEBARK

Brachychiton discolor

Most Kurrajongs or Brachychitons are denizens of the coastal brush forests. There are several species, and all are large-leaved tall trees with masses of bell-shaped flowers.

B. discolor has broad, deeply lobed, rather hairy leaves, which are semi-deciduous; the large pink or light-red flowers are 3–5 cm long and hairy both inside and out; they are deciduous, and form a lovely coloured carpet. This species occurs in brush land in Queensland and New South Wales. It flowers in spring.

BLACK-EYED SUSAN OR THYME PINKEYE

Tetratheca thymifolia

The Black-eyed Susans are so named on account of the dark, almost black anthers clustered together in the centre of the flower. The plants are under-shrubs. This species has purple-pink or white flowers with four or five free, loose petals about 2 cm long. The leaves are small, dark green, lanceolate, and usually in whorls of four. The ovary and capsule (fruit) are usually hairy. The species occurs in forest country on the coast and eastern edge of the tablelands of New South Wales, Victoria and Queensland. It flowers almost the whole of spring and summer.

EARLY NANCY

Anguillaria dioica

A tiny plant (25 cm is a tall specimen), which has narrow, sheathing leaves dilated at the base and reaching nearly to the height of the plant. The flexuose inflorescence stems arise from the sheathing base of the leaf. The number of flowers in each inflorescence varies from one to four. The flowers are white or purple, usually staminate or pistillate, but not perfect, the sepals and petals free and spreading. It occurs in rich soil in all the Australian States and flowers in spring. The stem of the specimen figured has been shortened for convenience.

PLATE 4

BORONIA FRASERI

LACEBARK
Brachychiton discolor

BLACK-EYED SUSAN
OR THYME PINKEYE
Tetratheca thymifolia

EARLY NANCY
Anguillaria dioica

PLATE 5

NARROW-LEAVED BITTER PEA
Daviesia corymbosa

MYRTLE ACACIA
Acacia myrtifolia

RUST PLANT OR RED VELVET BUSH
Lasiopetalum rufum

LARGE DUCK-ORCHID
Caleana major

PLATE 5

NARROW-LEAVED BITTER PEA
Daviesia corymbosa

Found on the coastal sandstone and hills of Queensland, New South Wales, Victoria, and South Australia, this shrub is 1.5–2 m high and so floriferous that the foliage is entirely concealed by the bright-yellow flowers. The leaves are usually long and narrow but sometimes broad and strongly veined. It flowers in spring.

MYRTLE ACACIA
Acacia myrtifolia

Wattles, or Acacias, with their 700-odd species in Australia alone, are found also in America, South Africa, Arabia, Egypt, and some islands in the Pacific. The Australian species, with several exceptions, do not occur elsewhere, and most of those with phyllodes are restricted to Australia. Wattles carry their blossoms in crowded balls or spikes in which the stamens are the most conspicuous part.

A. myrtifolia is a small, bushy, glabrous wattle of the coastal sandstone, flowering during July and August. It carries fluffy balls of rather pale colour, and long, thick, curved pods. It occurs in all the eastern States, while a variety occurs in Western Australia.

RUST PLANT OR RED VELVET BUSH
Lasiopetalum rufum

This small shrub of the sandy coast of New South Wales flowers in spring. The leaves are long and thin, dark-green, rusty below and rather pendulous. The small quaint flowers, greenish-yellow inside and covered with rusty hairs outside, add to the general rusty appearance of the plant. There are five sepals and no petals. It has a long flowering period through spring and summer.

LARGE DUCK-ORCHID
Caleana major

The peculiar arrangement of the floral parts is responsible for the popular name of this orchid. The stem is very smooth and slender, 20–60 cm high, with a single narrow, often reddish leaf at the base. The flowers are borne in short heads, one to four on a stem, always with a bud at the top which does not develop. They are reddish-brown, with the lower sepals green, the whole flower under 3 cm long. It occurs in the sandstone country close to the coast in all the eastern States of Australia and flowers in summer.

PLATE 6

GREEN SPIDER FLOWER
Grevillea mucronulata

Among the best known of the coastal bush flowers of both east and west are the Grevilleas. The flowers are small but very attractive and crowded into dense heads of red, pink, orange or grey. *G. mucronulata* is a spreading shrub about 1 m high; its rounded leaves are elongated to a sharp point, with rust-coloured hairs below. The heads are loose, containing only a very few greenish-brown flowers. It is common on the richer coastal land and Blue Mountains of New South Wales. It flowers in spring.

GREY SPIDER FLOWER
Grevillea buxifolia

The Grey Spider Flower is one of the best known of the flowers of the sandstone areas of the coast and Dividing Range of New South Wales. The shrub is bushy, 1–1.5 m high, with fairly broad leaves. The flowers are crowded into heads at the ends of the branches, and are covered with grey hairs, giving the plant a quaint and very attractive appearance. It flowers in late spring and early summer.

PENCIL ORCHID
Dendrobium beckleri

Many of the orchids, including the Dendrobiums, are epiphytes. The stems are slender, at first erect but bending over and almost pendulous. The leaves are cylindrical and fluted, 8–15 cm long. The flowers are solitary but numerous, in leaf axils, whitish, tinged with green, the labellum entirely white with a frilled margin, often striped with bright-purple. It grows in rain forest, along riverbanks of the coasts of New South Wales and Queensland and flowers in late spring.

WONGA WONGA VINE
Pandorea pandorana

The leaves of this woody climber are opposite, compound, and soft green. The flowers, borne in inflorescences in the leaf axils, are elongated, yellowish-white or deep-cream, tinged with red in the throat. They are about 2 cm long. The seed-pod is 4–8 cm long and tapering at each end, splitting to liberate numerous winged seeds. It is found on the coast and tablelands of eastern and South Australia and flowers in spring and summer.

PLATE 6

GREEN SPIDER FLOWER
Grevillea mucronulata

GREY SPIDER FLOWER
Grevillea buxifolia

PENCIL ORCHID
Dendrobium beckleri

WONGA WONGA VINE
Pandorea pandorana

PLATE 7

CONESTICKS
Petrophile sessilis

DRUMSTICKS OR NARROW-LEAF CONEBUSH
Isopogon anethifolius

PRICKLY SPIDER FLOWER
Grevillea juniperina

WILLOW GEEBUNG
Persoonia laevis

PLATE 7

CONESTICKS
Petrophile sessilis

The Petrophiles are rigid shrubs with stiff, usually divided leaves and crowded, sessile, yellow or white flowers with a cone-like appearance. The flowers are followed by tiny winged or hairy nuts which are produced in cones.

P. sessilis is very common on the barren sandstone hills of the coast of New South Wales. It grows to a height of 1–1.5 m, and has thinly divided leaves. The flowers are white, and covered with a soft down that gives them a creamy appearance. The fruits are conspicuous. It flowers in summer.

DRUMSTICKS OR NARROW-LEAF CONEBUSH
Isopogon anethifolius

The conical heads of the nuts, similar to those of *Petrophile*, have given this plant its common name. The plants are about 1 m high and have rigid, much-divided leaves. The flowers are bright-yellow, and produced in globular heads at the ends of the branches. This species is found commonly on sandy coastal soil and on the Blue Mountains of the Dividing Range in New South Wales. It flowers in summer, and continues in flower for many months.

PRICKLY SPIDER FLOWER
Grevillea juniperina

Unlike most of the Grevilleas this small bushy shrub, 1–1.5 m high, bears its flowers in short spikes, with only a few in each group. The leaves are smooth and very prickly. The flowers range in colour from yellow to pale-pink or deep-cream tinged with pink. It is common only in New South Wales, and is occasionally found on the coast, but more commonly on the Dividing Range, particularly in the south. Its flowering period is spring to summer.

WILLOW GEEBUNG
Persoonia laevis

The name "geebung" really belongs to the succulent, edible, though astringent, fruit. The flowers are small, yellow, and open, with four petals. The fruits are single-seeded, surrounded by sticky, succulent flesh.

This species is an erect shrub with thin, peeling bark and very broad, handsome, sickle-shaped leaves. The flowers are produced towards the ends of the branches. It occurs on the coast of New South Wales and Victoria, and flowers in summer.

7

PLATE 8

SMOOTH FLAX LILY
Dianella laevis

The ornamental "berries" of the Flax Lily are an intense deep blue, rather fleshy, and about 1 cm long. The leaves are smooth and narrow, 15–60 cm long. The pale-blue or occasionally white flowers are in large panicles: the six yellow stamens are conspicuous on account of their deep colour, large size, and protruding habit. It is common on the richer coastal soil of the eastern States and inland, flowering from spring to midsummer.

COCKSPUR FLOWER
Plectranthus parviflorus

This is a succulent, pubescent, erect herb, 30–100 cm high. The leaves are opposite, rounded, thick, 2–5 cm long, with toothed margins, and are borne on long petioles. The flowers are produced on erect stems, and are about 1 cm long, bluish-purple, slightly spurred at the base, with a four-lobed upper lip and an entire lower lip. It ranges from Queensland throughout New South Wales to Victoria and South Australia, in the coast district and on the Dividing Range. It also occurs in Hawaii. It flowers in summer, with a few blooms during the autumn.

WANDERING JEW
Commelina cyanea

In open grassland of the coast of Queensland and New South Wales this small plant is often seen and readily recognized by the clear blue of the small flowers. It is a procumbent, straggling little plant with soft light-green leaves, sheathing at the base, rounded, 4–5 cm long. There are three petals, free from each other and very readily falling. It flowers profusely from October to December, with occasional flowers for many months more.

KANGAROO APPLE
Solanum aviculare

An attractive shrub with pale- or deep-violet flowers, and eggshaped orange-red fruits about 2 cm in diameter. The upper leaves are large and undivided, the lower leaves lobed. The five petals are united and expanded, and the five bright-yellow anthers lie parallel and close together in the centre of the flower. It grows to a height of 1–2 m in the rich damp soils of the coast and elsewhere in Queensland, New South Wales, Victoria, South Australia and Tasmania. It flowers from October to December.

PLATE 8

SMOOTH FLAX LILY
Dianella laevis

COCKSPUR FLOWER
Plectranthus parviflorus

WANDERING JEW
Commelina cyanea

KANGAROO APPLE
Solanum aviculare

PLATE 9

COMMON BUTTERCUP
Ranunculus lappaceus

BULBINE LILY
Bulbine bulbosa

TALL YELLOWEYE
Xyris operculata

LONG-FLOWER MISTLETOE
Dendrophthoe vitellina

PLATE 9

COMMON BUTTERCUP

Ranunculus lappaceus

Buttercups, common all over Australia in marshy places, are at their best at high elevations. This species is common in all States, including Tasmania. It is a herb with hairy stems and leaves, the latter in a rosette as well as on the flowering stems. The flowers are glossy yellow with five or more petals, about 2 cm across. The fruits are numerous, in a globular head, each with a hooked beak. It flowers in spring and early summer.

BULBINE LILY

Bulbine bulbosa

The leaves of this plant are narrow and rather succulent. The open yellow star-like flowers, about 1.5 cm long and 2 cm across, are produced on a slender, leafless stem about 30 cm high. The stalks of the stamens have tufts of yellow hairs. It is found on the coast, tablelands, and plains of Queensland, New South Wales, Victoria, South Australia, and Tasmania. It flowers in spring and summer.

TALL YELLOWEYE

Xyris operculata

The bright-yellow papery flowers of this rush-like plant are produced in short inflorescences on wiry, flattened stems 30–40 cm high. The leaves are long, narrow, and flat, 15–45 cm long, with a brownish sheath at the base. At the base of the flower are dark bracts. The petals are about 1 cm long. It grows in the swampy land on the coast of Queensland, New South Wales, Victoria, South Australia, and Tasmania and flowers in summer.

LONG-FLOWER MISTLETOE

Dendrophthoe vitellina

This is a semi-parasitic plant with large rounded alternate leaves, and flowers produced in axillary inflorescences. The flowers are long and tubular with reversed tips, the tube is yellow and the tips red, the anthers yellow, long, and protruding. The fruit, a small sticky berry, is spread by birds. It occurs on many species of plants on the Queensland and New South Wales coasts, and flowers in summer.

PLATE 10

OLIVE-WOOD
Elaeodendron australe

A brush shrub or small tree of the coastal forests of Queensland and New South Wales, the Olive-wood has broad smooth bright-green leaves, small inconspicuous flowers, and bright-red fruit 1 cm long with a soft outer portion concealing a hard central "stone". It flowers in spring.

HEATH MILKWORT
Comesperma ericinum

This is a common eastern shrub with purple or pink flowers and heath-like leaves. The flowers are small, clustered in terminal heads, each flower having five petal-like sepals, two of which resemble the "wings" of pea flowers, with which it is often confused. It occurs on the sandy coast and the central and south-western slopes of the eastern States. It flowers in spring and early summer.

WEEPING BOTTLEBRUSH
Callistemon viminalis

There are many species of *Callistemon*, all characterized by the long showy heads of flowers with the appearance of a brush. The most conspicuous part of them is the stamens, usually red, though some are green, pink, or cream. One of the most popular is this weeping one, used effectively on the east coast as a street tree, though it is an inland species. It is variable in habit, ranging from 5–10 m, with slender pendulous branches, and flat thin leaves 4–8 cm long, the stamen filaments crimson. It grows along the riverbanks in Queensland and New South Wales and flowers in late spring.

THYME HONEY-MYRTLE
Melaleuca thymifolia

The Melaleucas rank among our most popular and decorative plants. Some of the daintiest are small shrubs, this one reaching a height of 60 cm–1 m. The leaves are opposite, fairly broad, and about 1 cm long. Flowers are in short lateral spikes, and the five bundles of purple stamens are incurved, giving a dainty, feathery appearance. It is a lover of the swamp lands and occurs in Queensland, New South Wales, and Victoria. It flowers in summer.

PLATE 10

OLIVE-WOOD
Elaeodendron australe

HEATH MILKWORT
Comesperma ericinum

WEEPING BOTTLEBRUSH
Callistemon viminalis

THYME HONEY-MYRTLE
Melaleuca thymifolia

PLATE 11

HOWITTIA TRILOCULARIS

LADY'S SLIPPER OR SLENDER VIOLET
Hybanthus filiformis

DOG ROSE
Bauera rubioides

LILAC LILY
Schelhammera undulata

PLATE 11

HOWITTIA TRILOCULARIS

In the moist, rich gullies of coastal New South Wales, Victoria, and South Australia this tall shrub is fairly abundant. Masses of purple or mauve-pink flowers about 2 cm across resemble small *Hibiscus* blossoms. The leaves are long and broadly heart-shaped. at the base. The three-chambered ovary is a distinguishing feature of the plant. It flowers in late spring. There appears to be only a single species of this genus recorded for Australia.

LADY'S SLIPPER OR SLENDER VIOLET
Hybanthus filiformis

Like its relatives the violets, this is a dainty little plant only a few centimetres high, with alternate slender leaves. The five petals are all very small with the exception of one which is elongated and slipper-shaped. The flowers are blue, two or three being produced on a slender thread-like stalk. It occurs in Queensland, New South Wales, and Victoria, mostly in moist situations, and flowers in summer. The stem in the specimen figured has been shortened for convenience.

DOG ROSE
Bauera rubioides

Bauera is a small genus of three species. It is reported that Banks so much admired the work of the artist brothers Bauer that he decided to perpetuate their memory in the name of the loveliest flower which next came under his notice.

B. rubioides is a very variable shrub, ranging from a scrambling plant to an erect shrub 2 m high, loving moist places. The open many-petalled pink or rarely white flowers are very dainty and attractive. It occurs in Queensland, New South Wales, Victoria, South Australia, and Tasmania, and flowers from spring to late summer.

LILAC LILY
Schelhammera undulata

A dainty little plant, this *Schelhammera* grows only about 15 cm high. It has broad wavy leaves 3–5 cm long, borne on short stems. The flowers are usually solitary, in the leaf axils, or in short, few-flowered inflorescences, pale-purple or pink, on slender stems about 2 cm long. The flowers are open and spreading, with five petals about 2 cm in diameter. It occurs in New South Wales and Victoria, and flowers in spring.

PLATE 12

WESTERN KURRAJONG (CURRAJONG)
Brachychiton populneum

This elegant tree with its somewhat swollen stem and well-balanced form is one of the more fortunate of our western trees, because its leaves make excellent fodder, and thus it is frequently saved from destruction. The foliage is light-green and very handsome. It bears very attractive creamy bell-shaped flowers with pink throats in summer. The large black seed-pods are quaintly attractive. It occurs in New South Wales, Victoria, and South Australia.

CHLOANTHES STOECHADIS

The flowers of this shrub are peculiar delicate-green forms with two lips, an upper of two lobes and a lower of three. The plant grows 45–60 cm high, with opposite narrow leaves, rough and coarse above and white-tomentose below. The flowers are produced singly in the leaf axils. It is fairly common in the coast districts and Dividing Range of Queensland and New South Wales. It flowers in summer.

NATIVE PLUM
Endiandra sieberi

This is a fair-sized tree of the brush forests and richer open coastlands of Queensland and New South Wales. The leaves are large and alternate, shining-green on both sides. The tiny greenish or cream flowers, 5–8 cm long, are inconspicuous, but the long oval berries are about 2 cm long, with a fragrance somewhat reminiscent of the nutmeg. It flowers from October to December.

KREYSSIGIA MULTIFLORA

The unbranched flexuose leafy stems of this small plant reach a height of about 45 cm. The leaves are somewhat heart-shaped, stem-clasping and pointed, 5–8 cm long, the veins very conspicuous. The flowers are in the leaf axils, on slender stems, mostly solitary but sometimes two or three together, with narrow bracts at the base, pale-purple in colour. The six small sepals and petals are free and spreading. The plant is found in the brush gullies of the coast of Queensland and northern New South Wales. It flowers in spring.

PLATE 12

WESTERN KURRAJONG
Brachychiton populneum

CHLOANTHES STOECHADIS

NATIVE PLUM
Endiandra sieberi

KREYSSIGIA MULTIFLORA

PLATE 13

HYACINTH ORCHID
Dipodium punctatum

HONEY FLOWER
Lambertia formosa

NATIVE CHERRY OR CHERRY BALLART
Exocarpos cupressiformis

MOLUCCA BRAMBLE
Rubus hillii

PLATE 13

HYACINTH ORCHID
Dipodium punctatum

No functional leaves are produced by this orchid, for it lives with a fungus which makes it unnecessary for it to manufacture its own food. There is an erect, leafless, fleshy stem bearing several beautiful flowers, pink spotted with carmine, or deeper in colour with deeper spots. Sepals and petals are nearly equal, 1–2 cm long. It is found in all the States except Western Australia, extending from the coast to the western slopes, commonly in sandy places. It flowers from late spring to late autumn. The stem in the drawing has been shortened for convenience.

HONEY FLOWER
Lambertia formosa

Sometimes this plant is called Mountain Devil, because of the curious form of the fruit. The tubular red flowers, which are usually grouped in heads of seven, have protruding styles and are full of honey, which attracts numerous small birds. The plant is stiff and rigid, and reaches a height of 1–2 m. It is extremely handsome in full flower. It grows on the coast and tablelands of New South Wales, blossoming profusely in the spring and sparingly all the year.

NATIVE CHERRY OR CHERRY BALLART
Exocarpos cupressiformis

This graceful cypress-like tree, 3–8 m high, has long pendulous branches bearing rudimentary leaves and tiny flowers borne in axillary clusters, and assumes a very stately and symmetrical form. The fruit is a small nut resting on a receptacle which looks like the berry itself. This receptacle is green at first, then yellow, and finally red. The tree is reputed to tap the roots of other plants for nourishment. It occurs on the coastal open country and inland in the eastern States. It flowers in late spring.

MOLUCCA BRAMBLE
Rubus hillii

This is a tall prickly scrambler with hooked spines, and simple lobed leaves that are hairy underneath. The flowers are open, with five free petals, red or rarely white. The red fruit is almost globular, with little flavour. It occurs in all the eastern Australian States, and flowers in the spring.

PLATE 14

PEACH-LEAF GROUNDSEL
Senecio amygdalifolius

The large, firm, acutely toothed leaves of this tall plant are characteristic. The individual flower-heads are yellow and small (about 2 cm across), and many are produced on a single stem. In full flower it makes a grand show. The plant is fairly common on the richer coastal lands of Queensland and New South Wales. It flowers in September and October.

PODOLEPIS JACEOIDES

This perennial grows 30–60 cm high, and has oblong or broad basal leaves 8–16 cm long, and narrow stem-clasping leaves usually shorter. The flower-heads are large, yellow, and terminal, with a centre of disc florets surrounded by long, strap-like, ray florets. The plant is widely distributed in Queensland, New South Wales, Victoria, South Australia, and Tasmania. It flowers in spring and summer.

PRICKLY MOSES
Acacia ulicifolia

This Wattle of the eastern coastal sand has short, sharp, prickly "leaves" and masses of pale yellow balls of flowers. The pods are long and thin, and become extremely contorted on opening, owing to the violent explosive action. The name is probably a mispronunciation of "Prickly Mimosa", the Acacias at one time being included in the genus *Mimosa*. It occurs in Queensland, New South Wales, Victoria, and Tasmania. It flowers profusely in August and September.

CURRAWANG OR SPEARWOOD
Acacia doratoxylon

This is an ashy-hued tall shrub of the inland areas, with long narrow "leaves", and short catkin-like spikes of golden-yellow flowers produced very abundantly. It is very attractive in full flower. It has a straight, narrow pod, slightly constricted between the seeds. It is a species of wide distribution, occurring in Queensland, New South Wales, and Victoria, flowering in late spring.

PLATE 14

PEACH-LEAF GROUNDSEL
Senecio amygdalifolius

PODOLEPIS JACEOIDES

PRICKLY MOSES
Acacia ulicifolia

CURRAWANG OR SPEARWOOD
Acacia doratoxylon

PLATE 15

GOLDEN GLORY PEA OR BROAD
WEDGE PEA
Gompholobium latifolium

NATIVE HOLLY
Oxylobium ilicifolium

DOUBLETAILS
Diuris aequalis

WHITE HONEYSUCKLE OR COAST BANKSIA
Banksia integrifolia

PLATE 15

GOLDEN GLORY PEA OR BROAD WEDGE PEA
Gompholobium latifolium

Here is truly the queen of the yellow peas. It well deserves its name, Golden Glory Pea, for the flowers glitter with a metallic brightness in the sunshine. The leaves are soft and narrow-lanceolate. Individual flowers are borne in leaf axils and are large, up to 4 cm across the standard. They are of a very delicate light-yellow, or sometimes deep-yellow. The keel is delicately ciliated. It has a small inflated pod. This plant and a related species (G. grandiflorum) would grace any garden. It is quite a common plant of the coastal sandstone of Queensland and New South Wales. It flowers in spring.

NATIVE HOLLY
Oxylobium ilicifolium

In August and September the richer hills and the moist gullies of New South Wales, Queensland, and Victoria are gay with the beautiful Native Holly, with its stiff deep-green elegant holly-like leaves, and its abundance of rich-yellow pea flowers, deepened by a tinge of red on the standard. The small brown pods are characteristic.

DOUBLETAILS
Diuris aequalis

The double-tailed orchids are so named on account of the long lower sepals which hang down from the flowers. Most of these orchids are yellow in colour, but a few are pink or purple.

The "tails" (lower sepals) of this Diuris are crossed and the labellum (lipped petal) is a little longer than the upper sepal and shorter than the other two petals. The flowers are orange. It is a New South Wales species, and is found on the coastal belt. It flowers in summer. The stem in the specimen figured has been shortened for convenience.

WHITE HONEYSUCKLE OR COAST BANKSIA
Banksia integrifolia

This species has a wide range from Queensland through New South Wales to Victoria, along the coast and tablelands. Pale-yellow flowers are produced in spikes. The leaves are fairly broad, 8–12 cm long, and covered with white down on the underside. The fruiting capsules are smooth when ripe. It flowers all the year, but more profusely in spring.

PLATE 16

RED SPIDER FLOWER
Grevillea speciosa syn. *G. punicea*

Although there are several red Grevilleas this species has claim to the name Red Spider Flower from long usage. It is common in the coastal area of New South Wales on the barren, sandy ridges. The leaves are short and round, and silky-hairy on the underside. The flowers are densely crowded in the head, and a bright-red colour. The long style, protruding to twice the length of the petals, is characteristic. It flowers for most of the year, but most abundantly in spring.

SHOWY MIRBELIA
Mirbelia speciosa

The reddish-purple flowers of this low shrub form terminal inflorescences which are quite conspicuous despite the plant's small size (often less than 15 cm high). The individual flowers are fairly large, and pea-type. Leaves are narrow, and produced in whorls of three. A handsome plant, it selects the moister, richer coastlands of Queensland and New South Wales. It flowers in late winter and early spring. Pods are short and smooth.

RED BEAN OR DUSKY CORAL PEA
Kennedia rubicunda

The Kennedias are creeping plants of fairly wide distribution, the flowers varying in colour from bright-red to almost black, according to the species. *K. rubicunda*, a common trailing pea plant of coastal districts of Australia, is sometimes confused with the Desert Pea, but the flowers of this species are not so brilliant, being smaller and of a more sombre red, without the contrast of the dark centred keel. It grows on coastal sandstone and headlands, coastal forests and sand dunes, flowering from spring through summer. The pods are long and hairy.

HOVEA LINEARIS

This is a shrub of coastal Queensland and New South Wales, attaining a height of about 60 cm at its best, and with long spikes of purple pea flowers. The individual flowers are quite small, solitary or 2–3 in the leaf axils. These flowering heads are erect and stiff, the stiffness being accentuated by the long narrow leaves, sometimes as much as 8 cm in length. It is a dainty little plant, flowering in spring. The pods are inflated.

PLATE 16

RED SPIDER FLOWER
Grevillea speciosa

SHOWY MIRBELIA
Mirbelia speciosa

RED BEAN OR DUSKY CORAL PEA
Kennedia rubicunda

HOVEA LINEARIS

PLATE 17

CRIMSON BOTTLEBRUSH
Callistemon citrinus

RED APPLE
Acmena australis

PINKIES OR PINK FINGERS
Caladenia carnea

NODDING GREENHOOD
Pterostylis nutans

PLATE 17

CRIMSON BOTTLEBRUSH
Callistemon citrinus

This is a somewhat straggling plant, very rarely more than 1.5 m high, except under cultivation, when it may be trained into a shapely bush. It has thickish acute leaves, variable in length. The spikes of deep-red flowers are 5–12 cm long, and the long red conspicuous stamens have dark anthers. It occurs in moist places on the coasts of New South Wales, Queensland, and Victoria. It flowers from spring into early or late summer.

RED APPLE
Acmena australis

The large red fruit of this species is its most attractive feature. It is a tree 6–10 m high, with oblong leaves about 12 cm long. The small reddish flowers are in clusters. The red globular fruits, about 2 cm in diameter and marked with the scar of the calyx, are very handsome. The plant is native to the rich coastal lands of Queensland and New South Wales. It flowers in the spring.

PINKIES OR PINK FINGERS
Caladenia carnea

This is a slender plant, growing to a height of about 4–6 cm, with a long narrow basal leaf. The flowers are solitary or two or three on a stem, delicately pink or white, and up to 5 cm in diameter. Sepals and petals are almost equal, except the labellum (lip), which is barred with red, three-lobed, the mid-lobe toothed and tipped with yellow, and bearing yellow club-shaped glands in two rows. It is distributed over the greater part of Australia except Western Australia, in the coastal and inland sandy patches. It flowers in early summer. The specimen stem figured has been shortened for convenience.

NODDING GREENHOOD
Pterostylis nutans

This dainty plant flowers in early winter, and is common in the coastal sandstone in all the eastern States except South Australia, where it occurs rarely. It grows 20–30 cm high, with a rosette of pale, smooth leaves. The flowers are bent forward, and curve over. The hood, consisting of two joined petals and one sepal, is rather narrow. The two lower sepals are narrow and somewhat bulging. The labellum (lip) is brownish, acute and much curved.

PLATE 18

BINDI-EYE
Calotis cuneifolia

Calotis is a genus confined to Australia, apart from two species from Annam and one from China. It has two kinds of florets, the outer ones being either white or purple. The fruits are unpleasantly prickly in this species, and called burrs or bindi-eyes.

C. cuneifolia is about 30 cm high, with wedge-shaped stem-clasping leaves, toothed along the apex, about 1.2 cm long. The flowers are blue or lavender, delicately thin, the ray florets very numerous and spirally curled back after opening. It is common in Queensland and New South Wales, mainly on the plains. It flowers in spring.

BRUNONIELLA AUSTRALIS

This perennial, 10–15 cm high, is very variable. The leaves are broad, pointed, 2–5 cm long. The flowers are blue, solitary in the leaf axils, about 2 cm in diameter, with five petals, tubular and expanded into an open platform. It is distributed widely throughout Queensland and New South Wales. Its flowering period is spring and summer.

FORKED SUNDEW
Drosera binata

Sundews are among the insect catchers of the plant world, and use their leaves to obtain nitrogen by this means. They are very beautiful, the glandular secretion on the leaves glistening in the sunlight with an almost unbelievable sparkle, and the delicate white or pink, papery, five-petalled flowers dancing on the slender stems with the first suspicion of movement in the air. This species is found in the eastern States and South Australia. It flowers in spring and early summer. The flower stem in the specimen figured has been shortened for convenience.

STRIPED HOOD
Cryptostylis erecta

This terrestrial orchid has a few elongated, rather rigid, radical leaves on long petioles. The inflorescence, which is 30–45 cm high, has a few sheathing scales. The flowers are reddish, the margins incurved, giving the appearance of being very narrow. The labellum is about 2 cm long, erect, and forming a broad hood conspicuously striped with dark veins. It is a Queensland, New South Wales, and Victorian species, occurring in the coastal sandy patches. It flowers in the summer months.

PLATE 18

BINDI-EYE
Calotis cuneifolia

BRUNONIELLA AUSTRALIS

FORKED SUNDEW
Drosera binata

STRIPED HOOD
Cryptostylis erecta

PLATE 19

AUSTRALIAN OR AUSTRAL BLUEBELL
Wahlenbergia stricta

BLUE DEVIL
Eryngium rostratum

CONOSPERMUM TENUIFOLIUM

PLATE 19

AUSTRALIAN OR AUSTRAL BLUEBELL
Wahlenbergia stricta

There are 22 species of Wahlenbergia (including naturalized), all commonly known as Australian Bluebells. They are closely related to the true northern hemisphere bluebells (Campanulas). Dainty, slender herbs with delicate blue nodding flowers, they are found in inland country and from coast to sub-alpine herb fields.

This species varies greatly in size and in depth of colour in the flower. It grows 15–45 cm high, with narrow light-green leaves. The pale- or sky-blue flowers vary from 2–2.5 cm in diameter, and are borne on long slender stems, several flowers to each. The five petals are united for part of their length to form a shallow cup. It is found in the open country, chiefly in the inland and highland districts of Queensland, New South Wales, Victoria, and South Australia. It flowers in summer and late spring.

BLUE DEVIL
Eryngium rostratum

A bluish colour prevails in this plant. It is a slender shrub up to 75 cm high, with radical leaves. The small flowers are in heads surrounded by spiny green or bluish bracts, giving a very beautiful misty appearance. It is found on the Dividing Range and the inland districts of all the eastern States, and also in temperate South America. It is a very hardy plant, being able to withstand considerable drought. It flowers in spring and summer.

CONOSPERMUM TENUIFOLIUM

Among the Conospermums are some very beautiful Western Australian species. There are several of them, on both sides of the continent, most of them with white flowers in crowded heads and fruits clustered together in cones.

Often lying almost flat along the ground, this slender, dainty shrub with its narrow, curling leaves produces its small bluish-white or white flowers on erect, fragile stalks in small heads. The plant is fairly common on the sandstone of coastal New South Wales, extending to the Blue Mountains. It flowers in late spring and summer.

PLATE 20

BORONIA LEDIFOLIA

All the flowers of the Boronias have four petals and eight stamens. This species is often called Sydney Boronia because it grows to great profusion on the sandstone of Sydney. The leaves are dark-green, simple but sometimes trifoliate, or pinnate, and highly aromatic. It is one of the earliest of the flowers to bloom, sometimes coming out as early as June and continuing in flower for some time. The flowers are a deep-pink and, unlike several other species, open widely. Later, the petals curl over the ripening fruit. It occurs on the sandy patches of the coast in Queensland and New South Wales.

BORONIA MOLLOYAE
syn. *B. elatior*

Taller than most species, this rather hairy Boronia reaches a height of about 1 m. It has delicately pinnate leaves, and deep-pink, often hairy, broad petals. The petals rarely open fully, and the flowers are inclined to be pendulous. It is a Western Australian species, a lover of damp sandy soil and flowers in spring.

BROWN BORONIA
Boronia megastigma

The very attractive strong perfume of this Boronia has made it one of the most popular. Comparatively easy to cultivate, it has been extensively grown in Melbourne and exported to the other States for distribution. The cultivation has, unfortunately, led to its being popularly known as "Melbourne Boronia" although it is a native of Western Australia only. The flowers are dark brown on the outside and yellowish-green inside. This Boronia has a dainty, attractive habit and an exquisitely aromatic and lingering perfume. It flowers in August and September. In cultivation its flowering period has been extended from a few weeks to several months.

BORONIA FALCIFOLIA

This very beautiful plant is common on the Queensland coast, and in the northern coastal districts of New South Wales. The twiggy habit and narrow leaflets distinguish it from the other Boronias. The flowers resemble those of the Native Rose very closely. The deep-pink flowers open fully and are very closely massed at the ends of the branches. It flowers in September and October.

PLATE 20

BORONIA LEDIFOLIA

BORONIA MOLLOYAE

BROWN BORONIA
Boronia megastig

BORONIA FALCIFOLIA

PLATE 21

PINK WAX FLOWER
Eriostemon australasius

PHILOTHECA SALSOLIFOLIA

OVAL-LEAF MINT BUSH
Prostanthera ovalifolia

CROWEA SALIGNA

PLATE 21

PINK WAX FLOWER
Eriostemon australasius syn. E. lanceolatus

The Wax Flowers are close relatives of the Boronias, having five petals, and ten free stamens clustered in the centre of the flower. The stamens have appendages on the anthers. The common Wax Flower of New South Wales, Victoria, and Queensland grows in the sandy coastal areas and some inland patches. It is a very attractive plant, with greyish-green leaves and large, starry pink or white flowers. During the flowering period, September to October, the weight of blossoms and leaves is sufficiently great to weigh down the flexible branches. This weeping habit adds to its attraction.

PHILOTHECA SALSOLIFOLIA

This is a small twiggy shrub with fairly large, starry, purplish flowers borne singly at the ends of the branches. It has five petals and ten stamens like the Eriostemons, but the stamens are joined and without anther appendages. It grows in sandy soils along the coasts of New South Wales and Queensland, flowering in late winter to late spring.

OVAL-LEAF MINT BUSH
Prostanthera ovalifolia

The strong aromatic odour emanating from the leaves of many species of Mint Bush makes their discovery in the field easy. The flowers of most species are purple, but some are white, red, or greenish, solitary or in inflorescences, with lipped tubular flowers.

In favourable places *P. ovalifolia* is a bushy shrub several feet high, with flat, oval leaves, slightly toothed or entire, about 1 cm long. The deep-purplish flowers are on slender stems in loose inflorescences. They are two-lipped, with two petals in the upper and three in the lower lip. It grows on the Dividing Range and into the interior of Queensland and New South Wales, flowering in spring.

CROWEA SALIGNA

The wide-open five-petalled flowers of this species are a deep, rich pink or red. The leaves are bright-green, glossy, thin, and somewhat like those of the willow. The plant is quite small, seldom reaching more than 45 cm, and the branches are very angular. It is found only in New South Wales, particularly in the Port Jackson area, growing in rocky, exposed situations on Hawkesbury sandstone. It flowers in mid-winter and continues into spring.

PLATE 22

GREVILLEA BANKSII

This is a tall shrub attaining 5–6 m in height, with softly-hairy young leaves and branches. The leaves are much divided and fern-like in appearance, 10–20 cm long and very silky-hairy below. The red, cream, or green flowers are crowded into long, dense heads as much as 15 cm in length. It occurs on open barren country in Queensland and flowers practically the whole year, being most prolific in the spring. It makes a very fine garden plant and is a great attraction to honey-eating birds.

GREVILLEA BAUERI

Although this species has a limited distribution, mainly confined to the ranges of central and southern New South Wales, it is fairly prolific in this restricted area. It grows 60–100 cm high. The young branches are slightly hairy and the flat blunt leaves are paler below. The flowers are yellowish-green, sometimes tinged with red, the petals quite smooth outside, but bearded inside. It flowers in spring.

HAKEA BAKERANA

The Hakeas are very well-known bush flowers of both the east and west. The flowers are usually white, occasionally pink, and though quite small are produced in such numbers and so close together that they are very showy.

H. bakerana is an attractive New South Wales shrub with narrow crowded leaves, and delicate pink flowers borne in crowded spikes well down from the ends of the branches. It flowers in spring.

GREVILLEA ROSMARINIFOLIA

This plant assumes a number of forms. It is found on the eastern coasts of New South Wales and Victoria. In the form illustrated the branches leave the main stem to form an obtuse angle above and an acute angle below. The plant is a small, variable, very bushy shrub 60 cm–2 m high, with narrow pointed leaves and loose heads of flowers. The flowers are a very delicate light-pink, and have long, protruding, red styles. It flowers in the spring for a long period.

PLATE 22

GREVILLEA BANKSII

GREVILLEA BAUERI

HAKEA BAKERANA

GREVILLEA ROSMARINIFOLIA

PLATE 23

NARROW-LEAF CONESTICKS
Petrophile linearis

WOODY PEAR
Xylomelum pyriforme

FIREWHEEL-TREE
Stenocarpus sinuatus

PINCUSHION FLOWER
Hakea laurina

PLATE 23

NARROW-LEAVED CONESTICKS
Petrophile linearis

This charming small plant inhabits the sandy coastal stretches of Western Australia. It reaches a height of about 60 cm, and has narrow thick leaves with recurved points. The flowers are pink with deep-grey tips, about 2 cm long and densely covered with soft grey hairs. The cones bearing the small nuts are rounded. It belongs to the same family as the Spider Flowers, and the other three plants shown on the same plate. It usually flowers in spring.

WOODY PEAR
Xylomelum pyriforme

The fruit of this plant is shaped like an elongated pear about 10 cm long, and has a beautiful velvety covering of hairs over the woody surface. It splits open to liberate two winged seeds. The flowers are small and velvety-brown, produced in long pendulous spikes in the leaf axils. The leaves are long and broad, the older ones toothed, the younger ones entire and frequently a rich red or bronze colour. It flowers in late spring and summer, and is found on open, sandy, somewhat elevated patches of the coast in Queensland and New South Wales.

FIREWHEEL-TREE
Stenocarpus sinuatus

Masses of crimson flowers produced on a central axis like the spokes of a wheel make this tall tree a magnificent sight. It inhabits the rich coastal brush gullies of Queensland and New South Wales and reaches a height of 12–15 m. The leaves are irregularly divided and very glossy. The quaint narrow seed-pods produce numbers of winged seeds. The tree is a favourite in cultivation. It flowers in late summer, autumn, and sometimes winter.

PINCUSHION FLOWER
Hakea laurina

Pink blossoms with cream stigmas projecting for some distance and the flowers in globular heads have earned the name for this most attractive plant from Western Australia. The leaves are broad and take on rich red shades when they become old and before they fall. It is easily cultivated on sandy or loamy soil. In full flower it is a magnificent sight. It flowers in spring.

PLATE 24

VERTICORDIA INSIGNIS

The flowers on this shrub, which reaches a height of 30–60 cm, are produced on long slender stalks, giving the plant a graceful appearance. They are pale-pink, the petals being fringed, as are the sepals. These fringed flowers, produced in heads, give a fluffy appearance to the plant. It is a native of Western Australia, inhabiting sandy or gravelly soil. It flowers in spring.

OVAL-LEAVED HONEY-MYRTLE

Melaleuca elliptica

The large showy red flowers of this plant make it one of the favourites among the Melaleucas. It is a smooth bushy plant with opposite leaves, and the flowers are produced in long spikes; each flower is about 2 cm long. The long, conspicuous stamens are the most attractive part of the flower. It is a native of Western Australia and blossoms in spring.

PINK PAPERBARK OR ROSY HONEY-MYRTLE

Melaleuca erubescens

This "pink"-flowering Melaleuca of the open sandy and shaly coastal lands of Queensland and New South Wales is a dainty, slender shrub 60–100 cm high. It has fine, closely set leaves about 1 cm long. The flower spikes are elongated, forming delightfully neat miniature bottlebrushes. The long fine stamens are pink, pinkish-purple, or light-red. It flowers in summer.

VERTICORDIA PENNIGERA

Among the many lovely Western Australian flowering shrubs the Verticordias hold a high place. The flowers are produced in dense clusters and are usually pink or purple, the delicately fringed calyx adding greatly to the beauty of the flower.

V. pennigera has pink flowers on stout stems. The leaves are usually narrow and fringed on the margins, and the flowers are borne in the upper axils. The plant is a native of Western Australia, and is found on sandy soil. It flowers in spring.

PLATE 24

VERTICORDIA INSIGNIS

OVAL-LEAF HONEY-MYRTLE
Melaleuca elliptica

PINK PAPERBARK OR
ROSY HONEY-MYRTLE
Melaleuca erubescens

VERTICORDIA PENNIGERA

PLATE 25

DWARF WATER GUM
Tristania neriifolia

GERALDTON WAX PLANT
Chamelaucium uncinatum

ROUND-LEAF TEA-TREE
Leptospermum scoparium
var. *rotundifolium*

PINK BUTTONS
Kunzea capitata

PLATE 25

DWARF WATER GUM
Tristania neriifolia

The name Water Gum explains itself. Although sometimes reaching the height of a tree it usually remains a shrub 2–3 m high. It has opposite, fairly broad, smooth dark-green leaves 4–8 cm long. The flowers are yellow and in terminal inflorescences. The petals are five in number, free, and form a flower about 0.5 cm in diameter. The numerous stamens, clustered in bundles of five, are longer. The Dwarf Water Gum inhabits the rocky creek-banks of coastal New South Wales and the Blue Mountains, flowering in summer.

GERALDTON WAX PLANT
Chamelaucium uncinatum

Almost everyone knows this Western Australian beauty. It is a handsome and delicate shrub 1–2 m high, very open in habit, and with fine narrow hooked leaves about 1 cm long. The flowers are borne in clusters in the leaf axils. It is common on the limestone hills of the coast of Western Australia, and is also one of the commonest of our natives in cultivation in the eastern States. It flowers in early spring and right through summer. The flowers vary in colour from very pale to very deep-pink.

ROUND-LEAF TEA-TREE
Leptospermum scoparium var. rotundifolium

This elegant, spreading species attains a height of 45–150 cm and produces masses of white or pale-pink open five-petalled blossoms 1-2 cm across. The rounded leaves are 0.5–1 cm in diameter. It occurs in New South Wales on the edge of the table-lands and coastal ranges and is common near Nowra on the south coast. It flowers from November to January.

PINK BUTTONS
Kunzea capitata

This erect twiggy shrub grows 60–100 cm high and bears narrow or broad leaves about 0.5 cm long. The flowers are in rounded heads, the petals and numerous stamens purplish-pink. The stamens are twice or three times as long as the petals. It occurs in the coastal areas, mostly on damp peaty soil, of Queensland, New South Wales, and Victoria, flowering in spring and summer.

PLATE 26

LILLY-PILLY
Acmena smithii

The common Lilly-pilly of northern Australia, Queensland, New South Wales, and Victoria loves the moist, rich parts of the coast. It is a small tree, 3–8 m high, with dark-green glossy leaves and rich pink young foliage. The five-petalled white flowers are not very conspicuous. The fruits are pale- or deep-purple, rarely quite white, about 1 cm in diameter, and make a grand show on a good tree. It flowers in spring and summer and the fruits are ripe in early winter. In healthy condition it is a prolific bearer.

TUCKEROO
Cupaniopsis anacardioides

This tree grows to a height of 12 m in the brush forests of Queensland and New South Wales. The leaves are compound, the leaflets rounded and dark-green. The flowers are small and inconspicuous. The fruit is a capsule covered with hairs on the outside and divided into three chambers. When the fruit splits open the attractive bright-red seeds are displayed. It flowers in early summer.

PURPLE BLADDERWORT OR FAIRIES' APRONS
Utricularia dichotoma

The basal leaves of this Bladderwort are rounded, 0.5–5 cm long, often with bladders and then elongated. The flowering stalk is 8–15 cm long, slender and carrying one to four fragile purple flowers, each with a small upper lip and a lower lip about 1 cm across. It is found in shallow water or moist patches in all the eastern States and Tasmania. The bladders catch small animals whose bodies are used as a supplementary nitrogen supply. It flowers in October and November.

SMALL-LEAF LILLY-PILLY
Syzygium luehmannii

The most attractive feature of this Lilly-pilly is the mass of pale-pink pendulous young foliage produced at the tips of the branches in the growing season. It may attain a height of 30 m and bears shiny dark-green leaves 4–5 cm long. The five white petals are fairly conspicuous and assist in attraction. The fruits are very handsome, being pear-shaped, about 2 cm long, and a rich bright-red. It occurs in the sandy soils on beaches on the coast of Queensland and New South Wales, flowering in late spring.

26

PLATE 26

LILLY-PILLY
Acmena smithii

TUCKEROO
Cupaniopsis anacardioides

PURPLE BLADDERWORT
Utricularia dichotoma

SMALL-LEAF LILLY-PILLY
Syzygium luehmannii

PLATE 27

CHORIZEMA CORDATUM

BIRD FLOWER
Crotalaria agatiflora

SUNSHINE WATTLE
Acacia terminalis

BRACHYSEMA LANCEOLATUM

PLATE 27

CHORIZEMA CORDATUM

The Chorizemas are all rather weak, straggling shrubs with slender branches. This one is a native of Western Australia. It has rough heart-shaped leaves, and small vivid orange-and-red pea flowers borne in slender inflorescences. The spreading petal at the back (standard) is kidney-shaped, the two side petals (wings) shorter, and the two central petals (forming the keel) very short. The species is a lover of the sandy country, flowering in spring. It makes an attractive scrambling border plant in cultivation.

BIRD FLOWER
Crotalaria agatiflora

The large greenish-yellow flowers of this plant rather resemble a bird with closed wings clinging to the stem by its beak. The plant is a shrub about 1 m high or, in favourable localities, a small tree with terete branches. The flowers are produced in terminal inflorescences. The spreading back petal (standard) is about 2 cm long when fully developed, and the central petals (forming the keel) as long. The side petals (wings) are much shorter. It is introduced from Africa, and is commonly cultivated. It flowers over a long period through winter into summer.

SUNSHINE WATTLE
Acacia terminalis syn. *A. botrycephala, A. discolor*

This plant is common in the coastal sandstone, and in some inland parts of Queensland, New South Wales, Victoria, and Tasmania. It is a spreading shrub or small tree with coarse feathery leaves and abundant clumps of pale- to deep-yellow flowers in balls. It is one of the most abundant and most beautiful of all the wattles. It often forms a shapely bush. It has a very long flowering period in New South Wales, from July to September.

BRACHYSEMA LANCEOLATUM

This plant bears deep-red pea flowers, solitary or in small groups in the leaf axils. It is a half-climbing shrub with silky-hairy young branches, and rounded simple leaves 3–5 cm long, attractively white, silky-hairy beneath. The spreading petal at the back (standard) is short and broad, the two side petals (wings) and the two central petals (forming the keel) elongated. The fruit is round. It is a native of the sandy soil of Western Australia, flowering in spring. It is a useful garden plant, flowering for a long period.

PLATE 28

FROGSMOUTH OR WOOLLY WATERLILY
Philydrum lanuginosum

The whole of this plant, including the inflorescence, is woolly, the woolliness being due to loose, soft, grey hair. It is rather a tall herb, up to 60 cm, with sword-shaped lower leaves about 30–45 cm long, the upper ones elongated. The flowers are yellow, hairy, solitary or in few-flowered inflorescences enclosed in bracts. The sepals are about 1 cm long, the petals shorter. It belongs to the swampy coastal lands of eastern Australia and flowers in late summer.

YELLOW MARSH FLOWER
Villarsia exaltata

This pretty little swamp plant grows to a height of 30–45 cm. The leaves are chiefly radical, on long stems. The inflorescences arise from the base of the plant. The flowers are about 2 cm in diameter; the five petals are very bearded inside at the base, free and spreading, giving the flower a starry appearance. It is found in the swamp lands on the coasts of Queensland and New South Wales, flowering in spring.

SHINY-LEAF GUINEA FLOWER
Hibbertia nitida

The Hibbertias are small erect or scrambling shrubs common in the coastal regions of Australia, especially on the eastern side. The flowers are open, with five free yellow petals. There are numerous stamens which are either arranged all round the centre of the flower or clustered in a group on one side. This is a small shrub with smooth glossy leaves. The flowers are 1–2 cm across. The calyx surrounds several bright-red seeds after the petals have fallen. It is found in fairly rich soil on the New South Wales coast. It flowers from July to November.

TWINING GUINEA FLOWER
Hibbertia scandens

The sand dunes of New South Wales and Queensland make the home of *H. scandens*. It bears large bright flowers commonly 5 cm across, and bright-red shiny seeds supported by the calyx. In full bloom it is spectacular. It flowers from July to November.

PLATE 28

FROGSMOUTH OR WOOLLY WATERLILY
Philydrum lanuginosum

YELLOW MARSH FLOWER
Villarsia exaltata

SHINY-LEAF GUINEA FLOWER
Hibbertia nitida

TWINING GUINEA FLOWER
Hibbertia scandens

PLATE 29

PINK FIVECORNERS
Styphelia triflora

DRACOPHYLLUM SECUNDUM

PINK SWAMP HEATH
Sprengelia incarnata

LONG-LEAVED FIVECORNERS
Styphelia longifolia

PLATE 29

PINK FIVECORNERS
Styphelia triflora

All the Styphelias are beautiful, but this excels. It grows to a height of 1 m with broad, closely set stiff leaves, very acute, about 2 cm long. The flowers are solitary or clustered in groups of three in the leaf axils, delicate pale-pink, or occasionally yellow, with five groups of soft, delicate yellow hairs just inside the tube, and long protruding stamens. It is a Queensland and New South Wales species of the sandy soil, flowering in winter and early spring.

DRACOPHYLLUM SECUNDUM

This is a small, rather weak shrub, belonging to the same family as the Fivecorners and Heaths, with rigid leaves 5–10 cm long. The flowers are short, tubular, cream or pink, in long loose inflorescences. It belongs to the moist shady rocks of Port Jackson and the Blue Mountains of New South Wales, flowering in spring and early summer.

PINK SWAMP HEATH
Sprengelia incarnata

Low-lying moist land may be covered with plants of this *Sprengelia* growing erect to a height of 60–100 cm, with stiff, pointed stem-clasping leaves. The pale-pink rather open five-petalled stiff flowers are borne singly on the ends of small shoots arranged in terminal clusters, surrounded by leafy bracts. It is found on the coast and tablelands in New South Wales, Victoria, South Australia, and Tasmania, flowering in late spring.

LONG-LEAVED FIVECORNERS
Styphelia longifolia

The peculiar greenish flowers of this plant are interesting in lack of conspicuousness against the green colour of the dense foliage. The tube is about 2 cm long, tufted inside. The shrub grows erect, up to 1–1.5 m, is somewhat hairy, and has narrow, stiff, pointed leaves. It occurs in the sandstone districts of Port Jackson, and flowers in winter and early spring.

Plate 30

KERAUDRENIA HILLII

This is a small shrub of the northern coastal districts of New South Wales and of Queensland. The whole plant, including the flowers, is covered with dense hairs. The flowers are in short, few-flowered inflorescences. The petals are wanting, but the sepals are large and spreading, and so assume the function of petals. After flowering the sepals enlarge and remain as a support to the developing fruit. It flowers in spring.

ISOTOMA AXILLARIS

This is quite a large *Isotoma*, an erect plant 30 cm high, with divided dainty pale-green leaves 2–8 cm long. The flowers are large, spreading to about 2 cm in diameter, blue inside and paler outside, with five equal petals. It occurs in arid rocky places of the coast and hills of Queensland, New South Wales, and Victoria. It flowers all the year.

PSEUDERANTHEMUM VARIABILE

This is a small variable plant ranging in height from several centimetres to over 30 cm, entirely smooth or minutely hairy. The leaves are rounded, stalked, 3 to 8 cm long. The white or purple flowers are solitary or in groups of two or three in the axils of small bracts. The slender tube formed by the five petals is 5 cm or a little longer, and the expanded portion nearly as long. It is widely distributed in Queensland and New South Wales. It flowers in summer and autumn.

AUSTRALIAN BUGLE

Ajuga australis

This small pubescent perennial has radical leaves, rounded and contracted into a long stem, and often toothed. The flowers are produced on an erect stem which also carries small sessile leaves. The flowers are usually blue or deep-purple, about 2 cm long, and nearly sessile. The corolla tube expands into a lipped form. It is common on sandy and rocky outcrops of the coast and inland in the eastern States, South Australia, and Tasmania. It flowers in spring and summer.

PLATE 30

KERAUDRENIA HILLII

ISOTOMA AXILLARIS

AUSTRALIAN BUGLE
Ajuga australis

PSEUDERANTHEMUM VARIABILE

PLATE 31

DAMPIERA STRICTA

LOVE CREEPER
Comesperma volubile

LEAFLESS MILKWORT
Comesperma defoliatum

LOBELIA GRACILIS

PLATE 31

DAMPIERA STRICTA

The rather angular habit of this small erect shrub and its toothed or smooth somewhat succulent dark-green narrow leaves make it easily recognizable. The flowers are blue, several on one flowering stem. The sepals are rusty-hairy. The petals are split down one side, the underside covered with rust-coloured hairs. It grows in poor sandy soil in the eastern States and Tasmania, flowering in spring and summer and sometimes into the winter.

LOVE CREEPER
Comesperma volubile

The flowers of this plant are similar in structure to those of *C. ericinum*. They are a delicate blue, purple, mauve, pink or white, and are produced in loose racemes. It is one of the most delicate of our bush flowers and is sometimes confused, at a casual glance, with the pea flowers. It is common in the sandy areas of the eastern coast and tablelands, and flowers in spring and summer.

LEAFLESS MILKWORT
Comesperma defoliatum

This is a slim erect plant found on heathy swamps in eastern Australia. The flowers are blue and the "wings" are only slightly longer than the other sepals, so that it does not closely resemble the pea types as do some other Comespermas. The stems are wiry and the leaves are very small. It flowers in spring and summer.

LOBELIA GRACILIS

The flowers of the Lobelias are deep-blue, purple, or almost white. They are slender, delicate plants, with three of the five petals much larger than the others.

L. gracilis is a slender herb up to 10 cm high, with rounded, deeply divided leaves and long loose spikes of flowers, a few on each stem. The central petal of the three large ones is very broad. It is found on the sandy coastal patches of Queensland and New South Wales, flowering in summer and autumn.

PLATE 32

MOSQUITO OR GNAT ORCHID
Acianthus reniformis

This terrestrial orchid is a small form usually under 30 cm high. The basal leaf is kidney-shaped, about 2 cm long, the stem about 20 cm high, with one to seven reddish flowers. The sepals and petals are all equal, narrow, except the labellum which is broad and flat, with a minute point, the raised portions dark-red. It occurs widely on the coast and inland in all States, and flowers in winter and early spring. The stem in the drawing has been shortened for convenience.

CLIMBING ORCHID
Galeola cassythoides

This is a saprophytic, leafless orchid, which climbs as high as 6 m up the stems of plants by means of sucker-like roots. The flowers are in much-branched inflorescences, very numerous, varying in colour from brown to a pale golden-yellow, the labellum always paler. The sepals and petals are about 1 cm long. The labellum is lobed, the central lobe being indented. It occurs in Queensland and New South Wales, flowering in spring.

SARCOCHILUS OLIVACEUS

The stems of this orchid are short, the leaves are flaccid, dark-green, rather broad and falcate. There are three to ten flowers in the inflorescence, with rather narrow segments, of a peculiar olive-green, almost as though coated with gold below the green, the labellum whitish with red markings. The flowers are faintly and delicately fragrant. It grows in brush forests of the coast of Queensland and New South Wales. It flowers in the late spring or early summer.

SPOTTED EMU BUSH
Eremophila maculata

This is a tall shrub of the western districts of Queensland, New South Wales, Victoria, and South Australia. It varies in height from 1-3 m, the branches hoary, with broad smooth leaves 2 cm long. The flowers are tubular, the stamens frequently protruding, two long and two short. The petals are reddish-brown, brown, pink, or whitish, smooth outside, often spotted with yellow, with pink or red spots on the inside of the tube, with an upper lip of four pointed petals and a lower lip of one blunt, reflexed petal. The fruit is succulent, smooth, and globular. It flowers in spring and summer.

PLATE 32

MOSQUITO OR GNAT ORCHID
Acianthus reniformis

CLIMBING ORCHID
Galeola cassythoides

SARCOCHILUS OLIVACEUS

SPOTTED EMU BUSH
Eremophila maculata

PLATE 33

BLACK OR SOUTHERN SASSAFRAS
Atherosperma moschatum

WILD GRAPE
Cissus antarctica

HIBISCUS HETEROPHYLLUS

COMMON FRINGE-MYRTLE
Calytrix tetragona

PLATE 33

BLACK OR SOUTHERN SASSAFRAS
Atherosperma moschatum

Sassafras is a tree up to 12 m high with a short-grained, black, aromatic bark. It has opposite entire leaves 4–8 cm long, with entire or irregularly toothed margins, shining above, greyish-green beneath and tiny cream-coloured flowers, pistillate or staminate, each enclosed in two pink bracts. Some flowers have stamens and pistils. After the flowers die the sepals persist round the several single-seeded reddish shining fruits. It grows in mountain gullies of Queensland, New South Wales, Victoria, and Tasmania, and flowers from August to October.

KANGAROO VINE OR WILD GRAPE
Cissus antarctica

In the richer jungle country of the coast of southern Queensland and New South Wales this climbing plant is common. It has a woody stem with simple rounded leaves, paler underneath, usually toothed. The flowers are small, in short, dense inflorescences, and covered with rusty hairs. The berries are round and black. It flowers in spring and summer.

HIBISCUS HETEROPHYLLUS

The native species of *Hibiscus* are soft-wooded types which commonly occur in the more sheltered regions of the open forest or in the brush country of all the States.

H. heterophyllus is a very beautiful shrub or small tree growing to 6 m with pale-pink or white flowers with a reddish-purple throat and a purple staminal tube. It is found in Queensland and New South Wales. The leaves vary considerably from one another, three-lobed when young, entire and lanceolate on flowering branches, and glabrous. It flowers in spring and summer.

COMMON FRINGE-MYRTLE
Calytrix tetragona

This is a dainty shrub up to 1.5 m in height, with attractive heath-like foliage. The flowers, borne in leafy clusters, are white or less commonly, delicate pink, star-shaped, with about twenty stamens and with the sepals extending into hair-like awns. The sepals remain and enlarge during the ripening of the fruit. They turn a rich bronze colour and are very attractive. The plant occurs throughout Australia (except in the north) on sandy soils. It flowers profusely in spring.

PLATE 34

CUT-LEAF MINT BUSH
Prostanthera incisa

This is a small bushy pubescent plant 1–2 m high, with rounded leaves, often toothed, 1–2 cm long. It has a pleasant aromatic scent. The violet or purple flowers are on short stalks, in terminal short few-flowered inflorescences, or solitary in the leaf axils. They are somewhat bell-shaped, with two lips, the lower lip of three, the upper lip of two petals. It occurs on the coast of Queensland, New South Wales, and Victoria, usually in moist land. It flowers in spring and is commonly found in gardens.

AUSTRALIAN BINDWEED
Convolvulus erubescens

All over the eastern side of Australia, in grasslands, this small flowered *Convolvulus* is to be found. It is prostrate or trailing, with narrow or heart-shaped variable leaves, and solitary bright-pink open flowers 1–2 cm long. It flowers throughout the summer and into autumn.

PURPLE VIOLET
Viola betonicifolia

Wild violets are among the daintiest of our plants, found growing in moist, shady places in all the eastern States.

The deep-purple of this comparatively large violet makes it specially attractive. The leaves are broad or rounded, 3–5 cm long, springing from the base of the plant. The five petals are nearly 1 cm long, the lateral ones bearded inside, the outer one shortly pouched. It flowers in spring and all summer, and occurs in the damp forest lands of all the eastern States.

SCALY BUTTONS
Leptorhynchus squamatus

A dainty little plant (35 cm is quite a tall specimen), it has cottony down thickly spread over the young parts and under-surface of leaves. The leaves are narrow and pointed, 1 to 2 cm or more in length. The tubular flowers are yellow, and surrounded by petal-like dry bracts, woolly, with small coloured smooth tips. It occurs in Queensland, New South Wales, Victoria, and South Australia on dry sandy open country of the inland. It flowers in spring.

PLATE 34

CUT-LEAF MINT BUSH
Prostanthera incisa

AUSTRALIAN BINDWEED
Convolvulus erubescens

PURPLE VIOLET
Viola betonicifolia

SCALY BUTTONS
Leptorhynchus squamatus

PLATE 35

NATIVE FUCHSIA
Correa reflexa

LARGE CHRISTMAS BELL
Blandfordia grandiflora

RED AND GREEN KANGAROO PAW
Anigozanthos manglesii

BLACK-EYED SUSAN OR HEATH PINKEYE
Tetratheca ericifolia

PLATE 35

NATIVE FUCHSIA
Correa reflexa

The name Native Fuchsia is also used for *Epacris longiflora* in New South Wales. *C. reflexa* is a small shrub with rough, opposite stem-clasping leaves and long, attractive bell-shaped flowers, red with yellow tips, or sometimes entirely green. There are four petals, and the stamens protrude beyond them. It occurs in sandy soil on the coast of all States though is limited to only the south-east of Western Australia. It flowers in late spring.

LARGE CHRISTMAS BELL
Blandfordia grandiflora

There are four species of Christmas Bells in Australia; three in New South Wales, two in Queensland and one in Tasmania. As many as twenty large flowers have been known on a single flowering stem of this magnificent species. The plant is bulbous, with long grass-like leaves often 30 cm or more in length coming from the base. The three sepals and the three petals are united to form a bell, narrow at the base and abruptly inflated. Christmas Bells are common in the swampy lands of the coast and parts of the Dividing Range of Queensland and New South Wales. This species is more commonly found in the northern parts of New South Wales, and sometimes extends to the tablelands. It flowers in summer.

RED AND GREEN KANGAROO PAW
Anigozanthos manglesii

This sedge-like plant has stems 60–100 cm high loosely covered with red wool. The smooth leaves, produced at the base of the plant, are 15–30 cm in length and 1 cm in width. The flowers are in inflorescences covered with green wool except at the base where it is red. They are about 8 cm long, narrow and slightly incurved, split open nearly to the base. It grows in sandy soil on the Western Australian coast, flowering in spring.

BLACK-EYED SUSAN OR HEATH PINKEYE
Tetratheca ericifolia

This is a small dainty shrub with narrow whorled leaves on long stalks, and open, delicate four-petalled purplish-red or pink flowers borne singly in the leaf axils. It is common in the coastal area of New South Wales between Port Jackson and Newcastle, flowering most of the spring and summer.

PLATE 36

HEATHY PARROT PEA
Dillwynia retorta

This is one of the commonest and most charming plants of the sandstone coastal land of all the Australian States except South and Western Australia. The leaves are fine and heath-like, and the flowers small, pea-shaped and so profuse that the small bushes, rarely more than 1 m high, are literally a mass of yellow during the flowering period. The large spreading petal at the back (standard) has a splash of red at the base, as have also the lateral or wing petals. It flowers in spring.

LARGE-LEAF BUSH PEA
Pultenaea daphnoides

The dense, compact heads of this species readily distinguish it from the large number of native yellow pea flowers. The leaves are flat, usually wedge-shaped and set close together. Each has a fine pungent point. The numerous yellow pea flowers in the head are so densely packed that they give the appearance of a single large bloom. It occurs in New South Wales, Victoria, South Australia, and Tasmania abundantly, on coastal sandstone and sometimes inland. It flowers during October and November.

GREEN BOTTLEBRUSH
Callistemon pinifolius

This is a small straggling rigid shrub 60–120 cm high. The leaves are narrow, 5–10 cm long. The flowering spikes are fairly short, 5–8 cm long and filaments of the stamens are green. It is now a rather rare plant, once occurring fairly commonly in the more or less open sandy parts of Liverpool, Randwick, and similar localities near Sydney, New South Wales. It flowers during October and November.

TOOTHED OR TWINING GUINEA FLOWER
Hibbertia dentata

This trailing shrub likes the brush forests and the richer open land of the coasts of Queensland, New South Wales, and Victoria, although it is also found occasionally on the open sandstone. The leaves are distinctly toothed, and the open yellow flowers are 4–10 cm across. There are five free petals, readily deciduous, and a large number of short stamens. The sepals remain round the developing fruits, which are red when ripe. It is very attractive, and flowers in spring and summer.

PLATE 36

HEATHY PARROT PEA
Dillwynia retorta

LARGE-LEAF BUSH PEA
Pultenaea daphnoides

GREEN BOTTLEBRUSH
Callistemon pinifolius

TOOTHED OR TWINING GUINEA FLOWER
Hibbertia dentata

PLATE 37

CASSIA FLORIBUNDA

GOODENIA STELLIGERA

FINE-LEAF GEEBUNG
Persoonia pinifolia

ACACIA FARNESIANA

PLATE 37

CASSIA FLORIBUNDA

Cassias have open five-petalled yellow flowers. Of wide distribution, several are cultivated in Australia for decorative purposes, their yellow flowers making a glorious display during autumn.

Like most Cassias this has compound leaves and bright-yellow flowers mostly borne in heads in the axils of the upper leaves. The flowers are about 4 cm across. A spring flowerer, this species of coastal Queensland and New South Wales has been introduced from tropical America.

GOODENIA STELLIGERA

Most Goodenias are yellow-flowering plants, entirely Australian, with five-winged petals, unequal and split to the base.

This *Goodenia* grows 30–45 cm high, with thick, narrow, smooth, entire or toothed leaves, radical, 5–15 cm long. The hairy yellow flowers are produced many on a single stem, opening from the base and remaining in flower for a long period. It is found on the coastal lands of Queensland, New South Wales, and Victoria, flowering in spring and early summer. The stem in the specimen figured has been shortened for convenience.

FINE-LEAF GEEBUNG
Persoonia pinifolia

This Geebung is recognized by its fine, delicate, pine-like foliage and supple, slender branches which frequently hang down when the additional weight of the fruits is given them. The hairy yellow tubular flowers are crowded together at the tops of the branches. The ovoid fruits are green in the early stages, ripening through a series of rich bronze and red tints. The plant grows in the sandy soil of the central coast of New South Wales, flowering in spring.

ACACIA FARNESIANA

The only wattle known to occur in both northern and southern hemispheres is this species, possibly introduced by early visitors from tropical America. It is found in Australia in the Northern Territory, Queensland, New South Wales and also in South Australia. It has a strangely inflated pod, which can float for many days without injury to the seed. It has fine feathery leaves with spiny sharp-pointed stipules, and deep-golden-yellow balls of flowers. From this species perfume is distilled. It flowers in spring.

PLATE 38

COASTAL MYALL
Acacia glaucescens

The Myall of the coast is a small spreading tree, truly magnificent in full bloom and extremely elegant at other times. It is one of the wattles. The glaucous foliage is soft and attractive. The "leaves" are 10–15 cm long, rather sickle-shaped, with three to five more prominent veins. The flowers are borne in long, delicate yellow catkin-like spikes, and have a delicate fragrance. The pods are narrow-linear and irregularly twisted. It occurs in Queensland, New South Wales, and Victoria on the coast and mountains, flowering in September and October.

BOSSIAEA HETEROPHYLLA

Here is one of the "Eggs and Bacon" or Yellow Pea tribe. This small shrub is readily distinguished by the somewhat flattened stems carrying leaves which vary considerably in size and shape. The flattened stems make it unnecessary for the plants to have many leaves, and, since it is through the leaf-surface that water is lost by evaporation, this modification enables the plant to live in poor sandy soil where water is scarce. The flowers are borne in the leaf axils. It is found in Queensland, New South Wales, and Victoria on the poor sandy stretches. The pea flowers are yellow with a brick-red keel, and are among the most beautiful of the group. It flowers from late winter to early spring.

HANDSOME FLAT-PEA
Platylobium formosum

This straggling plant is rather like Cinderella in the transformation which takes place when the blossoms appear. The flowers are yellow and solitary in the leaf axils, which are set rather far apart. The large flowers, up to 3 cm across the standard (large petal at the back), are well displayed against the harsh, coriaceous, stiff leaves. The touch of red at the back of the standard and on the wings and keel greatly enhances the richness of the blooms. The pod is flat and slightly winged. It is a common sandstone and gravel-country plant of Queensland, New South Wales, Victoria, and Tasmania and flowers in spring.

PLATE 38

COASTAL MYALL
Acacia glaucescens

BOSSIAEA HETEROPHYLLA

HANDSOME FLAT-PEA
Platylobium formosum

PLATE 39

WESTERN WONGA VINE
Pandorea pandorana

RED-FLOWERED GREENHOOD
Pterostylis coccinea

SMALL ST JOHN'S WORT
Hypericum gramineum

HYMENOSPORUM FLAVUM

PLATE 39

WESTERN WONGA VINE
Pandorea pandorana

Interior Queensland and New South Wales are the home of this woody shrub with twining branches. The leaves have nine to eleven narrow leaflets on narrow, somewhat jointed stems. The flowers, borne in terminal inflorescences, are tubular, the tube cream, the throat velvety-hairy and marked with brown streaks or blotches, and the expanded portion brownish. It flowers in spring. (Some botanists regard this form as another species, *P. oxleyi.*)

RED-FLOWERED GREENHOOD
Pterostylis coccinea

The rather unusual crimson or olive-red flowers of this species are sometimes green with darker stripes, solitary and 3–5 cm long, the upper tip tapering to a fine point which bends over the lower sepals for almost 3 cm, the single upper sepal much longer than the two upper petals. The lower lip has a broad space between the lobes, each sepal curving upwards in a long, fine point. The leaves are linear and bract-like, not arranged in a basal rosette. It is a New South Wales species of the highland, mainly on the Dividing Range, flowering in summer.

SMALL ST JOHN'S WORT
Hypericum gramineum

This is one of the native Hypericums, occurring throughout Australasia. Several other species, natives of Europe and Asia, have invaded Australia and infested the wheatlands, where it has been necessary to declare them noxious. The small species figured is a rather stiff, small perennial with stem-clasping leaves and small open five-petalled pale-yellow flowers about 1 cm in diameter. It flowers throughout the summer months. The stem in the specimen figured has been shortened for convenience.

HYMENOSPORUM FLAVUM

There is only one species of this genus. It occurs in New Guinea and Australia. It is a handsome, evergreen shrub or small tree with large yellow five-petalled flowers fading to white after pollination. The fruit is about 2 cm long, and is covered with silky hairs. It is found in Queensland and New South Wales, mostly in the rich coastal land. It flowers in early spring.

PLATE 40

CHRISTMAS BUSH
Ceratopetalum gummiferum

Two very beautiful Australian plants belong to the genus *Ceratopetalum*—the Christmas Bush and the Coachwood. They occur mainly in the rich gullies of the coast and the Dividing Range in New South Wales. Some other species occur in northern Queensland.

When the Christmas Bush is in flower in November and early December the bush is covered with a mass of tiny white flowers, very attractive to small flies and native bees. After pollination the five free calyx lobes commence to enlarge and colour and, in a short time, the bush is ablaze with its bright-red young fruits, resembling flowers because of the persistent calyces. It is one of the marvels of our bushland, and does well in cultivation.

PINK WEDDING BUSH
Ricinocarpos bowmanii

This is mainly an inland species of Queensland and New South Wales, occurring commonly on the hillsides. The leaves are narrow, usually under 2 cm long, and covered with whitish hairs on the under-surface. It has clusters of white or pale- or deep-pink open five-petalled starry flowers, making a most attractive display in spring and early summer.

MELASTOMA DENTICULATUM

This is a variable small shrub, more or less covered with bristles. The large purple or white flowers are produced in clusters and are about 7 cm across. They are very attractive. The fruit is round, about 1 cm in diameter, with a purplish flesh in which the seeds are embedded. It occurs in richer parts of the northern coasts of Queensland, New South Wales, Western Australia and the Northern Territory and flowers in spring and early summer.

BORONIA PINNATA

This feathery-leafed Boronia is frequently associated in the field with *B. ledifolia*. Its pinnate leaves and somewhat lighter coloured flowers, usually produced in groups of three, make it a daintier plant. It flowers in early spring, a little later than *B. ledifolia*. It occurs in Queensland, Victoria, and New South Wales, on the coast.

PLATE 40

CHRISTMAS BUSH
Ceratopetalum gummiferum

PINK WEDDING BUSH
Ricinocarpos bowmanii

MELASTOMA DENTICULATUM

BORONIA PINNATA

PLATE 41

DESERT ROSE
Gossypium sturtianum

FRINGED VIOLET OR COMMON FRINGE-LILY
Thysanotus tuberosus

FOREST DAISY-BUSH
Olearia cordata

DOTTED DOUBLETAILS
Diuris punctata

PLATE 41

DESERT ROSE

Gossypium sturtianum syn. Cienfuegosia gossypioides

This lovely plant has been well named, for it shows its magnificent open purple flowers, often up to 10 cm across, in some of the most arid areas of Queensland, New South Wales, South Australia, and Western Australia. It is about 1 m high, smooth and greyish-green, flowering in late winter and early spring. It is difficult to believe that the harshest conditions of our inland areas can produce a plant with such exquisite and delicate blooms.

FRINGED VIOLET OR COMMON FRINGE-LILY

Thysanotus tuberosus

The three delicate fringed petals of this plant, much larger and more conspicuous than the sepals, are a rich-purple. The leaves are basal, narrow and up to 15 cm long. Flowers are arranged irregularly on a flowering stalk 15–30 cm high. Common in grasslands all over Australia, except the far north, it flowers in spring and summer.

FOREST DAISY-BUSH

Olearia cordata syn. O. adenophora

This rather rare species belonging to the Dividing Range of Victoria may attain a height of 1.5 m. The leaves, a little over 2 cm long, are sticky, narrow, and blunt, with rolling margins. The flower-heads are solitary with thin, curling, purplish outer florets ("petals") and yellow central ones. It flowers in spring. The plant figured is not this species but one not yet named.

DOTTED DOUBLETAILS

Diuris punctata

The lower sepals of this beautiful terrestrial orchid are extended under the rest of the flower as long narrow tails. The painting was made from a rather unusual dark-coloured South Coast form with narrow petals and an exceptionally long labellum.

The pale-lilac or dark-purple colour of the flowers distinguishes it from other species. The plants are slender, and varying in height from 5–60 cm, with a few or as many as ten flowers in an inflorescence. There are generally two leaves, much shorter than the flower stem. Sometimes the flowers are very large, the lateral sepals as long as 8 cm. The labellum is often spotted with purple. This orchid is found in Queensland, New South Wales, Victoria, and South Australia, in the richer parts of the coast and inland, and on to the western slopes. It flowers in spring and early summer.

PLATE 42

(In these four figures the stem has been shortened for convenience in size.)

SCENTED FAN FLOWER
Scaevola calendulacea

The flowers of this widely distributed genus are white, blue, yellow, or red, the five petals nearly equal, split to the base and spreading. The succulent leaves of this species enable it to inhabit the sand dunes of all the eastern States. The pale-blue fan-shaped corolla is 1–2 cm long, very dainty in appearance and with a delicate light perfume. The fruits are conspicuous, being large purple, and succulent. It flowers in spring and summer with occasional blooms in winter and autumn.

BLUE OR TUFTED LILY
Stypandra caespitosa

The conspicuous bright-yellow stamens stand out against the deep-blue or purple of the open flowers, and make this plant very attractive. It is slender, 30–60 cm high, with basal narrow leaves 15–30 cm long. The flowers are produced in spreading inflorescences, the sepals and petals, three of each, are both coloured and spreading, up to 1 cm in length. It is found in sandstone country of the coast and Dividing Range of Queensland, New South Wales, Victoria, and Tasmania, flowering in late summer.

BURMANNIA DISTICHA

On the open coastal heath or swampy country of Queensland and northern New South Wales this richly coloured little plant has its home. It is slender and unbranched, about 30–60 cm high, smooth, with broad, pointed, radical leaves 2–6 cm long. The flowers are a rich deep-blue or purple in a slender inflorescence. There are three small petal-like sepals and three petals, the sepals winged and angular. It flowers in spring and summer.

AUSTRALIAN OR BLUE PINCUSHION
Brunonia australis

B. australis is a small perennial with radical, somewhat rounded leaves and massed heads of tiny azure-blue flowers 0.5–2 cm in diameter on long, leafless, unbranched stems. It abounds in the dry inland areas of all the eastern States, and is found, also, in some coastal situations. It flowers in November and December.

42

PLATE 42

SCENTED FAN FLOWER
Scaevola calendulacea

BLUE OR TUFTED LILY
Stypandra caespitosa

BURMANNIA DISTICHA

AUSTRALIAN OR BLUE PINCUSHION
Brunonia australis

PLATE 43

MORNING GLORY
Ipomoea cairica

WAX-LIP ORCHID
Glossodia major

FINGER FLOWER
Cheiranthera linearis

BLUE WATERLILY
Nymphaea gigantea

PLATE 43

MORNING GLORY

Ipomoea cairica syn. I. palmata

Occurring widely in tropical Asia, Africa, and America, and often regarded as a weed in many places, this resplendent climber with delicate radiating leaves and large purple flowers up to 10 cm across is common on the coast of Queensland and the North Coast of New South Wales. There are usually seven flowers produced on a single stem, mostly a delicate light-purple but sometimes pink or white. It flowers profusely during October and November, but continues more sparsely for many months.

WAX-LIP ORCHID

Glossodia major

The solitary purple or blue flowers of this orchid, on their slender stems, are very lovely. The plants range in height from 15–30 cm or more, with a basal broad leaf 5–10 cm long. The segments of the flowers, except the labellum (lip), are spreading and equal, and the flower has a diameter of 4–5 cm. The labellum is narrow at the base, broad in the centre, and narrow at the tip, about half as long as the other segments, with two pubescent prominences on the broad part, and a large narrow appendage with a yellow head at the base. It is common on the sandy soil of the coast and inland of all the eastern States. It flowers in early spring. The stem has been much shortened for convenience of size.

FINGER FLOWER

Cheiranthera linearis

The blue flowers, 2 cm across, of this shrubby plant, which is often under 30 cm high, make it most attractive. It likes the richer soil of the tablelands, though it occurs also in the inland areas of Queensland, New South Wales, Victoria, and South Australia. The leaves are narrow, minutely toothed, and flat. The flowers are produced two and three on a single slender stem. It flowers in late spring.

BLUE WATERLILY

Nymphaea gigantea

This is a Queensland and New South Wales waterlily with beautiful blue flowers raised well out of the water, and almost round leaves with a very deeply heart-shaped base. The petals are free and numerous, surrounding a large number of bright-yellow stamens. It flowers from February to April.

PLATE 44

ISOTOMA FLUVIATILIS

This tiny creeping plant is found in moist places, particularly at high elevations. The flowers are white or pale-blue, five-petalled, very dainty, several on a stem, the leaves small and rounded, sometimes irregularly toothed. It is found in Queensland, New South Wales, and Victoria and flowers all the year round.

VEINED SUN ORCHID
Thelymitra venosa

The labellum (lip) of *Thelymitra*, unlike most orchids, is scarcely different from the other sepals and petals, and all are free so that the open flower is not orchid-like in appearance. The plants are slender, 30–60 cm high, with a solitary, rather long, narrow leaf. The flowers are produced in an inflorescence of one to six, 2 cm or less in diameter, blue with dark veins. The margin of the labellum is slightly crisped. It is found commonly on the highlands of New South Wales, Victoria, South Australia, and Tasmania. It flowers in summer for a long period.

WILD IRIS OR LEAFY PURPLEFLAG
Patersonia glabrata

The stem of this plant grows to a height of 7–15 cm, with two rows of narrow, spreading leaves 5–18 cm long, hairy at the base. The flowers are enclosed in brown, hairy, sheathing bracts, solitary or two or three together, purple, with an expansion of 2–4 cm. The three petals are papery and very delicate. They open for a brief period on sunny days but soon fade. It grows on the coast of Queensland, New South Wales, and Victoria, flowering in spring.

GYMNOSTACHYS ANCEPS

The long, narrow, tough, rigid leaves, several feet in length, give this plant a sedge-like appearance. The flowering stem is about 1 m high, flattened, and with sharp, hard edges. The flowers are produced in long petal-like bracts of 5–7 cm, the individual flowers being very tiny and crowded. The berries, round, black and nearly 1 cm in diameter, are more conspicuous than the flowers. It is found on the edge of scrub country of the coast and Dividing Range of Queensland and New South Wales and flowers in spring.

PLATE 44

ISOTOMA FLUVIATILIS

VEINED SUN ORCHID
Thelymitra venosa

WILD IRIS OR LEAFY PURPLEFLAG
Patersonia glabrata

GYMNOSTACHYS ANCEPS

PLATE 45

OLIVE SPIDER FLOWER
Grevillea oleoides

WARATAH
Telopea speciosissima

FERN-LEAF SPIDER FLOWER
Grevillea longifolia

NARROW-LEAF BOTTLEBRUSH
Callistemon linearis

PLATE 45

OLIVE SPIDER FLOWER
Grevillea oleoides

A New South Wales species of Spider Flower on protected sandstone stretches of the central coast and Blue Mountains. It is an erect, rather sparse shrub, 60 cm–3 m high, with fairly broad leaves, silky-hairy on the lower surface. The flowers, which are deep-red and silky-hairy on the outside, are crowded into terminal heads, making them very conspicuous so that honey-eating birds visit freely. It flowers in spring and summer.

WARATAH
Telopea speciosissima

The gorgeous Waratah needs no introduction. The "flower" is a collection of small individual dark-red blossoms whose attraction is enhanced by the beautiful red floral bracts at the base of the head. The stiff elongated leaves greatly aid in the attraction of the plant. The flowers are followed by curved "pods" carrying winged seeds. Under cultivation the plants are frequently more robust and floriferous than in their native homes on the rich part of the coast and Dividing Range of New South Wales. Cultivated plants live for many years, often bearing a considerable number of their lovely flower-heads on a single bush.

FERN-LEAF SPIDER FLOWER
Grevillea longifolia

A tall, handsome, spreading shrub 1–2.5 m high, this is a plant of forest and woodland usually found along Blue Mountains streams and South Coast areas of New South Wales. Foliage is dainty and fern-like and the branches long and graceful, giving it a most attractive form, enhanced by the delicate rusty-brown of the young leaves and long spikes of rich red or rust-coloured flowers. It flowers in summer and early winter.

NARROW-LEAF BOTTLEBRUSH
Callistemon linearis

The channelling of the upper side of the stiff linear leaves of this species distinguishes it. The shrubs are straggling and the leaves 5–12 cm long. The spikes of flowers are 5–10 cm long, deep-red or green with dark anthers. It occurs on the coast of New South Wales in slightly protected areas, flowering in spring and summer. It does well in cultivation and may be trimmed to a shapely form.

PLATE 46

RED FIVECORNERS
Styphelia tubiflora

The colour of the flowers of *Styphelia* is often sufficient to distinguish them. This species has bright-red flowers with a narrow tube, nearly 2 cm long, and long, exserted stamens. It is an erect bushy shrub, with narrow pointed leaves about 1 cm long. This is a New South Wales species widespread on the coast and tablelands. It flowers in winter and early spring.

RUNNING POSTMAN OR SCARLET CORAL PEA
Kennedia prostrata

This is a delicate little trailing plant, with flowers similar in shape to those of *K. rubicunda*, but smaller in size and a brilliant scarlet in colour. The rounded three-lobed leaves and the small but numerous gay flowers make it most attractive. It grows in the slightly richer coastlands and some inland parts of New South Wales, Victoria, South Australia, Western Australia, and Tasmania. It flowers in spring.

PAVONIA HASTATA

This small shrub is found on the sandy coastal areas of Queensland, New South Wales, and South Australia, though it is comparatively rare. It bears delicate reddish five-petalled open flowers about 8 cm across, and is very floriferous. The peculiar arrow-shaped leaves are very characteristic and picturesque. It flowers in spring.

RED-BEAK ORCHID
Lyperanthus nigricans

The strange translucent flowers of this plant have reddish or deep-purple stripes. Flowers, leaves, and stem turn jet-black on drying. There is a single large rounded fleshy leaf, flat on the ground, 2–5 cm long, and a flowering stem 8–15 cm high, with two to eight flowers on a stem and a large bract at the back of each flower. The upper sepal, about 2 cm long, is incurved, the lower sepals narrow. The labellum is pale with dark stripes and the tip is three-lobed. It is common on the sandy stretches of the coast of all the eastern States except Queensland, the flowers rarely developing except in the season following a bushfire. It also occurs in Western Australia. It flowers in early summer.

PLATE 46

RED FIVECORNERS
Styphelia tubiflora

RUNNING POSTMAN OR SCARLET CORAL PEA
Kennedia prostrata

PAVONIA HASTATA

RED-BEAK ORCHID
Lyperanthus nigricans

PLATE 47

PITTOSPORUM REVOLUTUM

NATIVE PASSIONFLOWER
Passiflora herbertiana

CUCUMBER ORCHID
Dendrobium cucumerinum

FINE-LEAF BUSH PEA
Pultenaea stipularis

PLATE 47

PITTOSPORUM REVOLUTUM

This is a yellow-flowered tall shrub or small tree with orange-coloured fruits, bearing bright-red sticky seeds. The leaves are hairy on the under-surface and the young shoots are beset with rust-coloured hairs. The sticky seeds are attractive to birds. It occurs in Queensland, New South Wales, and Victoria, and flowers from September to October.

NATIVE PASSIONFLOWER
Passiflora herbertiana

The leaves of this species are soft, large, and very ornamental, and the large flowers, pale orange-yellow or greenish with bright-orange stamens, are most attractive. The fruits are green and oval, somewhat smaller than that of the cultivated passion, but otherwise very similar in appearance. The elongate fruits are edible, but probably only palatable to an acquired taste. It is found in the rich coastal areas of Queensland and New South Wales, flowering in spring.

CUCUMBER ORCHID
Dendrobium cucumerinum

The curious tubercular nature of the blunt, thick leaves of this orchid makes them appear like little cucumbers. The stems are creeping. The inflorescences, arising in the leaf axils, are short, bearing one to four flowers. Sepals and petals are 1–3 cm long, pale-green, yellow, or cream, with reddish streaks. Found in coastal valleys of Queensland and New South Wales, often on river oaks, it flowers in midsummer and sometimes again in autumn.

FINE-LEAF BUSH PEA
Pultenaea stipularis

This is an erect shrub of somewhat stiff appearance growing to a height of 60 cm–2 m, with fine leaves with conspicuous brown stipules at the base. The bright-yellow pea-flowers are borne in stalkless clusters at the top of the branches and make a brilliant display. It is very common on the sandy coastal soils of Queensland and New South Wales and flowers in spring.

PLATE 48

TRIGGER PLANT
Stylidium laricifolium

The pollination mechanism of these small Australian plants is so arranged that contact with the lower end of the column causes it to spring up suddenly, hitting the agent making contact. In young flowers pollen is exploded on the back of the agent. In older flowers, with spent pollen, the ripe, sticky stigma, now exposed, may collect pollen on contact with a visiting pollinator. The small bright-pink flowers are attractive to insects such as bees.

The leaves are crowded, very narrow and pointed, 1–3 cm long. Plants are found in Queensland and New South Wales on the coast and highlands and flower in September and October.

BLUE LILLY-PILLY
Syzygium coolminianum

Most of the Eugenias have pink or red fruits, but in this species they are almost blue. It is a tall shrub or small tree 2–3 m high. The leaves are opposite, smooth, broad and a dark, glossy green. The flowers are white, and not very conspicuous. The blue fruits are about 2 cm in diameter. It occurs in rich gullies on the New South Wales coast, flowering in summer.

PINK FLANNEL FLOWER
Actinotus forsythii

The so-called petals of the Flannel Flowers are bracts surrounding the many tiny flowers in the centre.

This is a much-branched, slender plant limited in distribution to certain patches on the Blue Mountains of New South Wales. The leaves are narrower than those of the better-known species, and the heads of flowers about 2 cm in diameter. The bracts are white and covered with soft hairs, and the tiny flowers in the centre are surrounded by reddish-brown hairs. It flowers in summer.

AUSTRAL LADIES' TRESSES
Spiranthes sinensis

The tiny flowers of this terrestrial orchid are produced in an inflorescence, but their deep-pink colour, with white labellum, makes them rather conspicuous. The plants are 20–45 cm high, with a few grass-like leaves. The inflorescence is spirally twisted. It is common in swampy, coastal, and elevated areas in all the Australian States except Western Australia, and northwards through Asia to Japan. It flowers in late summer.

48

PLATE 48

TRIGGER PLANT
Stylidium laricifolium

BLUE LILLY-PILLY
Syzygium coolminianum

PINK FLANNEL FLOWER
Actinotus forsythii

AUSTRAL LADIES' TRESSES
Spiranthes sinensis

PLATE 49

SPOTTED DOUBLETAILS
Diuris maculata

RIVER BUTTERCUP
Ranunculus inundatus

BORONIA BARKERANA

HAIRY NET-BUSH
Calothamnus villosus

PLATE 49

SPOTTED DOUBLETAILS
Diuris maculata

The yellow flowers of this orchid, borne two to eight on a slender, fragile stem, are covered with brownish spots. The plants are about 30 cm high, with two or three narrow leaves about one-third the length of the stem. The petals and lower sepals are much curved backwards, the lower sepals ("tails") are crossed and shorter than the petals. It is widely distributed in grasslands of the coast and inland in all States except Western Australia. It flowers in spring. The stem of the specimen figured has been shortened for convenience.

RIVER BUTTERCUP
Ranunculus inundatus

This buttercup is common in the eastern States and Tasmania, and grows in or near water. It has creeping stems. The smooth leaves are on long, slender stalks and have three major divisions. The flowers have five to twelve narrow, free, glistening yellow petals and numerous stamens. It flowers most of the year.

BORONIA BARKERANA

This is a New South Wales species found in deep gullies near Sydney and on the South Coast. It is somewhat like the Native Rose, with simple rounded leaves, which are not so rhomboid as those of the latter. The pink flowers, too, are more loosely arranged and open more widely. It flowers in spring.

HAIRY NET-BUSH
Calothamnus villosus

This more or less hairy shrub is fairly common in the open forest country of Western Australia. The plant is a low bushy shrub with crowded linear terete or slightly flattened leaves 1–2 cm long. The flowers are deep-red, in dense clusters along one side of the stems. The long red stamens, which form the most conspicuous part of the flower, are arranged in five bundles. The petals are small, papery, and deciduous. It flowers in spring.

PLATE 50

LIGHTWOOD
Acacia implexa

This wattle produces a useful cabinet-wood. It has slightly greenish-grey foliage, the "leaves" being rather broad, sickle-shaped and many-nerved. It has a handsome, spreading habit and produces dense heads of globular flowers from December to March. The pods are long, narrow, and much curved. It is widely spread, being found on the Queensland and New South Wales coast, particularly along the riverbanks, and scattered throughout Victoria.

QUEENSLAND SILVER WATTLE
Acacia podalyriifolia

This lovely wattle is one of the most commonly cultivated species. It is a tall shrub, mealy-glaucous all over, and covered with fine hairs. The "leaves" are small, ovate in shape, rather oblique, with a single central vein. The fluffy, globular flower-heads, of a delicate light golden-yellow, are produced in dense heads in springtime. They have a delicate fragrance. The pod is very flat and also mealy-glaucous, making an attractive show. It is a Queensland and northern New South Wales species.

BLACK WATTLE
Acacia decurrens

Among the tallest of the wattles, this fine species has dark-green bipinnate leaves with numerous glands along the common petiole. The leaflets are very numerous, and are smooth. The fragrant golden flowers are produced in long heads in spring. It occurs naturally only in New South Wales though it has been extensively planted in other States. It is considered to be one of the best of our wattles.

SWEET-SCENTED WATTLE
Acacia suaveolens

Growing in some of the most exposed sandstone areas, heath and dry forest of Queensland, New South Wales, Victorian and Tasmanian coasts, this is a charming and sweet-scented species. It grows to a height of about 1–2 m, slender, with grey-green "leaves" varying very much in size, sometimes being long and narrow, up to 10 cm in length, often being shorter and broader, but always rather thick. The flower-heads are pale-yellow, in fluffy balls, very sweetly scented and enclosed in numerous bracts in bud. The pod is oblong, flat, and leathery, grey-green and very blunt. It has varying flowering periods according to situation, but is most profuse in late winter or early spring.

PLATE 50

LIGHTWOOD
Acacia implexa

QUEENSLAND SILVER WATTLE
Acacia podalyriifolia

BLACK WATTLE
Acacia decurrens

SWEET-SCENTED WATTLE
Acacia suaveolens

PLATE 51

VANILLA PLANT OR RUSH-LILY
Sowerbaea juncea

HELMET ORCHID
Corybas aconitiflorus

HIBISCUS DIVERSIFOLIUS

Plate 51

VANILLA PLANT OR RUSH-LILY
Sowerbaea juncea

In the coastal swamps of Queensland, New South Wales, and Victoria this small rush-like herb is common. It is a charming plant, 30–60 cm high, with short, narrow, rush-like leaves 5–15 cm long coming from the base. The flowers are numerous on a single, unbranched stem. The individual flowers are small, surrounded by dry bracts, a few only opening at a time, of a delicate mauve shade and with a gentle vanilla perfume. There are three free petals and three free, coloured sepals. As the flowers die they hang down, the sepals and petals being persistent. It flowers in spring.

HELMET ORCHID
Corybas aconitiflorus

These queer hooded little orchids produce solitary flowers from a single flat heart-shaped leaf. The under-surface of the leaf is purple. This is a terrestrial orchid with a flowering stem about 2 cm high. The flower is purplish or white. The sepals and petals with the exception of the labellum (lip) are united to form a hood, shaped like an inverted boat or cradle. This hood completely conceals the labellum, except for its tip. The labellum is tubular below, with a broad blade and a fringed margin. The tube has two spines at the base. The plant is widely distributed along the coast of Queensland, New South Wales, Victoria, and Tasmania. It flowers in winter and into spring.

HIBISCUS DIVERSIFOLIUS

Queensland and New South Wales provide a home for this species, which has large yellow or pink five-petalled delicate flowers, with deep-red centres, in terminal racemes. The leaves differ considerably from one another, being oblong or orbicular, more or less five-lobed, and irregularly toothed. Short hairs are sparingly scattered over the leaves. The foliage is very handsome, and makes an attractive plant, even without flowers. It is a rather stiff shrub 1.5–2 m in height. It flowers in spring and summer.

PLATE 52

BURR DAISY
Calotis dentex

This hairy Burr Daisy sometimes attains a height of 60–100 cm, but is usually shorter. The leaves are rather narrow, usually pointed and remotely toothed 2–5 cm long, often dilated and stem-clasping. The flower-heads are about 2 cm across, light-blue or pale-lavender, the outer florets ("petals") numerous, spirally rolled back after expansion, the flowers in the centre yellow. It is found in Queensland and New South Wales, commonly in the grasslands, flowering in early summer.

AUSTRAL STORKSBILL
Pelargonium australe

Like most of its kind, this *Pelargonium* is a lover of sandy soils, and is found in the poor coastal country of all the eastern States and Tasmania. It is a pubescent shrub, covered with soft white hairs, and varies from about 5 cm in height to over 60 cm, with heart-shaped, shortly lobed, wavy leaves. The rosy-red flowers are produced in close inflorescences on long stems arising from the leaf axils. The calyx is produced at the base into a spur, which holds the honey. There are five unequal spreading soft petals. The stamens are conspicuous, protruding from the flower. There are ten altogether, but only five to seven bear anthers. The fruits are long and beaked, and separate when ripe into five parts, each bearing one seed. The plant flowers in summer.

FAIRY WAX FLOWER
Eriostemon obovalis

This has been called Fairy Wax Flower on account of its dainty habit. It flourishes on barren sandstone ridges in the mountainous coastal country of New South Wales. It has delicate pink or white flowers and greyish-green thick leaves, usually about 1 cm long, broad at the ends and narrowed at the base, and with conspicuous, raised tubercular glands on them. The flowers are open, with five petals and ten stamens. This form responds rather well to cultivation. Its flowering period is from late spring through early summer.

PLATE 52

BURR DAISY
Calotis dentex

AUSTRAL STORKSBILL
Pelargonium australe

FAIRY WAX FLOWER
Eriostemon obovalis

PLATE 53

FLAX-LEAF PAPERBARK
Melaleuca linariifolia

KUNZEA AMBIGUA

TANTOON TEA-TREE
Leptospermum flavescens

ZIERIA SMITHII

PLATE 53

FLAX-LEAF PAPERBARK
Melaleuca linariifolia

The Flax-leaf Paperbark loves the ill-drained swamps of the coast. It is a handsome small tree, even when not in bloom, 6–9 m high, with a white, papery bark. The long narrow leaves are opposite and 2–4 cm long. The flowers are white and borne in long fluffy spikes. The bundles of stamens, forming the most attractive part of the flower and giving it the fluffy appearance, are sometimes as much as 1 cm long. It occurs on the coast of Queensland and New South Wales and flowers in summer.

KUNZEA AMBIGUA

The tiny white clustered flowers of this species make it an attractive plant in full flower. It is 2–3 m in height. The narrow-linear leaves are often clustered. The flowers are sessile, the petals and stamens white, but the petals are small and concealed by the longer, numerous stamens when the flowers are open. It is a very common coastal plant of Queensland, New South Wales, Victoria, and Tasmania, often forming dense thickets, and flowering in spring.

YELLOW TEA-TREE OR TANTOON TEA-TREE
Leptospermum flavescens

This slender shrub grows usually 3–4 m high with flat oval leaves about 1–2 cm long. The flowers are pale-cream or white, up to 1 cm in diameter. The flowers are open, the calyx smooth, the corolla with five petals and numerous free stamens. It is one of the commonest species, occurring on the coast district and tablelands of Queensland and New South Wales and flowering from November to January.

ZIERIA SMITHII

The unpleasant name of Stinkwood is sometimes applied to this plant because of the very acrid nature of the aromatic oil produced. It has small, delicate white flowers borne profusely in loose clusters. The flowers have four petals and four stamens. It grows on the richer coastal soil of Queensland, New South Wales, and Victoria, flowering in late spring.

PLATE 54

TOOTH DAISY-BUSH
Olearia tomentosa syn. *O. dentata*

This handsome shrub is 60–90 cm high, rather coarse, with rough, toothed leaves of dark-green covered with rusty hairs when young. The solitary heads of purple or white flowers, 2–5 cm across, are produced in great numbers. The outer florets ("petals") are long and usually a bluish-purple; the inner florets in the centre of the head are yellow. It flowers in spring. It occurs in New South Wales and Victoria on the coast and highlands, often growing in exposed, rocky situations.

SNOW OR SILVER DAISY
Celmisia asteliifolia

The hill-slopes of Kosciusko and other highland areas are white with this lovely daisy in the summertime. The plants are small and matted, with narrow silvery-hairy leaves with broad sheathing bases. The flowering stems are about 45 cm in length, carrying a solitary head of white flowers 5 cm across. It is found in New South Wales, Victoria, and Tasmania.

LOVE FLOWER OR TALL EVERLASTING
Helichrysum elatum

Usually perennial, this plant attains a height of 0.5–2 m. It has broad woolly-hairy leaves, and large flower-heads 2–5 cm across, either solitary or two or three on a stalk. The bracts are white and papery. The flowers have a delicate fragrance. It is a New South Wales species, widely distributed in somewhat elevated land. It flowers in late spring and early summer.

ROUGH DAISY-BUSH
Olearia asterotricha

This is a blue or white flowering species of the fairly rich soil of the coasts of New South Wales, Victoria, and South Australia. It is a shrub about 1 m tall, with narrow, toothed leaves about 2 cm long, very rough on the upper surface. The flower-heads are large and solitary. It flowers in October and November.

var. *parvifolia*

This variety, with smaller and more sinuate leaves, about 1 cm long, is found less commonly in similar localities.

PLATE 54

TOOTH DAISY-BUSH
Olearia tomentosa

SNOW OR SILVER DAISY
Celmisia asteliifolia

LOVE FLOWER OR TALL EVERLASTING
Helichrysum elatum

ROUGH DAISY-BUSH
Olearia asterotricha var. *parvifolia*

PLATE 55

SYDNEY GOLDEN OR SALLOW WATTLE
Acacia longifolia

VARNISH WATTLE
Acacia verniciflua

UMBRELLA WATTLE
Acacia osswaldii

COOTAMUNDRA WATTLE
Acacia baileyana

PLATE 55

SYDNEY GOLDEN or SALLOW WATTLE
Acacia longifolia

This common wattle of the sandy coastal areas of New South Wales, Victoria, and South Australia, varies remarkably in relation to its habitats. On the sand dunes of the beaches it becomes a prostrate, straggling plant, and in the lee of the hills it will assume the erect habit of a stout tree up to 6 m or more in height. It is a rather angular plant, with broad oblong "leaves" 8–12 cm in length. The long rods of golden flowers are very conspicuous and sweet-smelling and are produced commonly from August to November, according to situation. The pods are long and narrow.

VARNISH WATTLE
Acacia verniciflua

This handsome inland species of wattle is a stout, sticky, smooth shrub, with rather angular branches. The "leaves" are 5–10 cm long, usually rather narrow and sickle-shaped. The flowers are bright-yellow, in single globular heads and the pods are long and thin, rather hairy. It is common on hills of the interior of New South Wales, Victoria, South Australia, and Tasmania. Its flowering period varies to some extent with the rainfall, but it commonly blooms profusely between July and September.

UMBRELLA WATTLE
Acacia osswaldii

Found only in arid parts of New South Wales, Victoria, South Australia, and the Northern Territory, this shrub reaches a height of 2–3 m. The "leaves" are long, markedly striated, silvery-grey when young but becoming smooth and dark-green with age. The bright-golden balls of flowers are borne as twins in the leaf axils. The pod is broad, twisted, and much coiled. It flowers in summer.

COOTAMUNDRA WATTLE
Acacia baileyana

This species is restricted to some inland areas of southern New South Wales. It is one of the feathery-leaved wattles, with grey-green leaves, and it grows to the height of a small tree. The bright clusters of globular flowers make a fine spectacle in spring or early summer. The pods are long and fairly thin. It is a very commonly cultivated species, growing well in a variety of soils and situations, and escaping into bushland in many places.

PLATE 56

BLUNT-LEAF HEATH
Epacris obtusifolia

This is a swamp-loving heath, a slender, stiff, erect plant, with elongated, blunt leaves about 1 cm long. The flowers are creamy-white, closely set between the leaves, shortly tubular, the petals spreading widely at the mouth. It is found in Queensland, New South Wales, Victoria and Tasmania, on the coast and mountain ranges. It flowers in spring and summer and has a light fragrance.

FIVECORNERS
Styphelia laeta

Among the Australian heaths the Fivecorners are the largest and most beautifully coloured. It is a small Australian genus with sessile, crowded leaves and solitary flowers. The flowers are tubular, and vary in colour from yellowish or light-red to cream. The ends of the petals are curled back to reveal soft hairs in the throat. The five-cornered, edible fruit is enclosed in the bracts.

This is a small, pubescent shrub, with rounded, closely set, pointed, stiff leaves, about 2 cm long. It is found on the coast of New South Wales, and in the Blue Mountains and flowers in winter and early spring.

ROCK SPRENGELIA
Sprengelia monticola

This *Sprengelia* is found commonly on rocks under dripping water. It is usually less than 60 cm high. The flowers are white, with broad, spreading lobes, giving the appearance of an open rather than a tubular flower. It is found in New South Wales in the Blue Mountains, and makes a charming picture. It flowers in spring and summer.

SWAMP HEATH
Epacris paludosa

This heath is distinguished by its narrow, pointed leaves, about 0.5 cm long and the crowding of the flowers towards the ends of the branches rather than in the elongated form of *E. obtusifolia*. The flowers are smaller than in *E. obtusifolia*, and have a characteristic fragrance. It is found on the coast and tablelands of New South Wales and Victoria, usually in swampy lands, flowering in spring.

PLATE 56

BLUNT-LEAF HEATH
Epacris obtusifolia

FIVECORNERS
Styphelia laeta

ROCK SPRENGELIA
Sprengelia monticola

SWAMP HEATH
Epacris paludosa

PLATE 57

MILKMAIDS
Burchardia umbellata

FLANNEL FLOWER
Actinotus helianthi

SWEET-SCENTED DOUBAH
Marsdenia suaveolens

PLATE 57

MILKMAIDS
Burchardia umbellata

This plant bears an unbranched stem 30–60 cm high, slender but rigid. The leaves are narrow, with a sheathing base, up to 15 cm long, mostly basal. The flowers are white and starry, in a terminal inflorescence, the three sepals and three petals free and about 1 cm long. It is a widespread species in Australia, found in all the States, including Tasmania, from the coast to the table-lands, in sandy places. It flowers in spring and summer.

FLANNEL FLOWER
Actinotus helianthi

The size of the attractive bracts of this well-known Flannel Flower, up to 8 cm across, suggested a resemblance to the Sunflower, and that explains the specific name *helianthi*. The leaves are divided and covered with a soft felt of hairs on the upper surface, giving a grey-green appearance, and a thick mat of white hairs on the under-surface. The bracts are numerous, white with a small green tip, and are also thickly covered with protective hairs. It grows profusely in the sandy coastal areas of New South Wales and Queensland, in arid, exposed, often rocky situations. It flowers from October to December.

SWEET-SCENTED DOUBAH
Marsdenia suaveolens

This is a somewhat inconspicuous twining plant with a very sweet perfume. The small clustered white flowers are produced in the leaf axils; the petals are united into a short tube and then expanded to form small starry flowers about 1 cm in diameter, bearded in the throat. The scent is heavier at night and attracts night-flying moths. The leaves are broad, shortly stalked and thick, so that the veining is inconspicuous. It is distributed throughout the coast and Blue Mountain areas of New South Wales and flowers in summer.

PLATE 58

COAST ROSEMARY
Westringia fruticosa syn. *W. rosmariniformis*

Not only the leaves but the general habit of the plant closely resemble that of the Rosemary of the northern hemisphere. The plant is a bushy, compact shrub 50–100 cm high, with narrow leaves 1–2 cm long, with recurved margins and a white pubescence below, produced in whorls of four. The flowers are white with purple spots in the throat, solitary, sessile, in the leaf axils, two-lipped with two petals in the upper and three in the lower lip. There are four stamens completely enclosed in the flower. It is found on the sea coasts, commonly on the exposed cliffs of Queensland and New South Wales. It flowers in spring and summer, with occasional flowers in autumn.

BRANCHING GRASSFLAG
Libertia paniculata

This is a small plant with narrow grass-like leaves 45 cm long arising from the base of the plant. The flowering stem, 45–60 cm high, arises from the base of the plant and produces branched, loose inflorescences of dainty white flowers. The three sepals are small and white, the three petals white, free, between 1–2 cm long, widely spread and giving the plant a star-like appearance. It is found in the coastal districts, usually the less exposed parts of Queensland, New South Wales, and Victoria and flowers in summer.

ORANGE BLOSSOM ORCHID
Sarcochilus falcatus

The short stems of this epiphytic orchid are covered with sheathing leaf-bases. It inhabits densely wooded country and often grows on the branches of trees and on rocks. The leaves are short and rather thin, but firm, and light-green. The inflorescences are about as long as the leaves with three to ten white flowers, the labellum streaked with orange and red on the lateral lobes. It is a very variable plant, ranging from Queensland through New South Wales to Victoria, on the coast and flowers throughout the spring.

PLATE 58

COAST ROSEMARY
Westringia fruticosa

BRANCHING GRASSFLAG
Libertia paniculata

ORANGE BLOSSOM ORCHID
Sarcochilus falcatus

PLATE 59

FIELD DAISY
Brachycome decipiens

TONGUE ORCHID
Dendrobium linguiforme

STURT'S DESERT PEA
Clianthus formosus

PLATE 59

FIELD DAISY
Brachycome decipiens

The closest approach in habit among our daisies to the well-known European Daisy (*Bellis perennis*) is this *Brachycome*. It is a smooth, tufted plant, with oval, basal, entire or slightly indented leaves 2–8 cm long. The heads are large, white or purple, with a yellow centre. It is found in Queensland, New South Wales, Victoria, South Australia, and Tasmania, on the fairly rich sand of the coast and the Dividing Range or inland and at elevations. It flowers in spring.

TONGUE ORCHID
Dendrobium linguiforme

The leaves of this species are thick and fleshy, flat, tongue-shaped, with longitudinal grooves, nearly 2 cm long. The fragrant snow-white flowers are borne in inflorescences in the leaf axils, four to twenty or more. The sepals and petals are very narrow, and about 2 cm long. The labellum is concave at the base, three-lobed, with raised longitudinal lines. A common and beautiful plant on the Queensland and New South Wales coast, it is occasionally found west of the Dividing Range. An epiphytic plant, often growing on trees or rocks in sheltered situations, it flowers in spring.

STURT'S DESERT PEA
Clianthus formosus

When the desert blossoms, this pea is one of its first products. Its handsome, densely hairy, grey, feathery foliage covers large areas of ground with great rapidity, and within a few weeks the noble blossoms, 8–10 cm in length, deep-red with an almost black patch at the base of the standard, appear. Occasionally the flowers produced are "sports", varying in colour from the type specimen. The one figured is such a sport. The standard (back petal) is pointed and sharply turned back. The pod is very hard, about 5–6 cm long, containing several flat kidney-shaped seeds. To germinate the seeds under cultivation it is advisable to file a portion of the very hard outer covering to liberate the seedling. The Desert Pea usually flowers in October, though its period is largely dependent on the rainfall. It has been recorded from the sandy plains of the interior of New South Wales, South Australia, and in northern and Western Australia.

PLATE 60

DARLING LILY
Crinum flaccidum

The leaves of this lily are 45–60 cm long and about 2 cm broad. The inflorescence stems grow to a height of 45–60 cm, bearing six to fifteen shortly stalked white flowers. The tube of the flowers is 8–10 cm long, the segments 1–2 cm broad and 6–8 cm long. There are three petals and three petal-like sepals. It has a characteristic heavy, but delightful, fragrance. It is a very beautiful plant, and grows in moist areas, principally along the banks of the inland rivers. It is found throughout Australia except in Tasmania, and flowers in late summer.

HAIRY-TAILS
Ptilotus exalatus **var.** *semilanatus*

This is a small grass-like perennial herb usually under 30 cm high found on the western plains of New South Wales and in the arid parts of Queensland and South Australia. The leaves are smooth, often wavy and narrow. Its reddish flowers, subtended by brown bracts, are borne in long hairy spikes which have earned for it the name of Hairy-tails, Pussy-tails, or Lambs'-tails. The individual flowers are small, 1–2 cm long, the inner ones woolly inside at the base and all of them red at the tips. It flowers in winter and early spring. It is a true desert plant, the cut flowers remaining unwithered, even without water, for many months.

WHITE SMOOTH DARLING PEA
Swainsona galegifolia

The Darling Pea hides its poison under the delicate cloak of pink, mauve, dark red or white blossoms. Its poisonous property is a protection against animals. The leaves are soft, smooth, and pinnate. The flowers are pea-shaped. The standard (back petal) is nearly orbicular, with prominent hard appendages just above its claw. The keel (formed of the two front petals) is broad. The pod is 2–5 cm long and inflated. It occurs in the inland parts of Queensland, New South Wales, and South Australia, sometimes extending to the coast. It flowers in late spring or early summer, though the period varies considerably with the rainfall.

PLATE 60

DARLING LILY
Crinum flaccidum

HAIRY-TAILS
Ptilotus exalatus

WHITE SMOOTH DARLING PEA
Swainsona galegifolia

PLATE 61

BLACK THORN
Bursaria spinosa

GUM VINE
Aphanopetalum resinosum

MOCK ORANGE
Pittosporum undulatum

TRAVELLERS' JOY
Clematis aristata

PLATE 61

BLACK THORN
Bursaria spinosa

This species occurs commonly in eastern Australia and Tasmania. In open country it becomes very susceptible to Indian Wax scale, which it transfers to more delicate plants. It is a variable, spreading shrub with masses of white flowers in November or December and January. The fruit is thin and purse-like.

GUM VINE
Aphanopetalum resinosum

Christmas Bush (*Ceratopetalum gummiferum*) and *Aphanopetalum* are very close relations. In *Aphanopetalum*, however, the small flowers are succeeded by less conspicuously enlarged sepals. The rich coastal areas of Queensland and New South Wales are commonly inhabited by this species and it occurs rarely in eastern Victoria. It flowers in spring and early summer. It is a straggling shrub with simple, opposite leaves and inconspicuous white flowers.

MOCK ORANGE
Pittosporum undulatum

The Pittosporums are handsome shrubs or small trees much cultivated on account of their heavily scented flowers, which are white, yellow, or purple, and their attractive fruits. The white-flowering species are moth-pollinated, and are very heavily scented at night. When the fruit or pod splits open it reveals a yellow or orange lining embedded in which are shining black or red seeds.

The citrus-like leaves and orange-coloured fruits of this species have earned it its popular name. It is common to all the eastern States of Australia, and flowers from August to September.

TRAVELLERS' JOY
Clematis aristata

Clematis is a charming climbing plant with large white flowers up to 2 cm across, borne in loose clusters. The soft, indented leaves are most attractive. It grows rapidly and covers large areas, scrambling on whatever support is available. When the flowers wither, the long bearded "seeds", even more beautiful, take their place, and are gradually carried on the wind with the aid of the long feathery style. It flowers from September to October, and is found on the coast district and tablelands of all the States with the exception of South Australia.

PLATE 62

WEDDING BUSH
Ricinocarpos pinifolius

This is a widely distributed genus with very conspicuous open five- or six-petalled attractive white flowers, that appear in masses and give this shrub its common name. It is a coastal species of the east, a lover of poor, sandy soil, and found in Queensland, New South Wales, and Victoria. It has two types of flowers, one bearing stamens only, the other bearing pistils only. It flowers in spring.

BUTTONS OR SLENDER RICE FLOWER
Pimelea linifolia

All the Pimeleas are small shrubby plants with white, pink, yellow, or (in one Queensland species) red flowers. *P. linifolia* grows in the open sandy country on the eastern coast. It is a slender shrub, sometimes as much as 1 m high, though usually shorter. The flowers are collected into a terminal head surrounded by four broad, smooth bracts, and are white, tinged with pink. The bright orange-coloured stamens protrude from tubular flowers, and add to their attraction. It flowers in winter and early spring.

PHEBALIUM DENTATUM

The numerous clusters of small, delicate five-petalled yellow flowers produced by this plant make it very attractive. It differs from the Eriostemons in the fact that it has valvate petals while Eriostemons have imbricate petals and the flowers are usually smaller. It frequents the richer gullies and creek beds of the coast of New South Wales from Illawarra in the south to Port Stephens and north-east to the Gibraltar Ranges. It flowers in late spring.

WHITE OR WILLOW BOTTLEBRUSH
Callistemon salignus

This is a small tree, varying in height from 4.5–9 m. It has flat, fairly narrow leaves 4–8 cm long. The cream flowers are in spikes 4–8 cm long. The bark is papery, and the young foliage is a beautiful rich-red. It occurs in the coastal districts, and the near inland areas in swamps and along creeks in Queensland, New South Wales, and Victoria. It flowers in October and November, the new pink foliage appearing shortly before the cream flowers. It is cultivated fairly extensively and responds well.

PLATE 62

WEDDING BUSH
Ricinocarpos pinifolius

BUTTONS OR SLENDER RICE FLOWER
Pimelea linifolia

PHEBALIUM DENTATUM

WHITE OR WILLOW BOTTLEBRUSH
Callistemon salignus

PLATE 63

NATIVE RASPBERRY
Rubus rosifolius

BLUEBERRY ASH
Elaeocarpus reticulatus

SCRAMBLING LILY
Geitonoplesium cymosum

CRINUM PEDUNCULATUM

PLATE 63

NATIVE RASPBERRY OR ROSE-LEAF BRAMBLE
Rubus rosifolius

The Native Raspberries are climbing or scrambling plants typical of the rich brush country of the eastern coast. They have open five-petalled white flowers, rosaceous in form. The flowers are followed by succulent red edible fruits.

Although this plant has a scrambling habit and the stems are thorny, it does not climb. The leaves are divided and sprinkled lightly with hairs. The fruits are dark-red and elongate. It flowers in spring and early summer.

BLUEBERRY ASH
Elaeocarpus reticulatus

A remnant of the "brush" flora which once extended over the whole of eastern Australia, this lovely shrub is found in sclerophyll forest right down that coast today. It is of handsome habit with shining bright-red young foliage and masses of white, shower-like, pendulous flowers in spring, and bright-blue "berries" in summer. The mature foliage is dark-green, shining, lighter beneath, and with a wavy and indented margin.

SCRAMBLING LILY
Geitonoplesium cymosum

This is a tall, scrambling, lily-like plant, smooth, with narrow leaves 5–8 cm long. The flowers are in loose, usually terminal, inflorescences with purplish sepals and petals, about 0.5 cm in diameter. The fruit is a conspicuous feature, being black and nearly globular, about 1 cm in diameter when mature. It is found in coastal sandstone gullies of Queensland, New South Wales, and Victoria. It flowers in summer.

CRINUM PEDUNCULATUM

The Crinums are fairly robust, lily-like, bulbous plants, with few flowers, in short inflorescences, usually within bracts, white, rarely reddish. The fruits split to release many large seeds.

Each plant has several thick, leafy stems, growing to a height of 60 cm, the leaves thick, grey-green, about 1 m long and over 10 cm broad at the centre, about fifteen on a single stem. The flowering stems, up to 60 cm long, are produced in the axils of the lower leaves. It is found in the coastal, swampy areas of Queensland and New South Wales and flowers in spring.

PLATE 64

PEACH BLOSSOM TEA-TREE
Leptospermum squarrosum

The Tea-trees were so named from the fact that during one of Cook's expeditions a concoction was made from the leaves of one of these plants. The plants are shrubs with open five-petalled flowers with many stamens, resembling superficially the flowers of a rose. The fruit is a round, flattened capsule opening by numerous longitudinal slits to allow the escape of the many tiny seeds.

The beautiful peach-like blossom of this *Leptospermum*, often 2 cm across, has given it its common name. The shrub reaches a height of 1–2 m, with pointed leaves 0.5–1 cm long. Masses of flowers are borne, mainly on the thick, leafy branches. It commonly occurs in the central coastal districts of New South Wales, and flowers from spring to late summer. It makes a handsome garden plant, continuing in flower for a long period.

DWARF APPLE
Angophora hispida syn. *A cordifolia*

Most Angophoras are trees. This is a shrub 1–3 m high, with rough, coarse branches and opposite, sessile leaves, very broad and whitish on the under-surface. The flowers are produced in short, compact inflorescences. There are five sepals, five free spreading petals and numerous long white stamens forming an attractive flower 2 cm in diameter and very similar to coarse Eucalypt blossom. It is a common plant of the most arid sandstone areas of New South Wales in the Sydney and Gosford districts. It flowers in summer.

IRONBARK ORCHID
Dendrobium aemulum

One is reminded very much of a diminutive rock lily when one examines this orchid. The swollen stems are only 8–25 cm long, each stem often bearing two leaves. From the leaf axils rise the short inflorescences, one to four from an axil. The flowers are very slender, three to twenty in a head; the petals and sepals about 2.5 cm long, white, the labellum being tinged or streaked with purplish-red. It has a fragrant perfume. It is an epiphyte growing in open forest country exclusively on ironbarks, and in the brush, usually on Brush Box, from Queensland to southern New South Wales. It flowers in early spring.

PLATE 64

PEACH BLOSSOM TEA-TREE
Leptospermum squarrosum

DWARF APPLE
Angophora hispida

IRONBARK ORCHID
Dendrobium aemulum

PLATE 65

BOX-LEAF WAX FLOWER
Eriostemon buxifolius

IVY-LEAF VIOLET
Viola hederacea

BLACKWATTLE
Callicoma serratifolia

PLATE 65

BOX-LEAF WAX FLOWER
Eriostemon buxifolius

Wax Flowers are so called on account of their waxy petals. They have open flowers very similar to the Boronias, but the flowers of most species are larger and, instead of four petals and eight stamens, they have five petals and ten stamens.

This is a New South Wales species, common on the sandy coastal hills of Port Jackson, Port Hacking, and Broken Bay. The plant is smaller than that of the common Wax Plant and so are the flowers, but the shrub is extremely floriferous. The mass of pink or white flowers against the dark-green foliage makes it a popular bush plant. It flowers throughout the spring and into early summer.

IVY-LEAF VIOLET
Viola hederacea

The flowers of this violet are smaller than those of the purple Wild Violet, and are a delicate lilac, bluish, or even white. The petals are free and arranged like those of the cultivated violets. The leaves are smooth and rounded, 0.5–2 cm long, but broader than long. It flowers sparsely all the year through, but is prolific in spring and summer. It loves moist ground, especially the banks of running streams, and grows in all the eastern States.

BLACKWATTLE
Callicoma serratifolia

The long fine stamens of *Callicoma* are its most conspicuous feature. The plants are trees with opposite leaves, with flowers made attractive by the numerous fine stamens, giving it a superficial resemblance to Wattle (*Acacia*).

It appears that the first wood to be used in Australia for the wattles of the wattle-and-daub huts was cut from the trees of this species, which were common round the shores of Sydney Cove. Blackwattle Bay received its name on account of the many *Callicoma* plants in this area. Later Acacias came to be used for the same purpose. The leaves are dark-green above, light below, and daintily serrated on the margins. It occurs in Queensland and New South Wales, and flowers in spring and early summer.

PLATE 66

CALADENIA CUCULLATA

There are a large number of Caladenias in Australia, most of them in the west and the south. They are slender terrestrial orchids with a single leaf, the stem and leaf hairy. The labellum is marked with conspicuous glands, often very beautiful. There is a wide range of colour in the flower of this genus.

The solitary leaf of *C. cucullata* is long and thin, and there are sheathing, leaf-like bracts about the centre of the flowering stem, which is about 30 cm high and bears two to five flowers. The flowers are white inside, brown or purple outside, rough, and about 2 cm in diameter. The upper sepal forms a hood. The labellum is short and broad, but elongated into toothed, purple tips and covered with tiny hairy glands in four rows. This is a dainty species of the inland parts of southern New South Wales and Victoria. It flowers in summer.

WILD PARSLEY
Lomatia silaifolia

The Lomatias are common sandstone and shale plants of eastern Australia and Tasmania, most of them with dainty divided leaves, creamy-white flowers, and seed-pods with winged seeds.

This is a small shrub with deeply toothed, divided leaves and long loose spikes of cream flowers. The leaves are extremely handsome and are responsible for the well-known common name for the plant. The individual flowers are often more than 1 cm long, with conspicuous protruding styles. The fruits are black, about 1 cm long, and open to expose several light-yellow winged seeds, beautifully and neatly packed. It grows in the sandstone coastal country of Queensland and New South Wales and flowers in November and December.

CORAL HEATH
Epacris microphylla

Among the plants of the barren sandy or swampy areas of the eastern coast of Queensland and New South Wales, this is one of the commonest. It is a shrub of variable habit, ranging in height from 0.5–1 m, with tiny sessile heart-shaped leaves usually under 0.5 cm long. The small white tubular flowers, with lobes as long as the tube, are produced for long distances down the stem. The flowering period is winter and early spring.

66

PLATE 66

CALADENIA CUCULLATA

WILD PARSLEY
Lomatia silaifolia

CORAL HEATH
Epacris microphylla

PLATE 67

NEEDLEBUSH
Hakea sericea

DUMPLINGS OR COMMON APPLE-BERRY
Billardiera scandens

SWAMP LILY
Ottelia ovalifolia

PLATE 67

NEEDLEBUSH
Hakea sericea

The Hakeas are well-known plants of the arid sandstone of both the eastern and western sides of the continent. The flowers are small, sometimes gathered together into dense heads, and the fruits are hard, woody structures which open to release two winged seeds.

Among the flora of the open coastal country where the soil is a little richer than the sandstone patches, this tall silky shrub is quite common in both New South Wales and Victoria. The leaves are long, narrow, and pointed, 2–8 cm long. The flowers are white, with a pinkish tinge, and so massed together that they make a grand display in the early spring. Sometimes the flowers are a rich-pink and most attractive.

DUMPLINGS OR COMMON APPLE-BERRY
Billardiera scandens

This quaint little climbing plant has earned the name of Dumplings from the children because of the shape of its fleshy, cylindrical fruit, which is acid and edible. It is a slender climber, with bell-shaped yellow five-petalled flowers about 2 cm long, and occurs in the sandy patches along the whole of the eastern coast of Australia. The leaves are ovate or linear, 1–5 cm long, often with wavy margins. It flowers in late spring and summer.

SWAMP LILY
Ottelia ovalifolia

Among shallow freshwater ponds throughout Australia, except Tasmania, this is very common. It has ovate to elliptical leaves on long stalks which rise to float the leaves on the surface. The large white or pale-yellow flowers are held in a two-lobed tubular six-ribbed spathe (bract) about 4 cm long. There are three sepals and three papery petals, eight to twelve stamens, and a much-divided stigma with six to eight lobes in the centre. It flowers in late summer.

PART II

KEY TO FAMILIES AND TECHNICAL DESCRIPTIONS
OF PLANTS

KEY TO THE FAMILIES OF PLANTS

(NOTE: This key covers only the species referred to in the text. See foreword for instructions as to use.)

CLASS 1: DICOTYLEDONS

Embryo with two cotyledons. Stem, when perennial, with distinct rings of wood and bark. Leaves net-veined. Parts of flower usually in fours or fives or multiples of these.

Petals free or absent. Stamens inserted below the ovary ......Sub-class 1
Petals free or absent. Stamens inserted away from the base of the ovary
......Sub-class 2
Petals united. Stamens inserted away from the base of the ovary
......Sub-class 3
Petals united. Stamens inserted below the ovary ......Sub-class 4

SUB-CLASS 1

Ovary of several carpels, not united ......Series 1
Ovary of one carpel ......Series 2
Ovary of several carpels, united ......Series 3

Series 1
Flowers perfect
   Terrestrial plants (*Ranunculus inundatus* sometimes aquatic)
      Calyx deciduous. Seeds without aril ......RANUNCULACEAE
      Calyx persistent. Seeds with aril ......DILLENIACEAE
   Aquatic plants ......NYMPHAEACEAE
Flowers imperfect, often unisexual. Petals absent
      Stamens definite. Carpels solitary ......LAURACEAE
      Stamens indefinite. Carpels several ......MONIMIACEAE

Series 2
Flowers regular
   Stamens indefinite. Leaves opposite ......HYPERICACEAE
   Stamens definite
      Leaves covered in glandular hairs ......DROSERACEAE
      Leaves not as above
         Flowers small, sessile within 2 scarious bracts ....AMARANTHACEAE

Flowers not as above
 Sepals and petals 4 or 5, stamens twice
  as many as petals . . . . . .TREMANDRACEAE
 Sepals, petals and stamens 5 . . . . . .PITTOSPORACEAE
Flowers irregular
 Sepals, petals and stamens 5 . . . . . .VIOLACEAE
 Sepals 5, petals 3, stamens 10 or less . . . . . .POLYGALACEAE

Series 3
Sepals imbricate in bud
 Ovary entire . . . . . .CELASTRACEAE
 Ovary lobed
  Leaves deeply dissected . . . . . .GERANIACEAE
  Leaves simple or pinnate but not dissected
   Leaves pellucidly dotted . . . . . .RUTACEAE
   Leaves not dotted . . . . . .SAPINDACEAE
Sepals valvate in bud
 Anthers one-celled. Stamens monadelphous . . . . . .MALVACEAE
 Anthers two-celled
  Stamens monadelphous or definite . . . . . .STERCULIACEAE
  Stamens free and indefinite . . . . . .ELAEOCARPACEAE
  Flowers unisexual. Ovary three-celled . . . . . .EUPHORBIACEAE

SUB-CLASS 2

Ovary of one or several carpels, not united . . . . . .Series 1
Ovary of several carpels, united . . . . . .Series 2

Series 1
Carpels usually quite free
 Carpels one
  Fruit dehiscent
   Corolla irregular
    Two lower petals united . . . . . .FABACEAE
    Petals all free . . . . . .CAESALPINIACEAE
   Corolla regular . . . . . .MIMOSACEAE
  Fruit indehiscent . . . . . .THYMELAEACEAE
 Carpels several. Stamens indefinite
  Flowers large and conspicuous . . . . . .ROSACEAE
  Flowers small . . . . . .CUNONIACEAE
Carpels usually connate, separating at maturity
 Ovules several in each cell . . . . . .BAUERACEAE
 Ovules one in each cell . . . . . .APIACEAE

Series 2
Stamens indefinite (species described here)
 Flowers perfect and regular . . . . . .MYRTACEAE
Stamens definite

72

Stamens twice as many as petals	. . . . . . MELASTOMATACEAE
Stamens as many as petals	. . . . . . VITACEAE

Calyx lobes very small and inconspicuous	. . . . . . Series 1
Calyx lobes conspicuously developed	. . . . . . Series 2

Series 1

Epiphytes	. . . . . . LORANTHACEAE
Terrestrial plants	
Ovary superior. Perianth of one whorl	. . . . . . PROTEACEAE
Ovary usually inferior. Perianth of sepals and petals. Root parasites	. . . . . . SANTALACEAE

Series 2

Climbing plants with tendrils. Anthers versatile	. . . . . . PASSIFLORACEAE
Erect plants	
Flowers in close heads surrounded by an involucre of bracts	. . . . . . ASTERACEAE (COMPOSITAE)
Flowers in dense globular heads intermixed with bracts. Stigma enclosed in an indusium	. . . . . . BRUNONIACEAE
Flowers in loose inflorescences with no involucral or intermixed bracts	
Stamens connate with style	. . . . . . STYLIDIACEAE
Stamens free from style	
Stigma enclosed in an indusium. Anthers free	. . . . . . GOODENIACEAE
Stigma without indusium	
Anthers connate	. . . . . . LOBELIACEAE
Anthers free	. . . . . . CAMPANULACEAE

Corolla regular	
Ovary one- or two-celled	. . . . . . Series 1
Ovary three- or five-celled	. . . . . . Series 2
Corolla irregular	
Ovary entire	. . . . . . Series 3
Ovary deeply lobed	. . . . . . Series 4

Series 1

Ovary one-celled	. . . . . . MENYANTHACEAE
Ovary two-celled	. . . . . . SOLANACEAE

Series 2

Anthers two-celled. Leaves net-veined	
Stamens opposite petals	. . . . . . SAPOTACEAE
Stamens alternate with petals	. . . . . . CONVOLVULACEAE
Anthers one-celled. Leaves apparently parallel-veined	. . . . . . EPACRIDACEAE

73

Series 3

Ovary one-celled. Water or marsh plants ......LENTIBULARIACEAE
Ovary two-celled
   Fruit dry
      Herbs with seeds borne on a spiny process ......ACANTHACEAE
      Herbs with small seeds not borne on a spiny process
......SCROPHULARIACEAE
   Woody climbers. Seeds winged ......BIGNONIACEAE
   Fruit succulent
      Leaves opposite ......VERBENACEAE
      Leaves alternate ......MYOPORACEAE

Series 4

Corolla irregular ......LAMIACEAE
Corolla regular ......ASCLEPIADACEAE

CLASS 2: MONOCOTYLEDONS

Embryo with one cotyledon, the radicle not forming a distinct tap root. Stem, when perennial, with scattered vascular bundles and no distinct bark. Leaves usually with parallel veins. Parts of flower usually in threes or multiples of three, calyx frequently petaloid.

Stamens inserted above the ovary ......Sub-class 1
Stamens inserted below the ovary ......Sub-class 2

SUB-CLASS 1

Flowers mostly irregular Stamen fewer than 3 ......ORCHIDACEAE
Flowers regular. Stamens 3 or more
   Aquatic plants ......HYDROCHARITACEAE
   Terrestrial plants
      Anther cells separated by broad connectives ......BURMANNIACEAE
      Anther cells not separated by broad connectives
         Flowers with 3 stamens. Style branched ......IRIDACEAE
         Flowers with 3–6 stamens. Style simple
            Stamens 6; flowers subtended by spathes
......AMARYLLIDACEAE

            Stamens 3–6; flowers without spathes
......HAEMODORACEAE

SUB-CLASS 2

Sepals and petals three. Flowers bisexual
   Flowers regular. Mostly terrestrial
      Sepals usually petaloid ......LILIACEAE

Sepals herbaceous ...... COMMELINACEAE
Flowers irregular. Mostly aquatic
    Erect herbs with sword-shaped leaves. Stamens one
        ...... PHILYDRACEAE
    Tufted herbs with narrow radical leaves. Stamens three
        ...... XYRIDACEAE
Sepals and petals less than three, scale-like. Inflorescence enclosed in a spadix
        ...... ARACEAE

75

TECHNICAL DESCRIPTIONS OF PLANTS

Family DILLENIACEAE

Trees, shrubs, climbers or herbs with alternate or rarely opposite leaves without stipules. They are found chiefly in Australia, Africa, and Central America. Most members have astringent properties. It is not an important economic family, though a few members yield timber of commercial value.

Flowers perfect, solitary or in inflorescences. Sepals 5, persistent, imbricate in bud. Petals 5, rarely fewer, deciduous, imbricate in bud. Stamens hypogynous, indefinite, few or many, rarely definitely 10, free or united in clusters. Ovary of several carpels, free and distinct, or cohering at the base, 1-celled, 1 or more ovules in each.

Fruits indehiscent succulent, or dehiscent, opening along the inner edge or in 2 valves.

HIBBERTIA Andr.

Small shrubs with alternate leaves, and yellow or white, open solitary flowers. Petals thin and slightly undulate. Fruiting carpels enclosed in the calyx. Seeds ovoid or sub-globular, usually reddish-brown, shining, with a jagged or frilled aril.

Distribution: Mainly tropical, in Africa, Central America, and Australia. About 90 in Australia: 24 in Queensland; 22 in New South Wales; 14 in Victoria; 11 in South Australia; 65 in Western Australia; 39 in the Northern Territory; 10 in Tasmania. (G. Hibbert, nineteenth-century botanist.)

Stamens all on one side of the carpels, and all fertile.
Leaves alternate, coriaceous, shining. Erect shrub.
H. nitida (R. Br. ex DC.) Benth.
(pl. 28)
(*nitida*, shining; in reference to the glossy leaves.)
Stamens all round the carpels. Trailing shrubs.
Leaves stem-clasping, entire, alternate, silky-hairy below. Stamens all fertile.
H. scandens (Willd.) Gilg
(pl. 28)
(*scandens*, climbing.)
Leaves distinctly toothed, glabrous except when very young, petiolate. Some stamens sterile. Trailing shrub.
H. dentata R. Br. ex DC.
(pl. 36)

76

(*dentata*, toothed; in reference to the leaves.)

Family AMARANTHACEAE

Herbs or undershrubs of wide distribution, mainly in the warm parts of the earth, including a great number of plants commonly distinguished as "weeds" and some showy garden plants. Leaves alternate or opposite, entire, without stipules.

Flowers usually perfect, in axillary or terminal spikes, each flower sessile within 2 scarious bracts and subtended by a scarious bract or a floral leaf. Perianth segments 5, imbricate in bud, rigid and scarious, or coloured. Stamens hypogynous, 5 or fewer, opposite the perianth segments, free or united at the base. Ovary 1-celled with 1 or several ovules, superior. Style simple or 2-3-fid.

Fruit membranous, indehiscent or circumsciss.

PTILOTUS R. Br

Herbs with alternate leaves and flowers in dense globular terminal spikes, with a woolly stem and scarious bracts. Perianth villous. Seeds usually shining.

Distribution: About 100 species, all restricted to Australia: 21 in Queensland; 15 in New South Wales; 5 in Victoria; 19 in South Australia; 60 in Western Australia; 19 in the Northern Territory.

(*ptilotus*, winged, feathered; in reference to the flowers.)

> Erect perennial with sepals tipped with red; inner sepals woolly at base.

P. exalatus Nees ex Lehm.

var. *semilanatus* (Lindl.) Maiden et Betche

(*exalatus*, tall.)

Family RANUNCULACEAE

A family of wide distribution, very numerous in Europe and northern Asia, and in all the temperate countries, but less common in the tropics. This family includes a number of garden plants well known in Australia, such as Anemone, Delphinium, Larkspur, Nigella. All members have an acrid sap which is poisonous in some species.

Herbs, either annual or with a perennial rootstock, or creeping stolons, with radical or alternate leaves, or climbers with opposite leaves. Leaves entire or divided, the petiole often dilated and sheathing at the base, more rarely with stipules.

Flowers regular, solitary or in inflorescences, usually terminal. Sepals 3, 4 or more, commonly 5, often petaloid and deciduous.

Petals same number as sepals, or more, sometimes wanting. Stamens indefinite, hypogynous, free. Ovary of several carpels, usually free.

Fruit of 1 or more indehiscent achenes or berries, or dehiscent follicles, the distinct styles persistent as short points or lengthened into long, bearded tails.

Climbers, usually woody, with opposite, divided leaves. Flowers with 4 petaloid sepals and no petals. Fruit a collection of achenes with bearded tails. *Clematis*.

Herbs with radical leaves. Flowers yellow, rarely white or red, with 5 petals. Fruit a collection of achenes.

Ranunculus.

RANUNCULUS L.

Herbs with alternate or radical leaves. Flowers solitary or axillary on leaf-opposed peduncles. Petals and sepals usually 5, sometimes more, often with a nectar-bearing pit at base. Petals white or yellow.

Distribution: A large genus in the temperate and colder regions of both hemispheres. 33 in Australia: 4 in Queensland; 22 in New South Wales; 19 in Victoria; 6 in South Australia; 4 in Western Australia; 15 in Tasmania.

(*ranunculus*, a little frog; in reference to the froggy places beloved by these plants.)

Villous land plant with deeply lobed radical ovate leaves on long petioles. Petals yellow. *R. lappaceus* Sm.
(pl. 9)

(*lappaceus*, like a burr; in reference to the fruiting head.)

Glabrous water plant with palmately divided leaves, usually with 3 segments on short petioles. Petals yellow.
R. inundatus DC.
(pl. 49)

(*inundatus*, overflowing; referring to its aquatic or river-bank habitat.)

CLEMATIS L.

Woody climbers with compound leaves. Sepals usually petaloid, 4, valvate in bud; petals none. Fruits dry, sessile, the style forming a long-plumed awn.

Distribution: A large genus in the temperate regions of both hemispheres. 6 in Australia: 3 in Queensland; 4 in New South Wales; 2 in Victoria; 1 in South Australia; 2 in Western Australia; 2 in Tasmania.

(*Clematis*, Greek name for plant.)
Leaves on long petioles, trifoliolate. Flowers white, in short clusters, male and female on separate plants.

C. aristata R. Br. ex DC.
(pl. 61)

(*aristata*, having ears of wheat, since the bearded fruit resembles these.)

Family LAURACEAE

Trees usually found in rain-forest areas with entire, alternate or rarely opposite leaves without stipules. Flowers small, in cymes, perfect. Perianth segments, usually 6, stamens 3, 6, 9, 12, or more, perigynous, the inner ones usually reduced to staminodes; filaments with a pair of large glands on the inner stamens, rarely on the outer; anthers adnate, 2-celled, opening in valves upwards. Ovary free, of 1 carpel, superior. Style simple, with a capitate or disc-shaped stigma.

Fruit a berry or a drupe, often nearly dry.

ENDIANDRA R. Br.

Trees with alternate penniveined leaves. Flowers small, in compound cymes. Fruit an oblong or globular berry.

Distribution: Indian Archipelago, India, Australia. About 20 in Australia: 14 in Queensland; 6 in New South Wales.

(*end-*, inner; *andros*, a man; the inner row of anthers only are fertile.)

Small glabrous tree, with ovate-lanceolate or oblong leaves with prominent veins. Flowers very small, in panicles.

E. sieberi Nees
(pl. 12)

(Sieber, a nineteenth-century botanist.)

Family MONIMIACEAE

A family found chiefly in Australia and South America. Trees, shrubs, or woody climbers with opposite leaves without stipules, usually coarsely serrate.

Flowers imperfect, often unisexual. Calyx lobed, with 4 or more lobes arranged in 2 or more rows. Petals absent. Stamens hypogynous, same number as calyx lobes or more, and opposite them. Carpels several, free, superior.

Fruits numerous, 1-seeded, seated on a disc-like expanded

calyx-tube or included in the enlarged calyx-tube.

Satinwood and Sassafras are well-known Australian members of the order.

ATHEROSPERMA Labill.

Aromatic trees with entire or toothed leaves and axillary, usually solitary, dioecious flowers. Calyx usually 8-cleft, stamens 8–20, carpels numerous.

Distribution: New Zealand and Australia. 1 in Australia: in Queensland, New South Wales and Victoria.

(*ather-*, awned; *spermum*, a seed.)

> Petals absent. Sepals forming a tube. Stamens with a wing-like appendage on each side.

A. moschatum Labill.
(pl. 33)

(*moschatum*, musk-scented.)

Family NYMPHAEACEAE

Aquatic plants with peltate or cordate leaves, and an underground stem attached to the muddy bed of shallow waters. They are distributed in quiet or slowly flowing waters all over the world, though more commonly in the northern hemisphere.

Flowers solitary, raised on long petioles to or above the surface of the water. Sepals 3–5. Petals 3 or more. Stamens hypogynous, 6 or more; all free or inner ones adnate to the ovary, or inserted on its summit; anthers adnate, the stamens opening in longitudinal slits. Ovary of 3 or more carpels, free and distinct, or sunken in the receptacle to form a compound ovary. Styles or stigmas free. Ovules solitary.

Fruit indehiscent, the seeds embedded in a fleshy or spongy arillus, or sometimes naked. The spongy material surrounding the seeds acts as a float and aids in dissemination.

NYMPHAEA L.

Leaves floating. Flowers axillary, usually solitary, with numerous perianth segments passing gradually into stamens. Carpels several, immersed in a ring on the fleshy receptacle. Fruit a spongy berry.

Distribution: Widely distributed in temperate and tropical regions. 5 in Australia: 5 in Queensland; 1 in New South Wales; 1 in the Northern Territory.

(Nymphe, the goddess of streams.)

Leaves cordate, up to 12 cm across. Flowers blue. Anthers
with appendages. *N. gigantea* Hook.
(pl. 43)
(*gigantea*, very large; in reference to the flowers.)

Family TREMANDRACEAE

A family strictly confined to Australia. Shrubs, commonly heath-like, often glandular-hairy, with small alternate opposite or verticillate leaves.

Flowers perfect, solitary, on axillary peduncles, usually dark-pink, occasionally pale-pink, white or purple, regular. Sepals usually 4 or 5, valvate in bud. Petals as many as sepals, free, spreading, induplicate-valvate in bud. Stamens twice as many as petals, hypogynous, free or joined in pairs at the base of the filament; filaments short; anthers oblong or linear, 4-celled, opening by terminal pores. Ovary 2-celled. Style filiform. Ovules 1, 2 or several in each cell.

Fruit a capsule, flattened, 2-celled, opening at the edges.

TETRATHECA Sm.

Small spreading often heath-like plants with solitary axillary deep-pink, purple or white flowers with 4–5 free spreading petals, and dark-coloured anthers.

Distribution: The genus is limited to Australia. About 40 in Australia: 1 in Queensland; about 16 in New South Wales; 7 in Victoria; 4 in South Australia; 20 in Western Australia and several in Tasmania.

(*tetra*, four; *theca*, a case; refers to the 4-chambered anther.)
Leaves verticillate, mostly in whorls of 4–6, linear, with
revolute margins. *T. ericifolia* Sm.
(pl. 35)
(*Erica*, the Heath; *folium*, a leaf.)
Leaves loosely revolute, recurved or rarely flat, verticillate
in whorls of 3–5 or 6, broadly to narrowly elliptical.
T. thymifolia Sm.
(pl. 4)
(*Thymus* or Thyme, name of a plant; *folium*, a leaf.)

Family HYPERICACEAE

Natives of humid and hot places, chiefly tropical South America, India, Africa Malagasy. Represented by only 2 genera in

81

Australia. The luscious Mangosteen is a member of the family and so is the Gamboge plant.

Trees or shrubs, exuding a yellow resinous juice. Leaves opposite, thickly coriaceous and entire. Flowers solitary or clustered, terminal or axillary.

Flowers regular, dioecious or perfect. Sepals 2–6, much imbricate or in decussate pairs. Petals 2–6, imbricate or contorted. Stamens in male flowers hypogynous, indefinite, free or united. Ovary sometimes developed in male flower but not fertile. Ovary of female flower 2 or more celled, with 1 or more ovaries in each cell.

Fruit fleshy or coriaceous, indehiscent or opening in as many valves as cells.

HYPERICUM L.

Herbs or shrubs with small, thin, usually entire exstipulate leaves. Yellow or white perfect flowers with 5 sepals and 5 twisted petals. Fruit a capsule.

Distribution: A large genus, distributed over the greater part of the globe. 2 in Australia: 2 in Queensland; 2 in New South Wales; 2 in Victoria; 2 in South Australia.

(*Hypericum*, old name of plant.)

Leaves, closely stem-clasping, ovate, with numerous oil dots. Capsule 1-celled with 3 valves.

H. gramineum Forst.
(pl. 39)

(*gramineum*, grass-like.)

Family VIOLACEAE

A family distributed all over the world. Herbs or shrubs with alternate, simple or lobed leaves with lateral stipules. Flowers perfect, axillary, solitary or in inflorescences. Pedicels with 2 bracteoles.

Flowers perfect. Sepals 5, imbricate. Petals 5, imbricate, equal or unequal, with the lower one larger, or spurred, or otherwise dissimilar. Stamens 5, hypogynous; anthers erect and connivent or connate round the pistil, sessile or on short filaments, the connective very broad, anther cells opening inwards. Ovary free, superior, sessile, 1-celled, usually with 3 parietal placentas and several or rarely 1 ovule to each placenta. Style simple.

Fruit a capsule opening in as many valves as placentas, or rarely an indehiscent berry.

82

Herbs with foliaceous and persistent stipules. Sepals with small backward prolongation (spur) below their insertion. Lower petal spurred or saccate.   *Viola*.
Herbs or shrubs usually with opposite narrow leaves and small narrow stipules. Sepals not spurred at the base. Lower petal saccate or gibbous at the base.
                                    Hybanthus (Ionidium).

VIOLA L.

Herbs often stoloniferous, radical or alternate leaves on long petioles, usually dilated in upper part. Capsule 3-valved, glabrous.

Distribution: A very large genus, mostly found in the temperate regions of the northern hemisphere. 5 in Australia: 2 in Queensland; 4 in New South Wales; 3 in Victoria; 3 in South Australia; 5 in Tasmania.

(*Viola*, Latin name.)

Leaves radical, lanceolate to ovate, entire, somewhat cordate. No stolons. Stipules linear, adnate. Flowers deep-purple.   *V. betonicifolia* Sm.
                                    (pl. 34)

(*Betonica* or Betony, a kind of plant; *folium*, a leaf.)

Leaves nearly orbicular, reniform or spathulate. Creeping stolons. Stipules free, lanceolate. Flowers lilac, pale-blue, or white.   *V. hederacea* Labill.
                                    (pl. 65)

(*hederacea*, like Ivy.)

HYBANTHUS Jacq.

Herbs or shrubs with alternate or, rarely, opposite subsessile leaves. Capsule 3-valved, glabrous.

Distribution: About 7 in Australia: 4 in Queensland; 4 in New South Wales; 3 in Victoria; 2 in South Australia; 4 in Western Australia; 3 in the Northern Territory.

(*hybos*, a bump; *anthos*, a flower; referring to the pouched flowers.)

Lowest petal usually much larger than others with a broad claw. Flowers deep-blue in slender, leafless racemes.   *H. filiformis* F. Muell.
                                    (pl. 11)

(*filiformis*, thread-like.)

Family PITTOSPORACEAE

A family almost exclusively Australian. Trees, shrubs, or undershrubs with flexuose, decumbent or twining branches. Leaves alternate, usually entire, without stipules. Flowers perfect, regular, solitary or in short inflorescences, terminal or axillary.

Flowers perfect, regular. Sepals 5, distinct and imbricate, or rarely connate at the base. Petals 5, imbricate, usually united into a tube, rarely spreading from the base. Stamens 5, hypogynous, free, alternating with the petals. Ovary superior, 1-celled, with 2 or rarely 3–5 parietal placentas, or divided into cells by the protrusion of the placentas. Style simple with an entire, dilated or capitate stigma. Ovules several, superimposed in 2 rows in each placenta.

Fruit a capsule opening loculicidally, or succulent and indehiscent. Seeds several or rarely 1 in each cell, dry or enveloped in pulp.

1. Fruit dry and splitting.
   2. Capsules with hard, thick valves.
      3. Seeds sticky, not winged.   *Pittosporum.*
      3. Seeds, not sticky, winged.   *Hymenosporum.*
   2. Capsules thin.
      4. Tall shrubs, glabrous, bushy. Flowers, small, white.
          Bursaria.
      4. Low, flexuose undershrubs. Flowers blue, showy.
          Cheiranthera.
1. Fruit succulent, not splitting.   *Billardiera.*

PITTOSPORUM Banks ex Gaertn.

Petals usually erect and united in the lower part with a spreading limb. Capsule hard, opening by valves.

Distribution: A large genus distributed over the warmer parts of Africa, Asia, Pacific Islands, New Zealand and Australia. About 10 in Australia: 9 in Queensland; 5 in New South Wales; 4 in Victoria; 1 in South Australia; 1 in Western Australia; 2 in the Northern Territory; 2 in Tasmania.

(*pitta*, resin; *sporos*, a seed; in reference to the sticky seeds.)

   Flowers white, in terminal clusters. A tree, glabrous, with oval-oblong or lanceolate, acuminate leaves with undulate margins. Fruit a capsule with red, sticky, angular seeds.   *P. undulatum* Vent.
               (pl. 61)

(*undulatum*, wavy; referring to the leaf margin.)

Flowers yellow, solitary. A tall shrub with tomentose young branches and ovate-elliptical, acuminate leaves.

P. revolutum Ait.

(pl. 47)

(*revolutum*, rolled back; referring to the petals.)

HYMENOSPORUM R. Br. ex F. Muell.

A small tree, with small flowers in terminal panicles. Petals erect at the base and cohering to above the middle. Capsules ovate, flattened, thick, coriaceous.

Distribution: The genus is limited to the single Australian species, in Queensland and New South Wales; also in New Guinea.

(*hymen*, a membrane; *sporos*, a seed.)

Glabrous tall shrub with ovate-oblong acuminate leaves, and yellow flowers in loose terminal panicles with small linear bracts. *H. flavum* (Hook.) F. Muell.

(pl. 39)

(*flavum*, yellow; referring to the colour of the flower.)

BURSARIA Cav.

Shrubs, often spiny. Flowers usually white. Petals small, spreading from the base. Capsule thin, coriaceous, with few seeds.

Distribution: The genus is confined to Australia. 4 in Australia: 3 in Queensland; 2 in New South Wales; 1 in Victoria, South Australia, Western Australia, and Tasmania.

(*bursa*, a purse; in reference to the fruit.)

Glabrous, bushy, thorny shrub with clustered, variable leaves, and numerous white flowers in terminal panicles. *B. spinosa* Cav.

(pl. 61)

(*spinosa*, thorny; alluding to the branches.)

BILLARDIERA Sm.

Woody climbers with entire, nearly sessile leaves and terminal flowers. Petals erect at the base, often cohering into a tube spreading at the top. Fruit an ovoid or oblong berry.

Distribution: A small genus, limited to Australia. 10 in Australia: 1 in Queensland; 3 in New South Wales; 3 in Victoria; 2 in South Australia; 4 in Western Australia; 2 in Tasmania.

(Labillardière, a renowned field botanist.)

Twining plant with obtuse variable leaves on short

85

petioles, and greenish or pale tubular flowers. Ovary
2-celled. Fruit a berry. *B. scandens* Sm.
(pl. 67)

(*scandens*, climbing.)

CHEIRANTHERA A. Cunn.

Glabrous undershrubs with twiggy branches and terminal
flowers. Petals spreading from near the base. Stamens all turned
towards one side, the anthers longer than the filaments. Fruit
a hard capsule.

Distribution: A genus of 4 species limited to Australia: 1 in
Queensland; 2 in New South Wales; 1 in Victoria; 2 in South
Australia; 3 in Western Australia.

(*cheir*, a hand; *anthos*, *anthera*, a flower.)

Low glabrous shrub with twiggy branches, linear leaves
with incurved margins, and dark-blue showy flowers.
Fruit a capsule. *C. linearis* A. Cunn.
(pl. 43)

(*linearis*, linear or narrow; in reference to the leaves.)

Family DROSERACEAE

This family is distributed in swamp lands of Europe, India,
China, South Africa, Madagascar, North and South America,
and Australia.

Herbs. Leaves covered with glandular hairs. The hairs are
sensitive and bend over to trap visiting insects which are attracted
to the leaves by the glistening tips of the hairs and/or the reddish
colour. Once caught the insect is digested by a sticky digestive
fluid poured out by the hairs. This novel method of obtaining
nitrogenous food enables such plants to live in soils deficient in
available nitrogen.

Flowers perfect, solitary or in 1-sided inflorescences, simple or
branching. Calyx free or shortly adnate to the base of the ovary,
divided to the base or nearly so into 4, 5 or rarely 8 sepals. Petals
as many as sepals, free. Stamens as many as petals, or rarely
twice as many, hypogynous, inserted with petals. Ovary 6-celled,
with 2–5 parietal placentas or 1 basal placenta, or 2–3 celled,
with several ovules to each placenta or cell. Styles as many as
placentas, simple or divided to the base so as to appear twice the
number, or variously branched or united.

Fruit a capsule, opening loculicidally in as many valves as
cells or placentas. Seeds several.

86

DROSERA L.

Glandular herbs growing in moist situations. Petals and sepals usually 5; petals papery, pink or white.

Distribution: A large genus, found in nearly all parts of the world. 60–70 in Australia: 11 in Queensland; 11 in New South Wales; 9 in Victoria; 8 in South Australia; 45 in Western Australia; 8 in the Northern Territory; 8 in Tasmania.

(*droseros*, dewy; referring to the glandular leaves.)

Leaves radical, on long petioles, the lamina divided at the base into 2 linear lobes. Flowers white, papery, in loose inflorescences. *D. binata* Labill.
(pl. 18)

(*binata*, paired: referring to the forked leaves.)

Family SAPINDACEAE

The family is abundantly represented in the tropics, with some members in the temperate regions of the northern hemisphere and a few in Australia.

Trees and shrubs, rarely herbs, frequently climbers, with alternate, compound leaves with a terminal odd leaflet, sometimes trifoliate or simple.

Flowers perfect, usually small. Sepals 4 or 5, free or united in a small, toothed or lobed calyx, imbricate or rarely valvate in bud. Petals as many as sepals or 1 fewer, sometimes absent, frequently each petal bearing a scale or tuft of hairs inside. Stamens 8 or 10, hypogynous; anthers versatile or erect. Ovary entire or lobed, 1–4 celled, most frequently 3-celled. Style simple with a simple stigma, more or less divided. Ovules 1 or 2 or rarely more in each cell.

Fruit dry or succulent, entire or separating into cocci.

CUPANIOPSIS Radlk.

Trees or tall shrubs with alternate, pinnate leaves and coriaceous, obovoid capsules. Fruit a capsule, coriaceous or hard; seeds usually with a hard aril.

Distribution: A large tropical genus. 5 in Australia: 5 in Queensland; 5 in New South Wales; 2 in the Northern Territory.

(*Cupania*, a genus of plants; *opsis*, appearance.)

Flowers in loose panicles. Sepals and petals 5. Stamens 10. Fruit a capsule, with 3 shining seeds with red arillus. *C. anacardioides* (A. Rich.) Radlk.
(pl. 26)

(*Anacardium*, a genus of plants; *oides*, like.)

Family POLYGALACEAE

A large family, widely distributed. Herbs, or small shrubs, climbers, or rarely trees, with alternate, entire leaves without stipules.

Flowers usually in terminal or axillary racemes with subtending bract and 2 bracteoles, perfect, irregular. Sepals 5, free, much imbricate, the 2 inner ones usually large and petal-like. Petals 3 or 5, rarely all free, most frequently 2 united at the base with the lower concave or helmet-shaped petal or keel. Stamens 10 or less, usually united to about the middle into a sheath open at the top. Anthers erect, 1- or 2-celled, usually opening by a terminal pore. Ovary free, 1–8 (usually 2)-celled. Style simple, usually curved at the top, with an entire or 2-lobed stigma. Ovules usually solitary in each cell.

Fruit a compressed capsule opening loculicidally.

COMESPERMA Labill.

Herbs or small shrubs, erect or twining, with alternate, small leaves, and flowers usually in terminal racemes.

Distribution: The genus is limited to Australia. About 25 in Australia: 9 in Queensland; 8 in New South Wales; 7 in Victoria; 5 in South Australia; 13 in Western Australia.

(*coma*, beard; *sperma*, a seed—all species have hairy seeds.)
1. Stems erect.
    2. Leaves few, reduced to minute scales. Erect plant with slender stems.   *C. defoliatum* F. Muell.
                          (pl. 31)

(*de*, without; *foliatum*, having leaves.)
    2. Leaves linear and crowded with recurved or revolute margins. Erect twiggy plant.   *C. ericinum* DC.
                          (pl. 10)

(*ericinum*, heath-like; referring to the leaves.)
1. Stems twining. Leaves linear, few and distant or absent.
                          C. volubile Labill.
                          (pl. 31)

(*volubile*, changing; referring to the twining habit.)

Family CELASTRACEAE

A large family distributed all over the world, but most abundant in the tropics. Trees, shrubs, or woody climbers, occasionally thorny. Leaves opposite or alternate, entire or toothed, with minute deciduous stipules or none.

Flowers perfect, regular, small, in inflorescences, terminal or axillary. Calyx small, persistent, with 4 or 5 sepals, rarely 3 or 6. Petals as many as sepals, spreading, imbricate or rarely valvate. Stamens as many as petals and alternate with them, hypogynous, filaments usually short, incurved; anthers short, 2-celled. Receptacle usually conspicuous, flat and fleshy, nearly free or adnate to the calyx at the base. Ovary sessile, 2–5 celled. Style short, with a simple or lobed stigma. Ovules usually 2 in each cell, occasionally several, rarely 1.

Fruit a capsule, berry, drupe, or samara, rarely divided into distinct carpels. Seeds usually enveloped in an aril, sometimes winged.

ELAEODENDRON Jacq.

Mostly small trees with opposite leaves and clustered flowers. Fruit a drupe; seeds without aril.

Distribution: A large genus distributed in east India, southern Africa and a few in tropical America and Australia. 3 in Australia: 3 in Queensland; 2 in New South Wales; 2 in the Northern Territory.

(*Elaia*, the Olive; *dendron*, a tree.)

Small glabrous tree with opposite, broad, acuminate, coriaceous leaves. Flowers in slender cymes. Fruit a bright-red globular or ovoid drupe with 1 seed.

E. australe Vent.

(pl. 10)

(*australe*, southern.)

Family RUTACEAE

A large family, ranging over the hotter and temperate regions of the whole world, but most abundant within the tropics and in South Africa and Australia.

Trees or shrubs with glandular dots on the leaves and other thin parts. Leaves opposite or alternate, simple or compound, usually entire, exstipulate.

Flowers axillary or terminal, solitary or clustered, regular, perfect, calyx small, 4–5 lobed. Petals the same number as sepals, rarely cohering. Stamens free (except *philotheca*), hypogynous, the same or double the number of sepals and petals; anthers versatile, with parallel cells opening longitudinally, the connective usually tipped by a gland or appendage. Receptacle usually thickened

89

into an entire or lobed disc. Ovary superior, of 4 or 5 cells, more or less united into a lobed ovary. Stigma terminal, entire or lobed. Ovules usually 2 in each cell (only one reaching maturity, the other aborting in most cases in Australian tribes).

Fruit separating into 2-valved or rarely indehiscent cocci, or the carpels united to form a capsule dehiscing loculicidally, an indehiscent berry or drupe. Seeds usually solitary in each cell.

1. Leaves opposite. Sepals and petals 4. Stamens four or eight.
  2. Petals free, spreading.
    3. Stamens four.   *Zieria.*
    3. Stamens eight.   *Boronia.*
  2. Petals united into a tube.   *Correa.*
1. Leaves alternate. Sepals and petals five. Stamens ten.
  4. Stamens free.
    5. Petals imbricate, not scaly.
      6. Stamens with inconspicuous appendages.
                                       Eriostemon.
      6. Stamens with conspicuous appendages.
                                       Crowea.
    5. Petals valvate, with inflexed tips, often scaly.
                                     Phebalium.
  4. Stamens united at the base.   *Philotheca.*

BORONIA Sm.

Shrubs or undershrubs with opposite, simple or compound leaves. Flowers small, solitary, or in cymes or racemes, usually with 2 bracts on the pedicel.

Distribution: The genus is confined to Australia. About 94 in Australia: 22 in Queensland; about 28 in New South Wales; 13 in Victoria; 5 in South Australia; 48 in Western Australia; 7 in the Northern Territory; 7 in Tasmania.

(Francesco Borone, Italian botanist.)

1. Petals pink or red.
  2. Petals valvate.
    3. Leaves simple, trifoliolate, or pinnate with 3–5 leaflets, glabrous or hispid, opposite. Flowers solitary, deep-pink, in axillary peduncles.
                      B. ledifolia (Vent.) J. Gay
                                (pl. 20)
(*Ledum*, a kind of plant; *folium*, a leaf.)
    3. Leaves are always pinnate. A glabrous shrub. Flowers in short umbels, deep-pink. Sepals very small.
                           B. fraseri Hook.

90

(*Fraser*, a nineteenth-century botanist.)
 2. Petals imbricate.
  4. Leaves pinnate.
   5. Plant glabrous.
    6. Leaves trifoliolate, crowded, with linear, terete, mucronate leaflets. Flowers 1–3, in loose cymes, deep-pink.   *B. falcifolia* A. Cunn. ex Lindl.
(pl. 20)

(*falcatus*, sickle-shaped; referring to the leaflets; *folium*, a leaf.)
    6. Leaves with 7–9 leaflets. Flowers 3–4 together, in loose cymes.   *B. pinnata* Sm.
(pl. 40)

(*pinnata*, winged; on account of the feathery leaves.)
   5. Plant hirsute.
    6. Leaves with 5–13 leaflets. Flowers usually solitary, pink.   *B. molloyae* (*B. elatior* Benth.)
(pl. 20)

(*elatior*, taller; referring to the fact that it is taller than usual in the genus.)
  4. Leaves simple.
    7. Leaves rhomboidal, serrulate, crowded. Flowers crowded in leafy terminal cymes.
         B. serrulata Sm.
(pl. 1)

(*serrulata*, with a little saw; referring to the leaf edges.)
    7. Leaves lanceolate, minutely toothed. Flowers 3–5 together.   *B. barkerana* F. Muell.
(pl. 49)

(Mrs C. A. Barker, local collector, Blue Mountains, N.S.W., about 1880.)
1. Petals yellow inside.
 Leaves usually trifoliolate, sessile. Flowers in axillary cymes, reddish-brown outside, greenish-yellow inside.
        B. megastigma Nees ex Bartl.
(pl. 20)

(*mega*, large; *stigma*, top of the pistil.)

ERIOSTEMON Sm.

Shrubs with thick, alternate, simple, subsessile leaves. Flowers usually solitary and axillary, pink or white.
 Distribution: An Australian genus. About 33 in Australia: about 7 in Queensland; about 12 in New South Wales; 4 in Victoria;

3 in South Australia; 10 in Western Australia; 2 in Tasmania.
(*erios*, wool; *stemon*, a stamen.)
> Leaves linear to lanceolate, thick, greyish-green. Flowers
> pale-pink or white, solitary, in leaf axils.
> > *E. australasius* Pers. (*E. lanceolatus* Gaertn.)
> > (pl. 21)

(*australasius*, Australasian.)
> Leaves cordate-ovate, thick, dark-green, mucronate.
> Flowers pale-pink or white, in short axillary racemes.
> > *E. buxifolius* Sm.
> > (pl. 65)

(*Buxus*, the ancient Box-tree; *folius*, leafy.)
> Leaves ovate-spathulate, thick, greyish-green. Flowers
> pale-pink or white, solitary, in leaf axils.
> > *E. obovalis* A. Cunn.
> > (pl. 52)

(*obovalis*, reversed oval—of the leaves in which the broader
part is outwards.)

CROWEA Sm.

Shrubs or undershrubs differing from *Eriostemon* principally in
the conspicuous appendages on the anthers.

Distribution: The genus is confined to Australia. 3 in Australia:
1 in Queensland; 2 in New South Wales, and Victoria; 1 in
Western Australia.

(J. Crowe, English botanist.)
> Branches angular. Leaves lanceolate, thin. Flowers red,
> solitary in leaf axils. Anther appendages narrow,
> bearded. *C. saligna* Andr.
> (pl. 21)

(*saligna*, willow-like; in reference to the leaves.)

CORREA Sm.

Stellate-hairy shrubs with simple, opposite, coriaceous, shortly
petiolate leaves. Flowers usually drooping, solitary, 2–3 together,
tubular in some species.

Distribution: The genus is confined to Australia. About 11 in
Australia: 1 in Queensland; 6 in New South Wales; 4 in Victoria;
7 in South Australia; 1 in Tasmania.

(Correa de Serra, Portuguese botanist.)
> Leaves opposite, simple, cordate-ovate to lanceolate.
> Flowers usually solitary on short, slender, terminal

peduncles. Corolla red with yellowish tips, or greenish-yellow all over, petals coherent into a cylindrical tube.

C. reflexa Labill.

(pl. 35)

(*reflexa*, turned back; in reference to tips of petals.)

ZIERIA Sm.

Shrubs with opposite, simple or trifoliate leaves. Flowers white or pink, axillary, usually in short cymes.

Distribution: The genus is confined to eastern coastal Australia from north-east Queensland through to South Australia and Tasmania. About 20 in Australia: 6 in Queensland; 7 in New South Wales; 5 in Victoria; 1 in South Australia; 3 in Tasmania; 1 New Zealand species.

(Zier, Polish botanist.)

Leaves opposite, trifoliolate, almost glabrous, lanceolate to ovate, flat. Anthers blunt with no appendages.

Z. smithii Andr.

(pl. 53)

(J.E. Smith, nineteenth-century Australian botanist.)

PHILOTHECA Rudge

Erect heath-like shrubs, usually glabrous. Flowers terminal, almost sessile, solitary.

Distribution: The genus is confined to Australia. 2 in Australia: 1 in Queensland; 1 in New South Wales; 1 in Western Australia.

(*psilos*, smooth; *theca*, a case or sheath; in reference to the stamens.)

Leaves almost terete, often channelled above. Flowers solitary, almost sessile, lilac, hoary. Styles united, hirsute in the middle.   *P. salsolifolia* (Sm.) Druce

(pl. 21)

(*salsolifolia*, Salsola-leafed; Salsola a kind of plant.)

PHEBALIUM Juss.

Shrubs, often glandular or scaly, with alternate, rigid, subsessile, simple leaves. Flowers small, white or yellow, solitary or crowded.

Distribution: Australia, with 1 species in New Zealand. About 44 in Australia: 7 in Queensland; 15 in New South Wales; 14 in Victoria; 6 in South Australia; 8 in Western Australia; 5 in Tasmania.

(*Phebalium*, appears to have been adopted from Greek name, *phibaleos*, for an early fig-tree.)

93

Leaves narrow-linear, elongated, with recurved and remotely denticulate margins, hoary underneath. Flowers yellow or white in leafy umbels.

P. dentatum Sm.
(pl. 62)

(*dentatum*, toothed; in reference to the leaves.)

Family MALVACEAE

Widely distributed in both hemispheres, being most abundant in tropical parts. To it belong several plants of economic importance, including the Cotton Plant (*Gossypium* sp.), Indian Hemp (*Hibiscus* sp.), while others yield mucilage of commercial importance. Many are ornamental and are widely cultivated, as the Queensland and Norfolk Island *Hibiscus* (*Langunaria patersonii*), the many tropical *Hibiscus*, the commonest being *H. rosa-sinensis*, which bears bright-red flowers. The very tenacious introduced pest plant Paddy's Lucerne (*Sida rhombifolia*) is also a member of the family.

Herbs or shrubs with alternate, petiolate, stipulate leaves and large showy flowers.

Flowers perfect. Calyx persistent, campanulate, with 5 lobes. Petals 5, hypogynous, often hairy at the base and twisted in bud. Stamens numerous, united in a tube, usually adnate to the base of the petals. Ovary of 2 to several carpels. Styles united at least in the lower half.

Fruit usually dry, the carpels separating and indehiscent, or 2-valved, or united to form a dehiscent capsule.

Fruit separating into fruitlets (small portions each containing a seed). Style branches twice as many as carpels.   *Pavonia.*
Fruit a 2- or 3-celled capsule.   *Howittia.*
Fruit a 5-celled capsule. Style branches as many as carpels.
  Stigmas capitate.   *Hibiscus.*
  Stigmas decurrent.   *Gossypium.*

PAVONIA Cav.

Herbs or shrubs. Calyx subtended by 5 or more bracteoles. Ovary of 5 carpels; style branches 10. Carpels separating from the axis, usually indehiscent.

Distribution: A tropical and sub-tropical genus with a single species found in South America and Australia; in Queensland, New South Wales, and South Australia.

(Pavon, Spanish botanist.)

94

Leaves ovate-cordate to oblong-hastate, crenate, 2–5 cm long. Flowers on axillary peduncles.   *P. hastata* Cav.
(pl. 46)
(*hastata*, spearlike; referring to the leaves.)

HIBISCUS L.

Herbs, shrubs, or trees. Calyx 5-lobed or 5-toothed, subtended by 5 or more bracteoles. Ovary of 5 carpels; style branches 5 sometimes very short with terminal stigmas. Fruit a 5-valved capsule.

Distribution: A large genus distributed throughout tropical and sub-tropical areas. About 50 in Australia: 28 in Queensland; 12 in New South Wales; 2 in Victoria; 9 in South Australia; 24 in Western Australia; 21 in the Northern Territory.

(*Hibiscum* or *Ibiscum*, old name for Marsh Mallow.)

Flowers yellow, usually with a crimson throat. Leaves broadly cordate, more or less 5-lobed and toothed.
H. diversifolius Jacq.
(pl. 51)
(*diversus*, different; *folium*, a leaf.)

Flowers white or pale-pink, usually with a deep-purple throat, on short peduncles in upper axils. Leaves entire or 3-lobed, irregularly toothed.   *H. heterophyllus* Vent.
(pl. 33)
(*heteros*, different; *phyllon*, a leaf.)

GOSSYPIUM L.

Shrubs or tall herbs. Calyx shortly truncate with 3 large cordate bracteoles. Ovary 4- or 5-celled; style club-shaped, furrowed. Fruit a 4- or 5-valved capsule.

Distribution: Found in Asia, America, and Australia. Contains the commercially useful cotton-bearing plants. 1 in Australia, in the western districts of Queensland, in New South Wales and South Australia.

Glabrous shrub. Leaves ovate or orbicular, mucronate, entire. Flowers purple or lavender with a reddish blotch at the base, partially enclosed in bud by 3 ovate-lanceolate many-veined bracteoles. Fruit an ovoid capsule.
G. sturtianum J. H. Willis. (*Cienfugosia gossypioides* (R. Br.) Hochr.)
(pl. 41)

95

(*gossypion*, according to Pliny the name of the African cotton-tree.)

(*sturtianum*, after Charles Sturt, explorer.)

HOWITTIA F. Muell.

Tall stellate-tomentose shrubs with violet flowers on short axillary peduncles. Calyx without bracteoles. Ovary of 3 carpels; styles connate with a 3-lobed stigma.

Distribution: The genus seems to be confined to the single species found in Australia: in New South Wales, Victoria, and South Australia.

(Howitt, a Melbourne physician.)

Leaves shortly petiolate, ovate-lanceolate to cordate, slightly toothed. Calyx small with no bracts. Flowers violet-purple, in short axillary inflorescences.

H. trilocularis F. Muell.
(pl. 11)

(*tri*, three; *locularis*, having cells; referring to the seeds being in three compartments.)

Family ELAEOCARPACEAE

This is a small family of only a few genera, most of which are confined to tropical regions. It is closely linked to the much larger family Tiliaceae (Lime or Linden family).

Trees and shrubs. Leaves alternate, rarely opposite, simple, pinnate or palmately veined, entire, often serrated. Flowers usually in short cymes, terminal or axillary.

Flowers regular, perfect. Sepals 5, free, usually valvate. Petals 4 or 5, often fringed or divided. Stamens indefinite, filaments free or slightly united at the base. Ovary 2–5 cells with a single style sometimes lobed at the apex and usually with 1 seed in each cell of the fruit.

Fruit a capsule opening loculicidally, or a drupe.

ELAEOCARPUS L.

Trees with alternate, rarely opposite, serrulate or serrate leaves in short petioles. Flowers usually white. Fruit a drupe, usually wrinkled.

Distribution: A large genus widely distributed throughout the tropics and in the Pacific Islands, New Caledonia, New Zealand and Australia. 14 in Australia: 14 in Queensland; 7 in New South Wales; 3 in Victoria.

(*Elaia*, the Olive; *carpos*, a fruit.)
A small glabrous tree with elliptical-oblong or oblong-lanceolate, acuminate, coriaceous, serrate leaves, 8–10 cm long. Fruit a globular or ovoid blue drupe.

E. reticulatus Sm.
(pl. 63)

(*reticulatus*, netted; referring to the veins.)

Family EUPHORBIACEAE

This is an extraordinary family, distributed over the whole world and with a tremendous number of species. Among them are many of commercial importance producing rubber, starches, tapioca, dyes, oils (castor, croton, and eboe), purgatives.

Shrubs or herbs, usually with simple stipulate leaves, and often exuding a milky juice.

Flowers mostly small, solitary or in inflorescences, unisexual, usually regular. Sepals and petals 4–6; petals sometimes wanting. Stamens 1 to many. Pistil superior, of 3 carpels united to form a 3-celled ovary. Styles as many as carpels.

Fruit usually a capsule, rarely succulent.

RICINOCARPOS Desf.

Small erect shrubs with alternate, entire leaves, and monoecious flowers in terminal clusters. Sepals and petals usually 5, stamens numerous, monadelphous; ovary 3-celled.

Distribution: The genus is confined to Australia. 17 in Australia: 4 in Queensland; 3 in New South Wales; 1 in Victoria; 10 in Western Australia; 2 in the Northern Territory.

(*Ricinus*, Castor-oil Plant; *carpos*, a fruit.)
Glabrous shrub with linear, mucronate leaves. Flowers on slender peduncles, usually 1 female with 3–6 males. Petals white, usually 6, about 1 cm long.

R. pinifolius Desf.
(pl. 62)

(*Pinus*, the Pine; *folium*, a leaf.)
Tomentose shrub with linear leaves with revolute margins and a dense white tomentum below. Flowers on slender peduncles, 3–6 in the clusters, females often solitary. Petals pink or white, usually 5, less than 1 cm long.

R. bowmanii F. Muell.
(pl. 40)

(E. M. Bowman, discoverer of the species.)

97

Family STERCULIACEAE

This is a family of world-wide, mainly tropical plants. Herbs, shrubs, or trees with alternate or irregularly opposite leaves, simple, palmately or pinnately veined, or digitate, mostly stipulate.

Flowers mostly in inflorescences, usually perfect. Calyx persistent, of 5, rarely 4, sepals. Petals 5, free or adhering to the staminal column, contorted, imbricate in bud, small and scale-like or wanting. Stamens united in a ring, 5–15, often hypogynous, alternating with staminodes. Ovary free, superior, 3–5 celled, carpels more or less united.

Fruit dry and splitting or the carpels free when ripe. Seeds sometimes hairy, often enveloped in pulp, testa coriaceous.

Stamens united into a column. *Brachychiton.*
Stamens 5, free or slightly united at the base.
Staminodes 5. *Keraudrenia.*
Staminodes absent. *Lasiopetalum.*

BRACHYCHITON Schott and Endl.

Tall trees with simple, lobed leaves. Flowers bell-shaped, usually in panicles. Sepals petaloid, petals absent.

Distribution: The genus is confined to Australia. About 10 in Australia: 10 in Queensland; 4 in New South Wales; 1 in Victoria; 1 in South Australia; 6 in Western Australia; 5 in the Northern Territory.

(*brachys*, short; *chiton*, a shirt or tunic; in reference to the coating of hairs over the seeds.)

Leaves ovate, entire or 3-lobed, acuminate, glabrous. Flowers creamy-white, mottled red inside.

B. populneum R. Br.
(pl. 12)

(*populneum*, poplar-like.)

Leaves deeply 3–7 lobed, broad, hairy on under-surface. Flowers reddish-pink, large. *B. discolor* F. Muell.
(pl. 4)

(*discolor*, variegated; in reference to the difference in colour of the two leaf surfaces.)

LASIOPETALUM Sm.

Stellate-tomentose shrubs with alternate, exstipulate leaves with white or rusty tomentum on the underside. Flowers in short axillary cymes. Petals minute or none.

Distribution: The genus is confined to Australia. About 30 in Australia: 9 in New South Wales; 6 in Victoria; 5 in South Australia; 19 in Western Australia; 3 in Tasmania.

(*lasios*, hairy; *petalon*, a leaf, hence petal.)
> Leaves rusty-tomentose on underside. Flowers in short inflorescences or solitary. Fruits simple, each bearing a single seed and splitting when ripe.
>
> *L. rufum* R. Br. ex Benth.
> (pl. 5)

(*rufum*, red.)

KERAUDRENIA J. Gay

Tall shrubs with rusty-tomentose young branches. Flowers in terminal or leaf-opposed cymes. Petals none.

Distribution: 1 species in Madagascar and 7 in Australia: 4 in Queensland; 2 in New South Wales; 3 in Western Australia; 2 in the Northern Territory.

(Keraudren, French nobleman.)
> Leaves linear-lanceolate, rusty or white below, coriaceous. Fruit a hirsute capsule, furrowed between the carpels.
>
> *K. hillii* F. Muell.
> (pl. 30)

(W. Hill, English botanist.)

Family FABACEAE

This is one of the largest and most successful of all plant families, being found in all parts of the world, but occurring most abundantly in tropical countries. Australia is well represented by this group. The family appears to owe its success largely to the presence of nitrogen-fixing bacteria in nodules on the roots, which makes it possible for the members to live in soils poor in nitrogen content. It is a family of economic importance, providing vegetables of many kinds (legumes, beans, peas, etc.), timbers, gums, perfumes, liquorice, indigo, fodder plants, and green manures.

The family contains trees, shrubs, herbs, creepers with alternate, often compound, stipulate leaves. Calyx of 5 lobes. Corolla 5 petals, irregular; the 2 lower petals united to form a keel, 2 lateral petals free, the dorsal petal always outside the others and embracing them in bud. Stamens usually 10 monadelphous or diadelphous, hypogynous or slightly perigynous, often united. Ovary superior, 1-celled, 10-many carpelled.

Fruit a legume.

99

1. Stamens all free.
    2. Leaves simple.
        3. Leaves alternate.
            4. Calyx lobes unequal, 2 upper ones usually united.
                5. Pod ovate.
                    6. Bracts wanting.
                        7. Flowers yellow or orange.   *Dillwynia.*
                        7. Flowers red.   *Brachysema.*
                    6. Bracts close under the calyx.   *Pultenaea.*
                5. Pod triangular.   *Daviesia.*
            4. Calyx lobes equal.   *Chorizema.*
        3. Leaves opposite or whorled.
                8. Fruit divided into 2 by a partition.
                                            Mirbelia.
                8. Fruit not divided into 2.   *Oxylobium.*
    2. Leaves trifoliolate or pinnate   *Gompholobium.*
1. Stamens united in a sheath open at the top.
            9. Flowers axillary.
                10. Anthers uniform. Petals yellow or red.
                    11. Pod flat and thin, winged.
                                            Platylobium.
                    11. Pod flat but not winged.   *Bossiaea.*
                10. Anthers alternately long and short.
                    Petals blue or purple.   *Hovea.*
            9. Flowers in terminal racemes.   *Crotalaria.*
1. Stamens united in a sheath, the upper stamen free.
                12. Herbs or shrubs, never climbing.
                    13. Petals acuminate. Trailing
                        plant.   *Clianthus.*
                    13. Petals obtuse. Erect plant.
                                            Swainsona.
                12. Climbing or trailing plants.
                                            Kennedia.

OXYLOBIUM Andr.

Shrubs or undershrubs occasionally climbing, with shortly petiolate leaves, mostly opposite or in whorls of 3. Flowers usually yellow, keel approximately equal in length to the wings.

Distribution: The genus is confined to Australia. About 30 in Australia: 5 in Queensland; 10 in New South Wales; 4 in Victoria; 14 in Western Australia; 2 in Tasmania.

(*oxys*, sharp; *lobos*, segment; in reference to the pointed lobes of the leaves.)

100

Shrub, almost glabrous, or with pubescent young branches and opposite, ovate-lanceolate pungent-pointed leaves bordered with a few distant pungent lobes with 1 on each side usually larger than the others. Flowers yellow with a darker keel. Stamens free. Ovary stipitate, silky, with 4–6 ovules.

O. ilicifolium (Andr.) Domin

(pl. 15)

(*ilicifolium*, holly-leafed.)

BOSSIAEA Vent.

Shrubs with simple, entire leaves, occasionally leafless; stipules usually small. Stems frequently flattened. Flowers yellow, axillary with imbricate bracts at the base of the peduncle.

Distribution: The genus is confined to Australia. About 42 in Australia: 11 in Queensland; 17 in New South Wales; 9 in Victoria; 3 in South Australia; 20 in Western Australia; 3 in the Northern Territory; 5 in Tasmania.

(Boissieu La Martinière, a companion of Laperouse.)

Low glabrous shrub, with stems considerably flattened. Leaves distant, the lower ones ovate, obtuse or nearly orbicular, the upper ones gradually narrower. Flowers yellow with a red keel.

B. heterophylla Vent.

(pl. 38)

(*heteros*, different; *phyllon*, a leaf.)

DAVIESIA Sm.

Shrubs or undershrubs with alternate, simple, rigid leaves; stipules minute or none. Flowers yellowish or red, usually axillary, sometimes with conspicuous bracts. Bracteoles absent. Pod oblique-triangular, usually flattened.

Distribution: The genus is confined to Australia. About 60 in Australia: 10 in Queensland; 14 in New South Wales; 7 in Victoria; 8 in South Australia; 52 in Western Australia; 1 in the Northern Territory; 2 in Tasmania.

(Davies, Welsh botanist.)

Glabrous shrub, branches slightly angular. Leaves usually lanceolate-linear with a short callous point, or quite blunt, rigid, strongly reticulate, stipules absent. Flowers in axillary, corymbose racemes.

D. corymbosa Sm.

(pl. 5)

(*corymbosa*, clustered; in reference to the flowers.)

101

PULTENAEA Sm.

Shrubs with simple, usually alternate leaves with narrow, scarious stipules. Flowers solitary and axillary but sometimes crowded at the ends of the branches and appearing as leafy clusters; bracteoles persistent, attached close under the calyx or adnate to it.

Distribution: The genus is confined to Australia. About 100 in Australia: 16 in Queensland; 54 in New South Wales; 47 in Victoria; 24 in South Australia; 28 in Western Australia; 15 in Tasmania.

(R. Pulteney, English botanist.)

Leaves flat with slightly recurved margins, glabrous, oblong-cuneate, mucronate, glabrous or slightly silky-hairy on the underside. Stipules usually very dark-brown and conspicuous. Flowers in terminal, sessile heads, at first surrounded by brown deciduous bracts. Petals yellow with scarlet keel. Pod ovate, pubescent.

P. daphnoides Wendl.
(pl. 36)

(*Daphne*, a well-known cultivated plant; *oides*, like.)

Leaves 2–3 cm long, linear, flat, crowded, with incurved margins, glabrous or sparingly hirsute; stipules long, brown, imbricate, conspicuous, concealing the branches. Flowers yellow in dense heads at the ends of the branches. Pod turgid, sparingly hairy.

P. stipularis Sm.
(pl. 47)

(*stipularis*, having stipules.)

PLATYLOBIUM Sm.

Shrubs with simple, reticulate leaves; stipules small. Flowers yellow, solitary on axillary peduncles with brown and scarious, imbricate bracts. Pod very flat, winged.

Distribution: The genus is limited to eastern Australia. 4 in Australia: 1 in Queensland; 1 in New South Wales; 4 in Victoria; 1 in South Australia; 3 in Tasmania.

(*platys*, broad; *lobos*, pod; in reference to the broad pod.)

Spreading shrub, glabrous or slightly pubescent. Leaves opposite, from broadly cordate to ovate, coriaceous, glabrous. Flowers large, yellow with a red keel. Stamens uniform in length except for 1 upper short one. Pod

102

stipitate.   *P. formosum* Sm.
                                                 (pl. 38)
(*formosum*, beautiful.)

GOMPHOLOBIUM Sm.

Shrubs or undershrubs with digitate leaves with 3 leaflets on a very short common peduncle, or pinnate; stipules small or none. Flowers terminal or in the upper leaf axils. Calyx dark-coloured. Pod turgid, almost globular, glabrous.

Distribution: The genus is confined to Australia. 26 in Australia: 4 in Queensland; 8 in New South Wales; 3 in Victoria; 1 in South Australia; 16 in Western Australia; 1 in Tasmania.

(*gomphos*, a nail-like fastening; *lobos*, a pod; in reference to the attachment of the pod.)

Glabrous shrub with erect virgate branches. Leaves trifoliolate, linear-lanceolate to linear-cuneate, with flat or slightly recurved margins. Stipules minute or absent. Flowers solitary, large, clear, yellow. Keel conspicuously ciliate on the margin. Seeds small. *G. latifolium* Sm.
                                                 (pl. 15)
(*latus*, broad; *folium*, a leaf.)

DILLWYNIA Sm.

Mostly erect shrubs with simple, alternate leaves without stipules and pubescent stems. Leaves usually narrow-linear. Stipules minute or absent. Flowers usually in short racemes or solitary, yellow or red.

Distribution: The genus is confined to Australia. 15 in Australia: 3 in Queensland; 11 in New South Wales; 6 in Victoria; 5 in South Australia; 6 in Western Australia; 3 in Tasmania.

(L. W. Dillwyn, botanist.)

Erect heath-like shrub. Leaves numerous, slender, alternate, terete, channelled above. Flowers yellow, rarely orange-red, in short inflorescences, almost sessile.
                                        D. retorta (Wendl.) Druce
                                                 (pl. 36)
(*retorta*, bent back, possibly in reference to the leaves.)

CHORIZEMA Labill.

Shrubs or undershrubs with simple, alternate leaves. Flowers in terminal racemes on short peduncles, orange or red.

Distribution: The genus is confined to Australia. About 20 in Australia: 1 in Queensland; 1 in New South Wales; 19 in

Western Australia.

(*chorizo*, to separate, and *nema*, a thread; in reference to the free and distinct filaments of the stamens.)

Glabrous shrub, with slender, weak branches. Leaves cordate-ovate to ovate-lanceolate. Flowers orange-red in loose axillary or terminal racemes.

C. cordatum Lindl.
(pl. 27)

(*cordatum*, heart-shaped; in reference to the leaves.)

CLIANTHUS Soland. ex Lindl.

Herbaceous perennials with pinnate leaves and large herbaceous stipules. Flowers large, showy, in umbel-like racemes on erect axillary peduncles. Pods flat.

Distribution: There are two species only, 1 in New Zealand and 1 in Australia: in Queensland, New South Wales, South Australia and Western Australia.

(*clio*, glory; *anthos*, a flower.)

Decumbent plant with 15–20 leaflets, sometimes ascending, densely villous with long, soft hairs. Leaves pinnate, obovate-elliptical or oblong, obtuse or almost acute. Flowers rich deep-red, black at base of keel, in dense inflorescences, rarely exceeding the leaves. Style bearded. *C. formosus* (G. Don) Ford et Vickery
(pl. 59)

(*formosus*, beautiful.)

SWAINSONA Salisb.

Perennial or, rarely, annual herbs with unequally pinnate leaves with herbaceous stipules. Flowers in axillary racemes in peduncles often longer than the leaves. Pods large.

Distribution: The genus is a large one, confined to Australia except for 1 New Zealand species. About 52 in Australia: 17 in Queensland; 26 in New South Wales; 11 in Victoria; 25 in South Australia; 27 in Western Australia; 6 in the Northern Territory; 1 in Tasmania.

(Swainson, scientist and plant cultivator.)

Glabrous perennial with erect flexuous branches. Leaflets 11–20 oblong or obtuse. Flowers variable in colour; red, purple, or white, in long terminal racemes much exceeding the leaves. Pods large.

S. galegifolia (Andr.) R. Br.
(pl. 60)

104

(*galega*, a genus of small, leguminous plants; *folium*, a leaf.)

KENNEDIA Vent.

Twining or prostrate herbs or undershrubs with 1-foliate or 3-foliate leaves with stipules, on long slender petioles. Flowers bracteate, axillary.

Distribution: The genus is confined to Australia. About 18 in Australia: 4 in Queensland; 4 in New South Wales; 2 in Victoria; 2 in South Australia; 11 in Western Australia; 1 in Tasmania.
(M. Kennedy, London nurseryman; one of the earliest cultivators of Australian plants.)

Flowers dull dark-red, in axillary racemes exceeding the leaves. Twining, pubescent plant; leaflets ovate, silky pubescent on both surfaces. Pod hairy, somewhat flattened. *K. rubicunda* Vent.
(pl. 16)

(*rubicunda*, reddish.)

Flowers scarlet, in short axillary racemes. Twining pubescent plant. Leaflets broadly ovate or orbicular, often undulate, pubescent. Pod hairy, subcylindrical. *K. prostrata* R. Br.
(pl. 46)

(*prostrata*, prostrate.)

MIRBELIA Sm.

Shrubs with simple leaves. Stipules minute or absent. Flowers sessile or on short peduncles, in axillary or terminal small clusters or short racemes. Pod turgid.

Distribution: The genus is confined to Australia. About 20 in Australia: 6 in Queensland; 7 in New South Wales; 1 in Victoria; 17 in Western Australia.
(C. F. B. Mirbel, French botanist.)

Erect shrub, virgate, often slightly pubescent. Leaves scattered or in whorls of 3, narrow-linear, with revolute margins. Stipules absent. Flowers bluish-purple, almost sessile in leaf axils. *M. speciosa* DC.
(pl. 16)

(*speciosa*, handsome.)

HOVEA R. Br.

Shrubs or undershrubs with simple, alternate, coriaceous leaves. Flowers blue in axillary clusters or very short racemes.

Distribution: The genus is confined to Australia. About 10 in

Australia: 5 in Queensland; 6 in New South Wales; 2 in Victoria; 2 in South Australia; 6 in Western Australia; 1 in the Northern Territory; 2 in Tasmania.

(A. P. Hove, Polish botanist.)

Low, erect shrub, closely tomentose when young, glabrous when old. Leaves narrow-linear, obtuse, coriaceous, with a small point. Flowers small, blue or purple, almost sessile, solitary or 2 or 3 together.   *H. linearis* R. Br.
(pl. 16)

(*linearis*, linear or narrow; referring to the leaves.)

CROTALARIA L.

Herbs or shrubs; leaves compound with 1–3 flat leaflets, the petiole more or less articulate near the summit. Flowers in simple, terminal racemes. Pod inflated.

Distribution: A genus widely distributed in tropical and subtropical regions: about 25 in Australia: 18 in Queensland; 6 in New South Wales; 4 in South Australia; 12 in Western Australia; 16 in the Northern Territory.

(*crotalum*, a rattle; alluding to the seeds in the pod.)

Glabrous shrub with rather slender, terete branches and soft, trifoliolate leaves. Flowers large, yellowish-green, in terminal or leaf-opposed racemes. An introduced plant.   *C. agatiflora* Schweinf.
(pl. 27)

(*agatiflora*, flowers like agate-greenish.)

BRACHYSEMA R. Br.

Small shrubs with simple leaves or leaves reduced to scales. Flowers usually red, terminal or axillary, solitary or several together, the pedicels usually recurved so that the keel is turned uppermost.

Distribution: The genus is confined to Australia. About 14 in Australia: 1 in Queensland; 1 in South Australia; 10 in Western Australia; 4 in the Northern Territory.

(*brachys*, short; *sema*, a sign—in this case the standard or large petal.)

Diffuse, procumbent or half-climbing shrub. Usually with alternate, ovate-obtuse, coriaceous leaves with recurved points. Flowers red, axillary, solitary or 2 or 3 together.   *B. lanceolatum* (Meissn.)
(pl. 27)

(*lanceolatum*, lance-shaped.)

Family MIMOSACEAE

A family closely related to Papilionaceae and at one time included with it as a sub-family of Leguminosae. Trees and shrubs with nitrogen-forming nodules on the roots. Widely distributed in the warmer regions of the globe. Leaves compound or reduced to phyllodes. Flowers regular; sepals and petals 4 or 5; stamens numerous. Fruit a legume.

ACACIA Mill

Trees or shrubs with bipinnate leaves or the leaves reduced to phyllodes; stipules small or absent, or represented by 2 spines. Flowers small, regular, yellow or white, in globular heads or cylindrical spikes, subtended by inconspicuous bracteoles.

Distribution: Over 700 in Australia; About 130 in Queensland; 180 in New South Wales; 106 in Victoria; 89 in South Australia; 350 in Western Australia; 100 in the Northern Territory; 20 in Tasmania.

(*Acacia*, an ancient name for some prickly Egyptian species.)
1. Leaves compound.
   2. Flower-heads in axillary racemes. Stipules wanting.
      3. Pinnae 2–4 pairs.
         4. Small tree. Leaflets scarcely paler on the underside. Prominent glands between each pair of pinnae. Pinnae very short, with linear, short, crowded leaflets, silvery-glaucous. Pods fairly long, flat, nearly straight.
            A. baileyana F. Muell.
            (pl. 55)

(F. M. Bailey, botanist.)
         4. Tall shrub. Leaflets much paler on the under-surface, oblong, under 1 cm long, firm, one-veined, not crowded. 10–15 pairs. Pods broad.
            A. terminalis (Salisb.) Court
            A. botrycephala (Vent.) Desf.
            A. discolor (Andr.) Willd.)
            (pl. 27)

(*terminalis*, terminal; referring to the flower-heads.)
      3. Pinnae in numerous pairs.

4. Small tree. Leaflets dark-green, 30–40 pairs, glabrous. Branches with very prominent angles decurrent from the petioles. Pod flat, nearly straight, much constricted between the seeds.

A. decurrens (Wendl.) Willd.
(pl. 50)

(*decurrens*, blade of leaf prolonged downwards along the stem.)

2. Tall shrub. Flower-heads on simple, solitary or clustered peduncles. Stipules spinescent. Pinnae 4–6 pairs, leaflets 10–20 pairs. Flowers fragrant. Pods thick, cylindrical, indehiscent.

A. farnesiana (L.) Willd.
(pl. 37)

(*Farnèse*, a palace in Rome.)

1. Leaves reduced to phyllodes.
5. Flowers in globular heads.
6. Phyllodes terete.

Bushy shrub. Phyllodes spreading, stiff, linear, pungent-pointed, rarely above 1 cm long. Pods falcate.

A. ulicifolia (Salisb.) Court
(pl. 14)

(*ulicifolium*, thorny-leafed.)

6. Phyllodes vertically flattened.
7. Phyllodes one- or rarely, two-veined.
8. Flower-heads in pairs.

Tall shrub. Phyllodes two-veined, acuminate, linear lanceloate, 5–10 cm long. Pod linear, straight, pubescent.

A. verniciflua A. Cunn.
(pl. 55)

(*verniciflua*, varnished; in reference to the leaves.)

8. Flower-heads in axillary racemes.
9. Phyllodes rarely above 4 cm long.
10. Racemes much longer than the phyllodes.

Small tree. Phyllodes obliquely

ovate, glaucous. Pods broad
and short.
A. podalyriifolia A. Gunn. ex G. Don
(pl. 50)
(*Podalyria*, a pea plant; *folium*, a leaf.)
10. Bushy shrub. Racemes not exceeding
the phyllodes. Phyllodes lanceolate, stiff, acute, with thickened edges and a prominent
gland below middle. Pods
linear, curved, thick.
A. myrtifolia (Sm.) Willd.
(pl. 5)
(*Myrtus*, Myrtle; *folium*, a leaf; referring to the similarity
between leaves of this and some European myrtles.)
9. Phyllodes about 4 cm long.
Slender shrub. Phyllodes glaucous, obtuse, mostly about 8 cm
long but very variable. Flowers
pale, covered in imbricate
scales in bud. Pods elliptical to
oblong, flat, glaucous, obtuse.
A. suaveolens (Sm.) Willd.
(pl. 50)
(*suaveolens*, sweet-scented.)
7. Phyllodes, several-veined.
11. Flower-heads in pairs.
Tall shrub. Phyllodes several-
veined, falcate-lanceolate to
linear, with a short, often
incurved, point. Flower-heads
nearly sessile. Pod hard, coriaceous, much twisted and coiled.
A. osswaldii F. Muell.
(pl. 55)
(Ferdinand Oswald, Adelaide collector for Baron von Mueller.)
11. Flower-heads in short axillary
racemes.
Tall shrub. Phyllodes falcate-
lanceolate with several veins,
rather thin, 7–15 cm long.
Branchlets nearly terete. Pods

109

rather narrow, curved or twisted, slightly constricted between seeds.

A. implexa Benth.
(pl. 50)

(*implexa*, entwined.)
    5. Flowers in cylindrical or rarely oblong spikes.
        12. Phyllodes elongated, not pungent.
           Shrub or small tree. Phyllodes elliptical-lanceolate, 5–15 cm long, coriaceous with several veins reticulate between them. Pods curved and twisted, somewhat constricted between seeds.

A. longifolia (Andr.) Willd.
(pl. 55)

(*longifolia*, long-leafed.)
        12. Phyllodes rather broad. Spikes dense.
           13. Young branches very angular. Tall shrub or small tree. Phyllodes slightly falcate, rather thick, often with recurved points. Pods very narrow, slightly constricted between seeds.

A. doratoxylon A. Cunn.
(pl. 14)

(*doru, dorata*, a spear; *xylon*, wood.)
           13. Young branches scarcely angular. Small tree. Phyllodes glaucous, pubescent, falcate-lanceolate, coriaceous, narrowed at both ends. Pods linear, straight.

A. glaucescens Willd.
(pl. 38)

(*glaucescens*, bluish-grey; in reference to the bloom on the leaves.)

Family CAESALPINIACEAE

A family closely related to Fabaceae and at one time included with it as a sub-family of Leguminosae. Trees and shrubs with compound leaves, rarely reduced to phyllodes. Flowers large, irregular, with 5 sepals, 5 petals, 10 stamens, some of them usually aborted. Fruit a legume.

CASSIA L.

Trees or shrubs with pinnate leaves, rarely reduced to phyllodes; stipules usually hard and deciduous. Flowers yellow, petals spreading. Pod usually 2-valved.

Distribution: 53 in Australia: 28 in Queensland; 17 in New South Wales; 3 in Victoria; 11 in South Australia; 28 in Western Australia; 23 in the Northern Territory.

(*Casia* or *Cassia*, from Hebrew *qaseah*, Cinnamon Laurel; in error.)

Erect glabrous shrub with compound leaves; leaflets 3–4 pairs, ovate to lanceolate, usually acuminate, with a slender gland between each pair. Pod membranous or somewhat coriaceous, cylindrical, and more or less inflated when ripe.   *C. floribunda* Cav.
(pl. 37)

(*floribunda*, rich in flowers.)

Family THYMELAEACEAE

This is a small order of about forty genera, a few of them in the temperate regions of the northern hemisphere, more common in the tropics, and most abundant in South Africa and Australia. Daphne is a well-known garden plant of the family.

Herbs or shrubs, with alternate or opposite, simple and entire leaves. Flowers in terminal or axillary clusters or inflorescences, surrounded by an involucre of 4 or more bracts.

Flowers perfect or rarely dioecious. Perianth simple, tubular or campanulate, usually regular, 4- or rarely 5-lobed. Stamens 2 or 4, or rarely 8 or 10, perigynous; anthers with 2 parallel cells opening longitudinally. Ovary superior, 1- or rarely 2-celled. Style simple with a terminal capitate or truncate stigma.

Fruit an indehiscent nut, berry, or drupe, or rarely a 2-valved capsule.

PIMELEA Banks and Soland. ex. Gaertn.

Shrubs or undershrubs with small tubular flowers. Sepals 4, petaloid. Petals wanting. Stamens 2, on short filaments. Ovary 1-celled. Fruit indehiscent, membranous.

Distribution: A genus belonging to Australia and New Zealand. About 80 in Australia: 20 in Queensland; 27 in New South Wales; 22 in Victoria; 22 in South Australia; 38 in Western Australia; 7 in the Northern Territory; 18 in Tasmania.

(*pimele*, fat; in reference to the oily seeds.)

Erect glabrous shrub, virgate, with opposite leaves, on very short petioles, linear-oblong or linear-spathulate. Fruit a nut. Very common in eastern New South Wales.

P. linifolia Sm.
(pl. 62)

(*Linum*, the Flax; *folium*, a leaf.)

Family MELASTOMATACEAE

This family is commonly distributed in the warm regions of India and America. It contains several plants with edible fruits. The beautiful garden shrub *Tibouchina* ("Lasiandra") is a member. Herbs, shrubs or, rarely, trees, with opposite leaves and flowers.

Flowers usually in terminal panicles or clusters. Sepals 3–5, or rarely 6. Petals as many as calyx lobes, imbricate, often contorted in bud. Stamens usually twice as many as petals, perigynous, the filaments curved down in bud; anthers 2-celled, opening in 1 or 2 pores at the top, or rarely in longitudinal slits. Ovary enclosed in the calyx tube, superior, with 2–6 or rarely more, cells. Style simple with a minute, capitate or peltate stigma. Ovules several in each cell.

Fruit succulent and indehiscent or bursting irregularly, or a capsule opening in as many valves as there are cells.

MELASTOMA L.

Shrubs with large showy flowers. Sepals and petals 5. Stamens 10, 5 large and 5 small. Ovary 5-celled. Fruit succulent, opening irregularly.

Distribution: A considerable genus extending over tropical Asia, the Pacific Islands and Australia. 1 in Australia: in Queensland, New South Wales, and the Northern Territory.

(*melas*, black; *stoma*, a mouth; alluding to the fact that the berries stain the mouth black.)

Small shrub, more or less clothed with bristles. Leaves

petiolate, ovate to oblong-lanceolate. Flowers usually 5–11, in terminal, almost sessile, cymes. Petals large, pale-purple or white. Fruit a succulent, nearly globular berry, pulp purple. *M. denticulatum* Labill.
(pl. 40)
(*denticulatum*, with small teeth; probably referring to the bracts at the back of the calyx.)

Family VITACEAE

A family most commonly found in the warmer regions and only poorly represented in Australia.

Woody climbers or rarely erect shrubs. Branches often articulate. Leaves alternate, or the lower ones opposite, simple or compound, the petiole usually articulate with the stem and expanded into a membranous stipule. Flowers small, in inflorescences.

Flowers regular, perfect or unisexual. Calyx small, entire or 4- or 5-toothed. Petals 4 or 5, free or cohering, valvate in bud. Stamens 4 or 5, epigynous. Ovary immersed in or surrounded by the disc, 2–6 celled. Style short and conical or subulate, or wanting; stigma small, capitate or lobed. Ovules 2 in each cell where there are 2 cells, 1 in each cell where there are more than 2.

Fruit a berry, seeds 1–6.

CISSUS L.

Woody climbers with articulate branches and leaf-opposed tendrils, and alternate, stipulate leaves. Flowers small, greenish, in cymes. Stamens free. Ovary 2-celled.

Distribution: A genus extending over the warmer regions of the earth. About 10 in Australia: 8 in Queensland; 4 in New South Wales; 1 in Victoria; 1 in Western Australia; 2 in the Northern Territory.

(*Kissos*, Ivy, e.g. climbing plant.)

Tall climber with rusty-tomentose young shoots. Leaves simple, ovate-oblong to nearly cordate, acuminate, thick, shining, glabrous, denticulate or nearly entire. Fruits globular, black. *C. antarctica* Vent.
(pl. 33)

(*antarctica*, of the antarctic; a misnomer.)

113

Family ROSACEAE

A very large and important family, chiefly of the temperate zones of the north, of very great economic importance, producing a great many edible fruits and ornamental flowering plants. Perhaps more than any order this has provided material for the breeder of plants of economic value.

Trees, shrubs, or herbs with alternate, simple or compound, usually stipulate, leaves. Flowers in axillary or terminal cymes or rarely racemes, sometimes solitary. Calyx 5- or 4-lobed, sometimes with accessory lobes. Petals as many as sepals. Stamens indefinite, perigynous or epigynous, or rarely hypogynous, free. Ovary superior, sometimes becoming inferior, of 1, 2, or more cells, usually distinct but later sometimes fused to the receptacle to form a 2–5 celled (then always inferior) fruit; ovules 1, 2 or, rarely, more in each cell. Style sessile, stigmas distinct.

Fruit a pome (apple), a drupe (peach), or a collection of small drupes (*Rubus*) or achenes on a fleshly receptacle (strawberry).

RUBUS L.

Weak, scrambling or prostrate shrubs, usually prickly, with pinnately or palmately divided leaves with toothed lobes. Flowers axillary or in terminal, leafy panicles. Fruit a head of succulent drupels.

Distribution: A fairly big genus found in most parts of the globe. About 13 in Australia: 7 in Queensland; 4 in New South Wales; 3 in Vic toria; 1 in South Australia; 1 in the Northern Territory; 2 in Tasmania.

(*Rubus*, the blackberry.)

> Tall, scrambling, woolly shrub. Leaves ovate to cordate-orbicular, toothed broadly 2–5 lobed, rusty underneath. Flowers red or white. Fruit red, nearly globular.
>
> *R. hillii* F. Muell.
> (pl. 13)

> Weak, creeping, glandular, pubescent shrub. Leaves ovate-lanceolate, green on both sides. Flowers white. Fruit ovoid or rarely globular, dark-red, of numerous small carpels.
>
> *R. rosifolius* Sm.
> (pl. 63)

(*Rosa*, the rose; *folium*, a leaf.)

Family CUNONIACEAE

Trees or shrubs, leaves trifoliolate or pinnate, rarely simple, mostly opposite; leaflets often glandular-sinuate. Stipules sometimes large, and united in pairs.

Flowers perfect or unisexual, solitary or in panicles. Petals 2–3 lobed, entire or toothed. Stamens perigynous, numerous, or few and alternate with the petals; filaments free; anthers 2-celled, opening longitudinally. Ovary superior or half-inferior, free, often 2–5 celled. Styles free. Ovules usually numerous.

Fruit dehiscent or indehiscent. A small family, mainly in the southern hemisphere.

> Twining plants. *Aphanopetalum.*
> Erect plants.
>> Flowers in loose inflorescences, sepals enlarging and colouring in fruit. *Ceratopetalum.*
>> Flowers in tight inflorescences. Sepals not enlarging on fruit. *Callicoma.*

APHANOPETALUM Endl.

Straggling or climbing shrubs, glabrous, with opposite, simple leaves; stipules minute. Flowers usually few in short cymes or leafy panicles. Fruit small, dry, surrounded by the wing-like calyx lobes.

Distribution: The genus is limited to Australia. 2 in Australia: 1 in Queensland, and New South Wales; and 1 in Western Australia.

(*aphanos*, invisible; *petalon*, a leaf or petal—since the petals are so tiny.)

> Tall, straggling or climbing glabrous shrub, with raised, resinous dots. Leaves ovate-lanceolate or elliptical, obtuse or scarcely acuminate, obscurely serrate, thinly coriaceous, smooth and shining. *A. resinosum* Endl.
> (pl. 61)

(*resinosum*, gum-bearing.)

CERATOPETALUM Sm.

Trees or tall shrubs, glabrous, with opposite, reticulate, coriaceous leaves; stipules minute. Flowers in terminal cymes or panicles.

Distribution: The genus is limited to Australia. 4 in Australia: 3 in Queensland; 2 in New South Wales.

(*ceratos*, horny; *petalon*, a leaf or petal.)

115

Tall shrub or small tree with smooth, trifoliolate, serrated leaves; leaflets lanceolate, shining. Petals and enlarged fruit laciniate. Enlarged calyx lobes deep-red. Fruit hard, indehiscent. *C. gummiferum* Sm. (pl. 40)

(*gummi*, gum; *ferum*, bearing.)

CALLICOMA Andr.

Trees with simple, opposite leaves; stipules ovate, very deciduous. Seeds tuberculate.

Distribution: The genus is limited to 1 Australian species, in Queensland and New South Wales.

(*calli*, beautiful; *come*, hair; in reference to the fine stamens.)
Tall shrub or small tree, young shoots often tomentose. Leaves elliptical-ovate to ovate-lanceolate, shortly acuminate, coarsely serrate, coriaceous, glabrous, white or rust-coloured below. Flowers small, numerous, in dense, yellow-globular heads. Fruit a tomentose capsule, separating into carpels. Follows watercourses. *C. serratifolia* Andr. (pl. 65)

(*serratus*, saw-edged; *folium*, a leaf.)

Family BAUERACEAE

A small order consisting of 1 genus only, confined to Australia. Small shrubs with small opposite sessile trifoliate leaves and regular, perfect flowers. Sepals 4–10, petals 4–10, free. Stamens 4–10, or more; perigynous; anthers opening by pore-like slits. Ovary superior, with 2 free styles, 2-celled.
Fruit a capsule free from the calyx.

BAUERA Banks

Low shrubs with opposite, sessile, trifoliate leaves, without stipules. Flowers solitary, axillary, with 4–10 spreading petals, usually rose-coloured. Stamens numerous. Ovary 2-celled. Fruit a truncate capsule opening loculicidally.

Distribution: The genus is confined to Australia. 3 in Australia: 2 in Queensland, New South Wales and Victoria; 1 in South Australia and Tasmania.

(Francis and Ferdinand Bauer, botanical artists.)
Graceful, slender shrub, branches terete. Leaves opposite, trifoliate; leaflets oblong or lanceolate, slightly serrate.

116

Flowers pink or white, on slender pedicels. Petals usually 8–9. Fruit a short capsule. Usually near water.

B. *rubioides* Andr.

(pl. 11)

(*Rubia*, a genus of plants; *oides*, like.)

Family APIACEAE

A numerous family found nearly all over the globe, especially in the temperate regions of the northern hemisphere.

Herbs or rarely shrubs with alternate, usually much-divided leaves, with the petiole dilated into a sheathing base but mostly without stipules. Flowers commonly small in terminal or lateral inflorescences (umbels) with bracts at the base of the umbel.

Flowers perfect or imperfect by the suppression of ovary or stamens. Calyx 5-toothed or lobed, the tube adnate to the ovary, often very small. Petals 5, usually inflexed at the tip, more or less imbricate (occasionally valvate) in bud. Stamens 5, epigynous, alternating with the petals and inserted with them round the disc at the summit of the adnate calyx tube; anthers versatile with parallel cells, opening longitudinally. Ovary inferior, 2-celled or occasionally 1-celled by abortion, with 1 ovule in each cell. Styles 2, with small, terminal stigmas.

Fruit usually separating into 2 indehiscent 1-seeded nuts called mericarps. Each carpel is marked with longitudinal ribs, normally 5 to each carpel, but some may be inconspicuous and, in some genera, others occur between. In many genera there are longitudinal glands (vittae) within the seed.

Flowers in simple umbels.   *Actinotus.*

Flowers in dense spikes.   *Eryngium.*

ACTINOTUS Labill.

Herbs usually with ternately divided leaves. Flowers numerous and crowded into simple umbels surrounded by radiating bracts. Fruit 1-seeded, ovate, dorsally compressed.

Distribution: The genus is confined to Australia. About 13 in Australia: 3 in Queensland; 5 in New South Wales; 7 in Western Australia; 3 in Tasmania.

(*actinotus*, furnished with rays; in reference to the floral arrangement.)

Leaves densely tomentose.

Erect perennial, thickly tomentose. Involucre of 10–18 softly tomentose bracts, white with green tips.

117

Flower-heads 5–8 cm across.   *A. helianthi* Labill.
(pl. 57)
(*Helianthus*, a composite genus including the Sunflower.)
  Leaves glabrous.
  Much branched annual or biennial. Leaves glabrous.
  Involucre of about 12 bracts, reddish-brown shading
  to white with long white silky hair. Flower-heads
  1–2 cm across.   *A. forsythii* Maiden et Betche
(pl. 48)
(Forsyth, one-time curator of Centennial Park.)

ERYNGIUM L.

Glabrous herbs with prickly, lobed leaves and flowers in compact
spikes or heads with narrow, pungent bracts, the outer ones
forming an involucre. Petals with a much inflexed, long apex.
Fruit turgid.

Distribution: A widely distributed genus, more common in the
northern hemisphere. 4 in Australia: 4 in Queensland; 4 in New
South Wales; 2 in Victoria; 4 in South Australia; 1 in Western
Australia; 2 in the Northern Territory and Tasmania.

(*Eryngium*, a kind of Thistle.)
  Erect herb. Radical leaves elongated, linear, pinnatifid,
  with entire or pinnatifid lobes, or in wet places the
  leaves quite entire, grass-like. Stem leaves only under
  the peduncles or branches, once or twice pinnatifid,
  very rigid and pungent. Flower-heads ovoid-globular.
  Fruit ovoid, scarcely compressed, ribs inconspicuous,
  vittae wanting.   *E. rostratum* Cav.
(pl. 19)
(*rostratum*, beaked; in reference to the beaked bracts.)

Family MYRTACEAE

This is a family represented in both northern and southern hemispheres and well represented in Australia. There are three major
divisions of the family, one with fleshy fruits and two with dry
fruits. The fleshy-fruited types are mesophytes, widely distributed
over the tropical regions of South America, the East Indies, and
north-eastern Australia. The dry-fruited types are mostly xerophytic and almost entirely Australian. Representative are
Eucalypts, Tea-trees, Bottlebrushes, and so many other genera
that it is one of the most important families of our open forest
country.

It is a significant family economically. Among the tropical species are found some bearing edible fruits (Guavas); others are used for spices (Allspice); another yields the cloves of commerce; another the volatile oil of Cajeput. Among the dry-fruited species we have some of the finest hardwood timbers including Turpentine, Stringybarks, Ironbarks, Boxes, and trees with a very high yield of the best essential oils.

Plants are trees or shrubs with simple, entire or rarely crenate leaves, opposite or alternate, without stipules and dotted with oil glands.

Flowers solitary or in inflorescences which are axillary or terminal. Bracteoles 2, at the base of the pedicel, often deciduous. Lower flowers sometimes aborted. Calyx tube adnate to the ovary at the base or at the insertion of the stamens; sepals 4 or 5, sometimes wanting. Petals as many as calyx lobes, much imbricate in bud, usually all equal, free, often small and deciduous, and, in several species sometimes wanting. Stamens indefinite, epigynous or perigynous, usually numerous, sometimes few and definite, in one or several rows on a disc; filaments free or united in a ring close round the summit of the ovary, or into as many bundles as there are calyx lobes; anthers 2-celled, versatile or basifixed. Ovary inferior or half-inferior, enclosed in the calyx tube; sometimes 1-celled, more commonly 2- or more celled. Style simple with a small stigma, usually capitate or peltate. Ovules 2 or more in each cell, in 2 or more rows.

Fruit inferior, adnate to the calyx tube, and crowned by the persistent limb, or marked by its scar when deciduous, or rarely partly superior and surrounded at the base by the persistent calyx tube. Fruit a succulent, 1- or many-seeded berry or a capsule opening loculicidally in as many valves as there are carpels.

1. Ovary 1-celled.
　　2. Sepals terminated by long awns.   *Calytrix.*
　　2. Sepals and petals fringed or digitate.   *Verticordia.*
1. Ovary 2-celled.
　　　3. Filaments connate into 5 bundles.
　　　　4. Flowers sessile. Arranged in spikes.
　　　　　5. Anthers erect.   *Calothamnus.*
　　　　　5. Anthers versatile.   *Melaleuca.*
　　　　4. Flowers pedunculate. Arranged in cymes.
　　　　　　　　　　　　　　　　　　　　　Tristania.
　　3. Stamens free.
　　　　6. Leaves alternate.

7. Stamens shorter or slightly longer than petals.
   Leptospermum.
7. Stamens over twice length of petals.
   8. Calyx lobes persistent to fruiting stage.
      Flowers in leafy spikes or compact heads.
      Kunzea.
   8. Calyx lobes falling before fruiting.
      Flowers in leafless spikes.
      Callistemon.
6. Leaves opposite.
   9. Fruit a berry.
      10. Fruit purplish-white, globular. Petals
         connate into a deciduous cap.
         Acmena.
      10. Fruit red or blue. Petals free, some-
         times deciduous.   *Syzygium.*
         11. Floral tube smooth.
            Tristania.
         11. Floral tube ribbed.
            Angophora.

LEPTOSPERMUM Forst

Shrubs or, rarely, small trees with alternate leaves. Flowers white, cream, red or pink, solitary and axillary, or terminating short, lateral branches; bracts usually broad and scarious. Fruit a capsule, opening at the top with numerous seeds.

Distribution: A large genus, common in the Indian Archipelago, New Zealand and Australia. About 60 in Australia; 25 in Queensland; 35 in New South Wales; 14 in Victoria; 5 in South Australia; 10 in Western Australia; 8 in Tasmania; 1 in the Northern Territory.

(*leptos*, narrow, *spermum*, a seed.)
   Leaves pungent-pointed, more or less clustered, concave, acute. Flowers pale-pink or peach-coloured, sessile, often produced on the main branches.
      L. squarrosum (Reichb.) Gaertn.
      (pl. 64)

(*squarrosum*, thickly crowded and rigid.)
   Leaves obtuse, with a grooved-recurved tip, broader than long, orbicular. Flowers white or pink.

L. scoparium Forst. var. *rotundifolium* Maiden & Betche
(pl. 25)
(*scoparium*, broom-like; *rotundus*, spherical; *folium*, a leaf.)
Leaves longer than broad, obtuse or acute, narrow-oblong
to obovate. Petals and filaments pale creamy-white or
white.
L. flavescens Sm.
(pl. 53)
(*flavescens*, yellow; in reference to the cream flowers.)

CALYTRIX Labill.

Small heath-like shrubs with small alternate stipulate leaves and
2 persistent narrow bracteoles at the base of the flower. Calyx
lobes produced into long hair-like awns.
Distribution: About 40 species, all Australian, mostly from
western and tropical parts. About 2 in Queensland; 2 in New
South Wales; 1 in Victoria; 2 in South Australia; 27 in Western
Australia; 1 in the Northern Territory; 1 in Tasmania.
(*kalyx*, a cup; *thrix*, a hair; referring to the awns on the sepals.)
Leaves alternate, linear, less than 1 cm long on very short
petioles. Flowers subsessile, solitary in the upper axils,
forming leafy heads, pink, white, or pale-yellow. Calyx
tube expanding after the petals have fallen.
C. tetragona Labill.
(pl. 33)
(*tetragona*, four-angled; referring to the leaves.)

VERTICORDIA DC.

Heath-like shrubs, glabrous, except for cilia on the edges of the
leaves; leaves small, entire, usually opposite. Flowers usually
pedicellate in the upper axils; the plumose, radiating calyx lobes,
often coloured.
Distribution: The genus is confined to Australia. 42 in Australia:
2 in Victoria; 2 in South Australia; 40 in Western Australia;
2 in the Northern Territory.
(*verto*, to turn; *cor, cordis*, heart; possibly in reference to the
inverted heart-shaped leaves of some species.)
Leaves broadly ovate or oblong and flat. Flowers pink, in
loose terminal clusters. Sepals fringed. *V. insignis* Endl.
(pl. 24)
(*insignis*, conspicuous.)
Leaves linear and subterete or oblong and concave.

121

Flowers in leafy racemes. Sepals plumose. Petals fringed
at end.   *V. pennigera* Endl.
                                                       (pl. 24)
(*pennigera*, winged.)

CHAMELAUCIUM Desf.

Heath-like shrubs with opposite or rarely, scattered, narrow,
sessile leaves. Flowers sessile or shortly pedicellate in the axils of
the upper stem leaves; bracteoles broad, thin, scarious. Fruit
formed by the hardened base of the persistent calyx.
  Distribution: A West Australian genus of about 10 species.
  (Probably from *chamelaia*, Greek name for a small, evergreen
    shrub of the daphne kind.)
        Heath-like shrubs with opposite, linear leaves, usually
          with a hooked point. Flowers 2–4, pale to deep-pink, in
          small terminal corymbs. Petals 5, spreading, orbicular.
                                              C. uncinatum Schau.
                                                       (pl. 25)
  (*uncinatum*, hooked; in reference to the leaves.)

CALOTHAMNUS Labill.

Shrubs, usually stout, with scattered, narrow, rigid or terete
leaves. Flowers showy, usually red, in lateral clusters or spikes,
mostly turned to one side; bracts none. Fruit a capsule enclosed
in the hardened and enlarged calyx tube.
  Distribution: A West Australian genus of about 18 species.
  (*calos*, beauty; *thamnos*, a shrub.)
        Low, bushy shrub, more or less hirsute with crowded,
          linear, terete or slightly flattened leaves. Petals 5.
          Stamens in 5 bundles, red. Capsules globular, usually
          truncate.   *C. villosus* R. Br.
                                                       (pl. 49)
(*villosus*, hairy.)

KUNZEA Reichb.

Shrubs, usually with alternate leaves. Flowers in terminal heads
or in the upper axils, usually with scale-like bracts. Fruit a
capsule, opening at the top.
  Distribution: The genus is limited to Australia. About 20 in
Australia: 2 in Queensland; 6 in New South Wales; 5 in Victoria;
1 in South Australia; 12 in Western Australia; 1 in Tasmania.
  (G. Kunze, German botanist.)
        Petals and filaments white.

122

Tall shrub. Leaves clustered, linear to narrow-lanceolate.
Flowers sessile, crowded along the leafy branches.
K. ambigua (Sm.) Druce.
(pl. 53)
(*ambigua*, doubtful.)
Petals and filaments purple.
Small shrub. Leaves ovate to narrow-elliptical.
Flowers few, in small terminal heads.
K. capitata Reichb.
(pl. 25)
(*capitata*, large-headed; in reference to the crowded flowers.)

CALLISTEMON R. Br.

Mostly tall shrubs with alternate, narrow, entire, coriaceous leaves. Flowers showy, closely sessile in dense cylindrical or oblong spikes. Buds usually enclosed in large scarious, caducous bracts. Fruits woody.

Distribution: The genus is confined to Australia. About 20 in Australia: 7 in Queensland; 11 in New South Wales; 8 in Victoria; 4 in South Australia; 1 in Western Australia; 2 in Tasmania.

(*calli*, beauty; *stemon*, a stamen; in reference to the coloured stamens.)
1. Filaments crimson.
2. Filaments quite free.
3. Leaves lanceolate, acute, rigid. Flower-spikes 5–10 cm long, not very dense. Filaments bright-crimson. Fruits truncate. C. citrinus (Curt.) Skeels
(pl. 17)
(*citrinus*, citron-like; probably in reference to the oil in the leaves.)
3. Leaves flat, linear, channelled. Filaments dark-crimson. Flower-spikes 5–12 cm long. Fruits much contracted at the summit. C. linearis DC.
(pl. 45)
(*linearis*, linear or narrow; in reference to the leaves.)
2. Filaments united at the base.
3. Leaves lanceolate, thin. Flowering spikes 5–8 cm long. Filaments bright-crimson. Fruits truncate. C. viminalis (Soland ex. Gaertn.) G. Don
(pl. 10)

(*viminalis*, bearing osiers, hence willow-like or drooping.)
1. Filaments yellowish, anthers yellow.
>4. Leaves flat, acute, distinctly veined. Flowers in loose short spikes about 5–8 cm long. Filaments cream. Fruits truncate. *C. salignus* (Sm.) DC.
>(pl. 62)

(*salignus*, willowy.)
>4. Leaves terete, rigid, channelled above. Filaments green. Flowering spikes 5–12 cm long, flowers not very densely packed. *C. pinifolius* DC.
>(pl. 36)

(*Pinus*, the Pine; *folium*, a leaf.)

ANGOPHORA Cav.

Trees or shrubs, usually with opposite leaves. Flowers white, in umbel-like cymes, forming corymbs; bracts very deciduous. Calyx 5-ribbed.

Distribution: The genus is limited to eastern Australia. 7 in Australia: 5 in Queensland; 7 in New South Wales; 1 in Victoria.
>(*angos*, a vessel; *phora*, bearing; in reference to the goblet-like fruits.)
>>Tall shrub with deciduous bark, branches and inflorescence densely hispid, with reddish hairs. Leaves opposite, obtuse, whitish underneath, sessile, cordate and stem-clasping. Flowers large in dense corymbs, creamy-white. Fruit a ribbed capsule.
>>*A. hispida* (Sm.) Blaxell (syn *A. cordifolia* Cav.)
>>(pl. 64)

(cor, *cordis*, the heart; *folium*, a leaf.)

MELALEUCA L.

Shrubs or trees with entire leaves. Flowers sessile in heads or cylindrical spikes, the axis usually growing through the inflorescence into a leafy shoot. Fruits usually forming woody clusters.

Distribution: The genus is a fairly large one, chiefly Australian but also in South-East Asia. About 150 in Australia, the majority in the south-west of Western Australia.
>(*melas*, black; *leucos*, white; alluding to the variation in the colour of the bark.)
>1. Leaves opposite, linear to linear-lanceolate, rigid.
>>2. Flowers white, fragrant, in pairs in dense spikes. Tall tree with slender branches, the bark papery, peeling off in layers, the young shoots and inflorescence pubescent,

124

the foliage glabrous, acute and often with a glaucous appearance. *M. linariifolia* Sm.
(pl. 53)
(*Linaria*, the Toad Flax; *folium*, a leaf.)
2. Flowers red or purple.
3. Leaves linear to lanceolate, usually veinless. Small, glabrous, spreading shrub. Flowers light-purple in short spikes. *M. thymifolia* Sm.
(pl. 10)
(*Thyme*, a kind of plant; *folium*, a leaf.)
3. Leaves ovate, obtuse, rather thin. Tall glabrous shrub with divaricate branches. Flowers large and showy, red, in oblong-cylindrical lateral spikes. *M. elliptica* Labill.
(p. 24)
(*elliptica*, elliptical; referring to the leaves.)
1. Leaves scattered, narrow-linear.
Variable shrub, virgate, glabrous. Leaves semi-tenete. Flowers in almost globular spikes, light-purple or reddish. *M. erubescens* Otto
(pl. 24)
(*erubescens*, reddish; in reference to the flowers.)

TRISTANIA R. Br.

Tall shrubs or trees, usually with fairly large entire leaves. Flowers usually in axillary cymes, pedunculate, often fragrant; bracts none or very deciduous. Capsule opening in 3 valves.
Distribution: There are a few species in South-East Asia and New Caledonia. About 11 in Australia: 6 in Queensland; 4 in New South Wales; 1 in Victoria; 1 in the Northern Territory.
(M. Tristan, French botanist.)
Tall shrub or small tree with opposite, lanceolate, acute, glabrous leaves. Flowers yellow, in a terminal corymb. Stamens erect, much exserted. Capsule small, not protruding from the persistent calyx.
T. neriifolia (Sm.)
R. Br. (pl. 25)
(*Nerium*, the Oleander; *folium*, a leaf.)

EUGENIA L.
(Including ACMENA DC.
and SYZYGIUM Gaertn.)

Note: The true genus *Eugenia* may not occur in Australia. Two closely related genera, *Acmena* and *Syzygium*, do. They differ from

125

Eugenia in certain details of seed structure and behaviour in germination and in the fact that the calyx-tube is produced above the ovary, whereas in *Eugenia* proper the calyx-tube is not produced above the ovary.

These two genera, *Acmena* and *Syzygium*, are so closely related that for purposes of identification they are considered here together. They may be distinguished from each other by the following key.

Anther loculi parallel. Truncate calyx on fruit   SYZYGIUM
Anther loculi diverging. Remains of lobed calyx on fruit

                   ACMENA

(*Acmena*, nymph of Venus.)

(*Syzygium*, joining together, perhaps referring to the seed-leaves in some species.)

Distribution: Two genera spread over the tropical and sub-tropical regions of the world. About 50 in Australia: about 40 in Queensland; 20 in New South Wales; 1 in Victoria; 7 in the Northern Territory.

   1. Fruit white or light-purple.
      2. Glabrous tree with leaves ovate to ovate-oblong or ovate-lanceolate, usually obtuse, narrowed at the base, smooth and shining. Flowers small and numerous in a terminal panicle.

     Acmena smithii (Poir.), Merrill et Perry (*E. smithii* Poir.)

                                (pl. 26)

(J. E. Smith, eighteenth- and nineteenth-century botanist.)

      2. Small tree with white bark and opposite, acuminate, narrow-lanceolate to ovate leaves. Flowers in inflorescences at the ends of the branches or in the upper leaf axils. Fruit globose or urn-shaped; purplish-blue.

     Syzygium coolminianum (C. Moore) L. Johnson

                                  (pl. 48)

(*coolminianum*, in reference to the aboriginal name for the tree *Coolmin*.)

   1. Fruit red or dark-purple.
      3. Leaves elliptical, tapering at both ends, glossy. Tree with smooth, grey bark. Flowers in inflorescences at the ends of the branches. Fruit globular.

     Acmena australis (C. Moore) L. Johnson

                                  (pl. 17)

(*australis*, southern.)

3. Leaves ovate or lanceolate.
   4. Stamens long (about 1 cm).
      Small tree. Leaves cuneate. Flowers in short axillary panicles. Fruit ovoid or nearly globular.

S. paniculatum Gaertn.
(pl. 1)

(*paniculatum*, paniculate; flowers arranged in a loose inflorescence.)
   4. Stamens short (about 0.5 cm).
      Tree with grey or brown bark. Leaves acuminate, glossy on the upper surface. Flowers in small inflorescences at the ends of branches or in the forks of the upper leaves. Fruit red, somewhat pear-shaped.

S. luehmannii (F. Muell.) L. Johnson
(pl. 26)

(J. G. Luehmann, one-time Government botanist of Victoria.)

Family LENTIBULARIACEAE

Herbs growing in marshy places or in water, with radical, floating leaves or none. Flowers solitary or several in a leafless, slender raceme.

Flowers perfect. Calyx free, 2–5 sepals. Corolla irregular, the tube usually projecting into a spur or pouch at the base, the limb 2-lipped, of 5 petals. Stamens 3, hypogynous, included in the corolla tube. Anthers 1-celled. Ovary superior, 1-celled, with several ovules attached to a free-central placenta. Style short with a 2-lipped stigma.

Fruit a capsule.

UTRICULARIA L.

Herbs with floating or submerged root-like leaves, deeply divided and interspersed with tiny bladders.

Distribution: A widely distributed genus in both northern and southern hemispheres. About 37 in Australia: 16 in Queensland; 7 in New South Wales; 3 in Victoria; 2 in South Australia; 7 in Western Australia; 6 in the Northern Territory; 6 in Tasmania.

(*utricularia*, with leathern bottles; referring to the bladders.)
   Slender herb with radical, petiolate, linear or ovate leaves. Flower purple or lilac, in slender, terminal inflorscences.

U. dichotoma Labill.
(pl. 26)

(*dichotoma*, cut in two; referring to the disposition of the flowers.)

Family SANTALACEAE

Herbs or shrubs, rarely trees, with alternate or rarely opposite, entire, exstipulate leaves. Flowers usually small, sometimes minute, in terminal or lateral heads, cymes or spikes, or, rarely, solitary.

Flowers perfect, sometimes dioecious. Sepals 3–5, rarely 6, valvate in bud. Petals 3–5. Stamens as many as petals, perigynous; anthers 2-celled, opening longitudinally. Ovary inferior, or, if superior, attached by a broad base, usually 1-celled with 2–5 ovules.

Fruit an indehiscent nut, drupe, or berry.

EXOCARPOS Labill.

Trees or shrubs with leaves reduced to minute scales. Flowers minute, in axillary inflorescences. Petals 4 or 5. Fruit a nut, resting on the succulent, enlarged pedicel.

Distribution: A genus practically confined to Australia. About 11 in Australia: 5 in Queensland; 7 in New South Wales; 5 in Victoria; 4 in South Australia; 4 in Western Australia; 2 in the Northern Territory; 4 in Tasmania.

(*ex*, outside; *carpos*, a fruit.)

Small tree of drooping habit, believed to be partially parasitic on the roots of other plants. Leaves reduced to minute scales. Fruit ovoid, globular, the enlarged pedicel red and fleshy. *E. cupressiformis* Labill. (pl. 13)

(*Cupressus*, Cypress Pine; *formis*, shape.)

Family LORANTHACEAE

Branching shrubs, partially parasitic on the branches of trees. Leaves opposite or rarely alternate, thick and leathery, or rarely fleshy, sometimes reduced to minute scales or wanting.

Sepals 4–6, the tube adnate to the ovary. Petals 4–6, free or united, valvate in bud. Stamens 4–6, epigynous. Ovary inferior, 1-celled with 1 ovule.

Fruit a succulent drupe or berry.

DENDROPHTHOE Mart.

Parasitic shrubs usually with opposite leaves. Flowers racemose

128

or spicate with short pedicels. Long and brightly coloured. Fruit a berry.

Distribution: A genus of wide distribution in the tropics and sub-tropics. There are 6 species in Australia, mainly in Queensland and the Northern Territory.

(*dendron*, a tree; *phthoe*, to destroy.)

Leaves broadly ovate to ovate-lanceolate, obtuse, narrowed at the base, alternate, thick. Flowers large in short dense axillary racemes, pedicellate; tube yellow, petals joined, expanded petals red.   *D. vitellina* Tiegh.
(pl. 9)

(*vitellinus*, like the yolk of an egg.)

AMYEMA Tiegh.

Parasitic shrubs with opposite leaves. Flowers cymose, long and brightly coloured. Fruit a berry.

Distribution: A genus of wide distribution in the tropics and sub-tropics. There are about 30 species in Australia, in all states.

(*amyema*, meaning obscure.)

Leaves obovate or oblong-cuneate, mostly opposite. Flowers mostly yellow.
A. congener (Sieb. ex Schult. et f.) Tiegh.
(pl. 2)

(*congener*, of the same race; referring to its similarity, sometimes, to its host.)

Family PROTEACEAE

Plants of this family are represented chiefly in South Africa and in Australia, with a few types in eastern Asia and South America, most of them being xerophytic with special modifications to enable them to withstand drought conditions or regions where the available water-supply is low. They have little economic value, though many are cultivated for their decorative habit and attractive flowers. On account of the great diversity of floral form found in the family the name Proteaceae (Proteus—the Sea God alleged to be able to change his form at will) was given to it.

Trees or shrubs with alternate or scattered leaves, rarely opposite or verticillate, sometimes crowded under the inflorescence, usually coriaceous, often vertically placed, without stipules. Flowers axillary or terminal, solitary or, more commonly, in crowded inflorescences, occasionally subtended by conspicuous floral bracts, the pedicels without bracteoles.

129

Flowers perfect. Perianth of one whorl only; 4 petals or petaloid sepals usually deciduous, valvate and united in bud, forming a cylindrical tube often dilated below the middle, perianth segments separating when fully expanded. Stamens 4, often perigynous, opposite the perianth segments and usually sessile in their tips or adnate with the filaments, free after a short distance, or, rarely, the stamens entirely free. Ovary 1-celled, sessile or stalked with a single, terminal, undivided style with a small terminal oblique or lateral stigma. Ovules solitary, 2, or many.

Fruit an indehiscent nut or drupe or a woody follicle, 1-celled and 1-seeded or 1-celled to many-seeded.

1. Leaves alternate.
  2. Flowers sessile.
    3. Leaves divided. Flowers in dense, cone-like heads.
      4. Flower spikes longer than broad. Perianth tube splitting to base.   *Petrophile.*
      4. Flower spikes globular, elongating slightly as fruits ripen. Perianth tube not splitting.   *Isopogon.*
    3. Leaves undivided.
      5. Style prominently exserted. Fruit a woody follicle.   *Banksia.*
      5. Style inconspicuous. Flat hairy, flat-topped achene.   *Conospermum.*
  2. Flowers pedicellate.
      6. Flowers solitary or in pairs or clusters in leaf or bract axils.
        7. Perianth segments spreading equally.   *Persoonia.*
        7. Perianth segments rolled back to one side. Fruit a woody follicle.   *Hakea.*
      6. Flowers in elongated or short dense racemes or umbels.
        8. Floral bracts small, inconspicuous or absent.
          9. Racemes 1-sided or short, dense and umbel-like.
            10. Floral gland 1, horseshoe-shaped. Seeds 2, wingless.   *Grevillea.*
            10. Floral glands 3, separate. Seeds more than 2, winged.   *Lomatia.*
        8. Floral bracts large and coloured.   *Telopea.*

1. Leaves opposite or whorled.
          11. Leaves broad flat coriaceous.
               12. Fruit a woody follicle, pear-shaped.   *Xylomelum.*
               12. Fruit coriaceous.   *Stenocarpus.*
          11. Leaves narrow, stiff with recurved margins.
               12. Fruit a woody follicle, horned.
                                   Lambertia.

TELOPEA R. Br.

Tall shrubs with alternate, coriaceous leaves. Flowers crowded in a large terminal, crimson, head-like raceme surrounded by large coloured bracts. Fruit coriaceous with several winged seeds with yellow powdery substance between them.

Distribution: The genus is confined to Australia. 4 in Australia: 3 in New South Wales; 1 in Victoria; 1 in Tasmania.

(*tele*, far; *opsis*, sight; hence—seen from afar.)

    Tall glabrous handsome shrub with cuneate-oblong or almost obovate, penniveined, rigid leaves, usually sinuate-toothed in the upper part. Flower-head surrounded by large red bracts.   *T. speciosissima* R. Br.
                                          (pl. 45)

(*speciosissima*, most beautiful.)

HAKEA Schrad.

Erect shrubs or, rarely, trees, with alternate leaves. Flowers usually white or cream, in axillary clusters or racemes. Fruit woody with 2 winged seeds.

Distribution: The genus is limited to Australia. About 100 in Australia: 20 in Queensland; 20 in New South Wales; 12 in Victoria; 15 in South Australia; 80 in Western Australia; 14 in the Northern Territory; 7 in Tasmania.

(After Baron Hake.)

    Tall shrub. Leaves flat, lanceolate, obliquely twisted. Flowers in globular sessile inflorescences, pink with protruding cream styles. Fruit narrow, crested.
                                     H. laurina R. Br.
                                        (pl. 23)

(*laurina*, laurel-like.)

    Tall shrub. Leaves narrow, crowded, slightly pungent. Branches slightly hairy. Flowers on short stalks in leaf axils, pink. Fruit ovoid-globular, oblique beaked.
                       H. bakerana F. Muell. et Maiden
                                        (pl. 22)

(After R. T. Baker, biochemist.)
    Tall shrub. Leaves terete, glabrous, pungent-pointed. Branches and young foliage glabrous or silky-hairy. Flowers in axillary sessile clusters. Fruit ovoid-globular, with a small smooth beak.   *H. sericea* Schrad.
(pl. 67)
(*serikon*, silk; since the plant is silky-hairy.)

BANKSIA L.f.

Trees or shrubs with alterate leaves. Flowers usually silky-pubescent, sessile on the thick stem of a large, dense, terminal spike. Fruits woody, consolidated with the stem into a cone-like mass.

Distribution: The genus is limited to Australia. About 50 in Australia; 6 in Queensland; 10 in New South Wales; 5 in Victoria; 2 in South Australia; 43 in Western Australia; 1 in the Northern Territory.

(After Sir Joseph Banks, Father of Australia.)
    Variable tree with closely tomentose young branches and scattered, sometimes irregularly verticillate, oblong-cuneate or lanceolate, entire or irregularly toothed leaves. Flowers in oblong or cylindrical spikes. Fruit an oblong-cylindrical cone of several follicles.
B. integrifolia L.
(pl. 15)
(*integer*, whole; *folium*, a leaf; alluding to the unbroken leaf edges.)

XYLOMELUM Sm.

Small trees with opposite, large leaves. Flowers in dense spikes, axillary or apparently terminal; bracts very deciduous. Fruit woody, large, with 2 flat, winged seeds.

Distribution: The genus is confined to Australia. 5 in Australia: 3 in Queensland; 2 in New South Wales; 2 in Western Australia.

(*xylon*, wood; *melum*, a fruit.)
    Slender tree, young shoots rusty-tomentose, with entire or prickly, toothed, lanceolate, coriaceous leaves. Flowers dense, woolly. Fruit a large pyriform follicle, with 2 winged seeds.   *X. pyriforme* Sm.
(pl. 23)
(*pyriforme*, pear-shaped.)

132

PERSOONIA Sm.

Shrubs or small trees with entire, opposite or alternate leaves, usually narrowed into a short petiole. Flowers mostly yellow, perianth segments spreading and recurved, usually solitary in leaf axils.

Distribution: With the exception of 1 species in New Zealand, the genus is Australian. About 80 in Australia: 12 in Queensland; 32 in New South Wales; 8 in Victoria; 1 in South Australia; 23 in Western Australia; 3 in the Northern Territory; 2 in Tasmania.

(After C. H. Persoon, great botanist and father of mycology—the study of fungi.)

Tall shrub, with drooping habit. Leaves narrow, terete, linear, filiform, glabrous. Branches and young leaves pubescent. *P. pinifolia* R. Br. (pl. 37)

(*Pinus*, the Pine; *folium*, a leaf.)

Tall, erect shrub. Leaves broad, lanceolate, mostly falcate, flat, almost vertical, distinctly veined, glabrous when full grown. *P. levis* (Cav.) Domin (pl. 7)

(*levis*, smooth; referring to the leaves and shoots.)

PETROPHILE R. Br.

Shrubs with rigid leaves, usually much divided. Flowers crowded, in cone-like heads, with spreading perianth segments and persistent scales at the base of the flowers. Fruit a small nut.

Distribution: The genus is confined to Australia. About 40 in Australia: 4 in Queensland; 4 in New South Wales; 1 in South Australia; 30 in Western Australia.

(*petra*, rock; *philos*, loving; in reference to the habitat of most species.)

Glabrous shrub. Leaves divided, twice or thrice pinnate, segments numerous, terete, divaricate, slender, blunt, grooved above. Perianth silky-hairy, yellow. *P. sessilis* Sieber ex Schult. et f. (pl. 7)

(*sessilis*, sessile; alluding to the stalkless flower-heads.)

Erect shrub. Leaves entire, linear, flat, thick, incurved towards the end. Perianth pinkish with dark-grey tips, densely hairy. *P. linearis* R. Br. (pl. 23)

(*linearis*, linear or narrow; in reference to the leaves.)

ISOPOGON R. Br

Shrubs with rigid, usually much-divided leaves. Flowers crowded in cone-like heads with a slender perianth and deciduous scales at the base of the flowers. Fruit a small nut.

Distribution: The genus is confined to Australia. About 36 in Australia: 2 in Queensland; 6 in New South Wales; 2 in Victoria; 1 in South Australia; 24 in Western Australia; 1 in Tasmania.

(*isos*, equal; *pogon*, a beard; in reference to the hairs on the fruit.)

Glabrous shrub. Leaves compound, much dissected, branches terete. Inflorescences almost sessile, solitary or in clusters of 2 or 3 at the ends of the branches, nearly globular. Fruit a nut.   *I. anethifolius* (Salisb.) Knight
(pl. 7)

(*Anethum*, a plant of the Flannel Flower family; *folium*, a leaf.)

STENOCARPUS R. Br.

Glabrous trees with alternate leaves. Flowers in umbels without bracts. Fruit narrow, coriaceous with winged seeds.

Distribution: New Caledonia and Australia. 5 in Australia: 4 in Queensland; 2 in New South Wales, Western Australia and Northern Territory.

(*stenos*, narrow; *carpos*, a fruit.)

Glabrous tree with sinuate or divided glossy leaves. Inflorescences terminal, 2 or more together in a general umbel of bright-red flowers. Fruit a long narrow follicle with numerous winged seeds.   *S. sinuatus* Endl.
(pl. 23)

(*sinuatus*, wavy; alluding to the wavy leaf margins.)

GREVILLEA R. Br.

Trees or shrubs with alternate leaves. Flowers in racemes, often umbel-like; bracts very deciduous. Stamens sessile in the tips of the perianth segments. Fruit coriaceous, usually oblique, with 2 seeds, usually wingless.

Distribution: The genus is practically confined to Australia. About 230 in Australia: 30 in Queensland; 50 in New South Wales; 20 in Victoria; 15 in South Australia; 140 in Western Australia; 6 in the Northern Territory; 1 in Tasmania.

(C. F. Greville, a keen horticulturist and patron of botany.)

1. Leaves divided.
   2. Tall, delicate, silvery-white, tomentose shrub with narrow-lanceolate leaves. Inflorescence

134

a long terminal one-sided raceme of reddish flowers.   *G. longifolia* R. Br.
(pl. 45)
(Note: Known for some time as *G. aspleniifolia*.)
(*longus*, long; *folium*, a leaf.)
2. Tall, softly rusty-tomentose shrub with deeply divided leaves. Flowers red, cream, or green, terminal, dense, softly hairy outside in racemes 5–10 cm long, solitary or 2 or 3 together.   *G. banksii* R. Br.
(pl. 22)
(Sir Joseph Banks, Father of Australia.)
1. Leaves entire.
   3. Ovary villous.
      4. Perianth dilated below the middle.
         5. Perianth glabrous outside, bearded within. Bushy shrub with oblong, glabrous leaves. Perianth red with greenish-yellow apex. Flowers in short inflorescences.
G. baueri R. Br.
(pl. 22)
(Ferdinand Bauer, botanical artist.)
         5. Perianth hairy outside. Bushy shrub with acutely acuminate, ovate or lanceolate leaves. Flowers greenish-brown in short, loose, few-flowered inflorescences.
G. mucronulata R. Br.
(pl. 6)
(*mucronulatus*, with little points; in reference to the leaves.)
      4. Perianth not dilated, villous inside and outside. Shrub with ovate or broadly lanceolate leaves, usually about 1 cm long, but very variable with recurved margins. Flowers grey, rather large, hairy, in short dense inflorescences.   *G. buxifolia* (Sm.) R. Br.
(pl. 6)
(*Buxus*, the ancient Box-wood; *folium*, a leaf.)
   3. Ovary glabrous, rarely with a few basal hairs.
      6. Ovary not stipitate. Shrub with slender, velvety branches and sessile, linear to narrow-lanceolate, pointed

135

leaves with revolute margins. Flowers
pink, short, in racemes, often nodding.

G. *rosmarinifolia* A. Cunn.

(pl. 22)

(*Rosmarinus*, Rosemary; *folium*, a leaf.)
      6. Ovary stipitate.
         7. Style much longer than the corolla.
            8. Leaves 2–5 cm long.
               Small tomentose shrub with oblong-
elliptical or almost oval obtuse leaves.
Flowers red, in short and dense racemes.

G. *speciosa* (Knight) D. McGillivray

(syn. G. *punicea*)

(pl. 16)

(*speciosa*, beautiful.)
            8. Leaves 8–10 cm long.
               Erect, tomentose shrub, with stiff, broad,
linear-oval dark-green leaves, with re-
curved margins. Flowers red in short,
dense, spreading racemes.

G. *oleoides* Sieb. ex Schult. et f.

(pl. 45)

(*Olea*, the Olive; *oides*, like; in reference to the leaves.)
         7. Style only slightly longer than perianth.
            Erect, bushy. tomentose shrub with linear-
subulate, spreading pungent-pointed leaves
nearly 2 cm long. Flowers red or yellow,
in short loose racemes.

G. *juniperina* R. Br.

(pl. 7)

(*juniperina*, juniper-like.)

LOMATIA R. Br.

Shrubs or trees with alternate leaves. Flowers long cohering in
loose axillary or terminal racemes with very deciduous bracts.
Fruit coriaceous with several winged seeds with a yellow powdery
substance between them.

Distribution: South America and Australia. About 7 in Australia: 3 in Queensland; 4 in New South Wales; 3 in Victoria; 3
in Tasmania.

(*loma*, a border; in reference to the winged seeds.)
     A glabrous shrub with leaves twice or thrice pinnate, seg-

136

ments sessile and decurrent, linear or lanceolate, deeply and sharply toothed, the whole leaf 15–20 cm long. Flowers cream, in terminal long loose racemes.

L. silaifolia (Sm.) R. Br.

(pl. 66)

(*Silaus*, a northern plant of the Flannel Flower family; *folium*, a leaf.)

CONOSPERMUM Sm.

Shrubs or undershrubs sparingly branched, with entire leaves. Perianth unequally 4-lobed, the upper lobe usually broad. Flowers white or bluish in short dense spikes.

Distribution: The genus is confined to Australia. About 40 in Australia: 2 in Queensland; 6 in New South Wales; 3 in Victoria; 2 in South Australia; 27 in Western Australia.

(*conos*, a cone; *spermum*, a seed.)

Low procumbent shrub with narrow-linear, almost terete, slender leaves, grooved above. Flowers in small inflorescences on long slender pedicels, purple or creamy-white, slender.

C. tenuifolium R. Br.

(pl. 19)

(*tenuis*, slender; *folium*, a leaf.)

LAMBERTIA Sm.

Shrubs, usually with leaves in whorls of 3. Flowers sessile within an involucre of coloured bracts. Perianth elongated, the lobes narrow spirally revolute. Anthers also revolute. Fruits sessile, woody, with horn-like projections and winged seeds.

Distribution: The genus is confined to Australia. 8 in Australia: 1 in New South Wales; 7 in Western Australia.

(A. B. Lambert, an English country gentleman who devoted his life to botany.)

Bushy shrub with linear to narrow-lanceolate, coriaceous, rigid, mucronate leaves. Flowers sessile, in an involucre of red bracts. Inflorescence usually of 7 bright-red flowers.

L. formosa Sm.

(pl. 13)

(*formosus*, beautiful.)

Family ASTERACEAE

A very large family, containing about 20,000 species and distributed all over the world. It contains many ornamental species

137

such as Aster, Cosmos and Dahlia; a few useful species such as the Jerusalem Artichoke which yields edible tubers, the artichoke which gives edible involucral bracts and the annual sunflower whose seeds yield oil, chicory from the roots of another, and insect powder from the crushed heads of another.

Herbs, shrubs, or, very rarely, small trees, with alternate or opposite leaves without stipules. Flower-heads terminal or rarely axillary, solitary or in panicles.

Flowers (or florets) collected together in a head (capitulum) surrounded by a number of involucral bracts, in one or several rows, the whole having the appearance of a single flower. The receptacle on which the florets are inserted is either naked or bearing scales or bristles between florets. In each floret the calyx is missing or converted into a pappus or ring of hairs or scales on the top of the ovary. Flowers either perfect, tubular and 5-toothed, or perfect with 5 petals united into a strap-shaped corolla, or those of the centre or disc tubular and perfect or staminate, and those of the circumference (ray florets) strap-shaped and pistillate or neuter. Stamens 5, epigynous, inserted in the tube of the corolla, the anthers linear and united in a sheath round the style, opening inwards, the connective usually produced at the top into a small, erect appendage. Ovules inferior with a single, erect ovule. Style filiform, often divided at the top into 2 branches. Fruit a small seed-like nut or achene.

1. Florets all of one type. (Perfect flowers.)
  2. Receptacle with bracts. Flowers all yellow.
    3. Involucral bracts appressed, thin and scarious or membranous. *Leptorhynchus.*
    3. Involucral bracts thin and transparent, not radiating. *Podolepis.*
  2. Receptacle without bracts. Involucral bracts white or coloured, papery or scarious.
    4. Pappus hairs with plumes from the base. *Helipterum.*
    4. Pappus hairs simple, barbellate or plumose at the end. *Helichrysum.*
1. Florets of 2 types. (Perfect or pistillate.)
    5. Style branches flattened, produced into papillose tips.
      6. Pappus none or very short. Achenes truncate. *Brachycome.*
      6. Pappus present.
        7. Pappus of short rigid awns or spines. *Calotis.*

7. Pappus of long capillary bristles.
    8. Erect shrubs with woody stems.   *Olearia.*
    8. Herbs with radical leaves.   *Celmisia.*
5. Style branches truncate. Pappus of capillary
    bristles.   *Senecio.*

CALOTIS R. Br.

Herbs with alternate leaves. Flower-heads radiate. Involucral bracts with scarious margins. Fruiting heads usually globular and burr-like.

Distribution: The genus is almost entirely confined to Australia. About 22 in Australia: 15 in Queensland; 16 in New South Wales; 10 in Victoria; 13 in South Australia; 8 in Western Australia; 7 in the Northern Territory.

(*calos*, beautiful; *ous, otis*, an ear—from the ear-shaped scales of the pappus of some species.)

Leaves linear-lanceolate, remotely toothed, small, erect. Perennial, pubescent or hispid, usually with acute leaves often dilated and stem-clasping. Pappus bristles almost united into a fringed cup. Ray florets blue.
C. dentex R. Br.
(pl. 52)

(*dens, dentis*, a tooth.)

Leaves cuneate or spathulate, toothed at the end. Erect or branching perennial, hoary or hirsute, with stem-clasping leaves. Pappus scales broader than long. Ray florets blue.   *C. cuneifolia* R. Br.
(pl. 18)

(*cuneus*, a wedge; *folium*, a leaf.)

BRACHYCOME Cass.

Herbs with alternate or radical leaves. Flowers terminal, the rays white or bluish, rarely yellow. Involucre usually hemispherical, the bracts of nearly equal length with scarious margins.

Distribution: The genus is practically confined to Australia, with a few in New Zealand. About 55 in Australia: 20 in Queensland; 37 in New South Wales; 35 in Victoria; 26 in South Australia; 14 in Western Australia; 14 in Tasmania; 4 in the Northern Territory.

(*brachys*, short; *come*, hair; in reference to the short or absent pappus on the fruit.)

Leaves all radical.

Leaves obovate-oblong, entire or remotely and shortly
toothed or crenate, narrowed into a short, broad
petiole. Ray florets white or pale. Small herb.
Flower-heads borne on long, naked stems.

B. decipiens Hook.

(pl. 59)

(*decipiens*, deceiving; since this plant so closely resembles the
European Daisy.)
Leaves on the stems.
Small glabrous shrub with thin leaves, the lower ones
ovate-lanceolate, acute. Flower-heads solitary, often
axillary. Ray florets purple or white.

B. angustifolia A. Cunn ex. DC.

(pl. 3)

(*angustus*, narrow; *folium*, a leaf.)

OLEARIA Moench

Shrubs or undershrubs with alternate or clustered leaves. Flower-
heads terminal or apparently axillary owing to the contraction of
the flowering branches. Flower-heads radiate.

Distribution: The genus is confined to Australia and New
Zealand. About 75 in Australia: 16 in Queensland; 39 in New
South Wales; 38 in Victoria; 27 in South Australia; 25 in Western
Australia; 3 in the Northern Territory; 22 in Tasmania.

(*Olea*, the Olive; in reference to the leaves of some species.)
Tall shrub with alternate, elliptical, cordate-ovate leaves,
toothed, thick, and coarsely hairy beneath. Flower-
heads large and few in a terminal inflorescence. Ray
florets numerous, usually blue or purple, sometimes
white. *O. tomentosa* (Wendl.) DC. (*O. dentata* Moench)

(pl. 54)

(*tomentosa*, woolly.)
A small shrub with alternate, oblong-linear, sinuate-
toothed, rough leaves. Flower-heads large, or few
together, terminal. Ray florets purple.

O. asterotricha F. Muell. ex Benth.

(*aster*, star; *trichos*, a hair.)
Leaves small. var. *parvifolia* Benth.

(pl. 54)

(*parvus*, small; *folium*, a leaf.)
Glandular shrub with leaves crowded, linear, obtuse,
entire. Flower-heads large, solitary, or a few together

140

on short stalks. Ray florets numerous, white.

O. cordata N. Lander (syn O. adenophora F. Muell.)

(pl. 41)

(*cordata*, heart-shaped.)

CELMISIA Cass.

Shrubs and undershrubs with densely tufted leaves. Flower-heads terminal and radiate. Fruit somewhat striate.

Distribution: The genus is confined to Australia, New Zealand, and Antarctica. 3 in Australia: 1 in New South Wales; 2 in Victoria.

(Celmisius, a Greek; son of nymph Alciope.)

> Low, tufted perennial covered with loose white silky hairs. Leaves mostly radical, linear to linear-lanceolate, dark-green, base broad and sheathing, acute. Ray florets numerous, white, sometimes tipped with pink or purple, in a single row.

C. asteliifolia Hook.

(pl. 54)

(*astelia*, kind of plant; *folium*, a leaf.)

LEPTORHYNCHUS Less.

Herbs or undershrubs with alternate, entire leaves. Flower-heads on long peduncles and usually yellow, all tubular. Fruit somewhat compressed.

Distribution: The genus is confined to Australia. 9 in Australia: 3 in Queensland; 7 in New South Wales; 6 in Victoria; 7 in South Australia; 3 in Western Australia; 3 in Tasmania.

(*leptos*, slender; *rhynchos*, a beak; in reference to the beaked fruit.)

> Perennial, slightly woolly, with linear-lanceolate acute leaves. Involucre almost hemispherical, the bracts imbricate in several rows. Receptacle flat, without scales. Florets yellow.

L. squamatus Less.

(pl. 34)

(*squamatus*, scaly.)

PODOLEPIS Labill.

Erect, rigid herbs with alternate, entire leaves. Flower-heads terminal, usually solitary; flowers yellow. Fruit cylindrical or terete.

Distribution: The genus is confined to Australia. About 18 in

Australia: 5 in Queensland; 9 in New South Wales; 5 in Victoria; 6 in South Australia; 11 in Western Australia; 3 in the Northern Territory; 1 in Tasmania.

(*pous*, *podis*, foot; *lepis*, a scale; in reference to the stalked scales at the base of the flower-head.)

> Tufted perennial with radical, petiolate, oblong or lanceolate leaves. Flower-heads large. Involucre hemispherical, the bracts dry, acute, and smooth.
>
> *P. jaceoides* (Sims) Druce
> (pl. 14)

(*jaceoides*, Jacea-like, Jacea, a kind of plant.)

SENECIO L.

Herbs with alternate leaves. Flower-heads terminal, radiate. Involucral bracts, green. Fruit terete and striate.

Distribution: A very large genus, ranging over almost the whole world. About 32 in Australia: 13 in Queensland; 20 in New South Wales; 14 in Victoria; 15 in South Australia; 8 in Western Australia; 2 in the Northern Territory; 10 in Tasmania.

(*senex*, an old man; in reference to the white "beard" on the fruits.)

> 1. Ray florets 3–6.
> A tall, erect, glabrous, branching shrub with petiolate, ovate-lanceolate, coarsely serrate, acute leaves. Achenes glabrous, slightly longer than the involucre.
>
> *S. amygdalifolius* F. Muell.
> (pl. 14)

(*Amygdalus*, the Almond; *folium*, a leaf.)

> 1. Ray florets 10–15.
> A glabrous perennial with petiolate, lanceolate, flaccid leaves, deeply cut and lobed, the middle lobe longer than the others.
>
> *S. vagus* F. Muell.
> (pl. 2)

(*vagus*, rambling; in reference to its spreading habit of growth.)

HELICHRYSUM Mill corr. Pers.

Herbs or shrubs, usually with alternate leaves. Flower-heads terminal; flowers all tubular, with several rows of involucral bracts, often scarious. Fruit scarcely compressed.

Distribution: About 100 in Australia: 18 in Queensland; 41 in New South Wales; 24 in Victoria; 24 in South Australia; 26 in Western Australia; 11 in the Northern Territory; 32 in Tasmania.

142

(*helios*, the sun; *chrysos*, gold; in reference to the bright-golden flowers of many species.)
   1. Bracts yellow.
      2. Leaves glabrous.
         An annual or perennial with oblong-linear leaves. Heads large and solitary with a semi-globular involucre.   *H. bracteatum* (Vent.) Andr.
(pl. 2)
(*bracteatum*, bearing bracts.)
      2. Leaves woolly.
         A branching perennial with linear or narrow-lanceolate leaves, on short petioles. Flower-heads small, in dense terminal inflorescences. Involucres nearly globose.   *H. semipapposum* (Labill.) DC.
(pl. 2)
(*semi*, half; *pappus*, a cluster of hairs; in reference to the leaves.)
   1. Bracts white.
      Perennial with lanceolate or ovate-lanceolate leaves, contracted into a petiole, stem-clasping. Flower-heads large, solitary or loosely paniculate. Involucre hemispherical, spreading.
H. elatum A. Cunn. ex DC.
(pl. 54)
(*elatum*, tall.)

Family PASSIFLORACEAE

Climbers or, rarely, erect herbs or shrubs with alternate, entire or divided, stipulate leaves, and with axillary tendrils. Calyx tube short, 4–5 parts, valvate, or slightly imbricate in bud, often coloured inside. Petals as many as the calyx lobes, inserted at their base and alternating with them. Stamens as many as the calyx lobes, rarely twice as many, perigynous. The disc often produced into numerous filiform segments forming a large corona. Ovary stalked, 1-celled, with 3 or 5 placentas each with several ovules. Styles divided into as many segments as there are placentas, with terminal stigmas.

Fruit a berry, rarely dry, opening in valves between the placentas. A family dispersed over the tropics and sub-tropics.

PASSIFLORA L.

Climbers with axillary tendrils. Calyx petaloid. Corona of several rings of coloured threads. Stamens united, styles 3, spreading,

143

with capitate stigmas. Fruit succulent, indehiscent.

Distribution: A large genus distributed in tropical and subtropical America, with a few in Africa, Asia, Pacific Islands and Australia. 8 in Australia: 8 in Queensland; 4 in New South Wales; 1 in Victoria.

(*passus*, spread out; *flos, floris*, flower.)

> Tall, stout, slightly pubescent climber with axillary tendrils and broad, truncate or slightly cordate leaves with 3 broad, triangular, almost acute lobes. Flowers solitary or in pairs, rather large. Calyx petaloid, corona of several rings of coloured threads. Fruit a green succulent berry. *P. herbertiana* Lindl.
> (pl. 47)

(Herbert, after Lady Carnarvon.)

Family LOBELIACEAE

Herbs with milky juice. Leaves alternate, without stipules. Flowers solitary or clustered, perfect or unisexual. Corolla usually blue or white, tubular, with 5, often irregular, lobes, often slit to the base or notched. Stamens 5, anthers connate round the style; filaments often joined to the corolla tube at the base.

Ovary inferior, 2–3 celled with numerous seeds. Fruit a capsule, indehiscent, rather fleshy.

> Corolla split open to the base, 2-lipped. *Lobelia.*
> Corolla entire, nearly regular. *Isotoma.*

LOBELIA L.

Herbs with alternate leaves. Corolla-tube split open to the base on the upper side, the lobes unequal. Anthers united in a ring round the style. Fruit dry or succulent.

Distribution: The genus is a large one, widely spread over the globe but most abundant in North America, South Africa, and Australia. About 30 in Australia: 11 in Queensland; 13 in New South Wales; 5 in Victoria; 5 in South Australia; 11 in Western Australia; 4 in the Northern Territory; 11 in Tasmania.

(Lobel, Flemish seventeenth-century botanist.)

> Smooth annual, erect, with leaves small, the lowest ovate and deeply cut, the others lanceolate, cut or entire, and all narrowed at the base. Flowers deep-blue. Capsule tiny. *L. gracilis* Andr.
> (pl. 31)

(*gracilis*, slender.)

144

ISOTOMA R. Br.

Herbs with alternate leaves. Corolla-tube entirely or, rarely, shortly split, the lobes nearly equal, spreading. Stamens inserted near the summit of the corolla-tube; anthers united in a ring round the style. Fruit dry.

Distribution: A small genus, fairly widely distributed in temperate regions. 7 in Australia: 4 in Queensland; 3 in New South Wales; 2 in Victoria; 3 in South Australia; 4 in Western Australia; 2 in the Northern Territory; 1 in Tasmania.

(*isos*, equal; *toma*, a cutting, in reference to the equally cut petals.)

An erect branching herb. Leaves deeply cut.

Glabrous erect perennial with linear leaves, irregularly divided. Flowers large, bluish-purple, sometimes yellowish-green outside; sometimes very pale.

I. axillaris Lindl.
(pl. 30)

(*axillaris*, axillary; referring to the position of the flowers.)

A creeping or prostrate perennial. Leaves ovate.

Small prostrate or creeping perennial, usually pubescent, with oblong-ovate, or sometimes linear, leaves, slightly toothed. Flowers bluish.

I. fluviatilis (R. Br.) F. Muell. ex Benth.
(pl. 44)

(*fluviatilis*, belonging to a river; on account of the habitat of the plants.)

Family CAMPANULACEAE

Herbs with fleshy or almost woody rootstocks or underground stems. Leaves alternate or opposite. Flowers solitary on long stalks. Sepals 4–5; corolla regular, tubular, usually with 5 petals. Stamens 5, free. Ovary inferior with 2–3 cells and 3-fid style. Fruit a capsule.

WAHLENBERGIA DC.

Herbs with alternate leaves. Corolla regular, campanulate, the lobes equal. Stamens free. Fruit dry.

Distribution: A fairly large genus, widely distributed but most abundant in South Africa. About 22 (1 naturalized) species in Australia, widely distributed in all States. At present under review.

(G. Wahlenberg, nineteenth-century Swedish botanist.)
Variable, small herb, with obovate to lanceolate, or almost linear leaves. Flowers solitary, blue, campanulate. *W. stricta* Sweet
(pl. 19)
(*stricta*, straight.)

Family GOODENIACEAE

Herbs, undershrubs or rarely shrubs, with alternate or radical leaves, entire, toothed or rarely divided.

Flowers perfect, axillary or in terminal inflorescences. Bracts and bracteoles when present, opposite. Corolla usually yellow, blue, or white. Calyx of 5 sepals, adnate to the ovary or rarely free, the rim of 5 persistent lobes, sometimes minute. Corolla usually irregular, 5 petals, valvate in bud, margins usually induplicate and expanding into glabrous wings as the flower opens. Stamens 5, alternate with the petals, epigynous; anthers 2-celled, free or united in a ring round the style. Ovary inferior, 1–2 celled, ovules 1 or more in each cell. Style simple and undivided with a cup-shaped or lipped dilation (indusium) at the top enclosing the stigma.

Fruit an indehiscent nut or drupe or a capsule. The family is almost exclusively Australian.

1. Corolla-tube entire. Flowers crowded into a head.
   Brunonia.
1. Corolla-tube split down 1 side. Flowers in loose inflorescences.
   2. Anthers connate round style. *Dampiera.*
   2. Anthers free.
      3. Fruit indehiscent. *Scaevola.*
      3. Fruit dehiscent. *Goodenia.*

Family BRUNONIACEAE

BRUNONIA Sm.

Herbs with radical leaves. Flowers numerous in a terminal dense head interspersed with bracts on long, leafless, unbranched stems. Fruit small, dry, indehiscent.

Distribution: One species widely distributed throughout Australia.

(Robert Brown, eighteenth- and nineteenth-century botanist.)
Tufted, comose perennial, with radical, obovate to linear-

146

cuneate, entire leaves. Flowers blue, in dense globular heads. Stigma enclosed in an indusium. Fruit is a small nut enclosed in the hardened calyx tube.

B. australis Sm.
(pl. 42)
(*australis*, southern.)

SCAEVOLA L.

Herbs or shrubs. Flowers solitary. Corolla-tube hairy inside, split open to the base, the lobes with membranous margins. Fruit indehiscent, dry or succulent.

Distribution: Pacific Islands and sea coasts of northern hemisphere and Australia. About 80 in Australia: 15 in Queensland; 7 in New South Wales; 6 in Victoria; 13 in South Australia; 47 in Western Australia; 12 in the Northern Territory; 4 in Tasmania.

(*scaevola*, left-handed; on account of the spreading flowers.)

Prostrate, usually pubescent undershrub with ovate to ovate-spathulate, petiolate, thick and fleshy, entire leaves. Flowers blue or lilac. Fruit a succulent drupe.

S. calendulacea (Kennedy) Druce
(pl.42)
(*calendulacea*, resembling Calendula, a plant of the daisy family.)

DAMPIERA R. Br.

Erect or rarely spreading shrubs or undershrubs. Flowers usually blue or purple on peduncles mostly in the upper axils. Corolla split down one side, the lobes usually very tomentose outside except the membranous margins. Fruit dry, indehiscent.

Distribution: The genus is confined to Australia. About 58 in Australia: 6 in Queensland; 8 in New South Wales; 5 in Victoria; 5 in South Australia; 25 in Western Australia; 3 in the Northern Territory; 1 in Tasmania.

(G. W. Dampier, seventeenth-century navigator.)

Rigid glabrous perennial with broadly angular stems. Leaves sessile, broadly ovate or obovate-cuneate to oblong or linear. Flowers blue, solitary or irregularly clustered in the upper axils, densely covered on the outside with rust-coloured appressed stellate hairs. Fruit a small nut.

D. stricta (Sm.) R. Br.
(pl. 31)

147

(*stricta*, rigid; in reference to the upright habit of the plant.)

GOODENIA Sm.

Herbs or, rarely, shrubs. Flowers usually yellow. Corolla-tube split open to the base, the lobes usually forming an upper and lower set with membranous margins. Fruit dry, dehiscent.

Distribution: The genus is confined to Australia. About 125 in Australia: 31 in Queensland; 29 in New South Wales; 19 in Victoria; 28 in South Australia; 60 in Western Australia; 27 in the Northern Territory; 7 in Tasmania.

(Goodenough, eighteenth-century English botanist.)

Tufted glabrous perennial with erect, almost leafless stems and radical, petiolate, linear or linear-cuneate obtuse, rather thick, entire or sparsely toothed leaves. Flowers yellow, sessile, in distant clusters of 2–3, the upper ones solitary. Fruit a capsule, opening in 2 valves.

G. stelligera R. Br.
(pl. 37)

(*stelligera*, starry.)

Family STYLIDIACEAE

Herbs or shrubs with radical, scattered or tufted leaves usually without stipules.

Flowers perfect, in terminal inflorescences. Calyx-tube adnate to the ovary, 5 sepals, free and 2-lipped. Corolla usually irregular, deeply 5-lobed, the lowest one smaller and differing from the others markedly. Stamens 2, the filaments connate with the style in a column; anthers sessile at the top of the column, 2-celled. Stigmas often concealed beneath the anthers in the early stages, later, as they shrivel, protruding between them. Ovary 2- or rarely 1-celled.

Fruit a capsule.

STYLIDIUM Sw.

Herbs with narrow leaves, petals 5, in the form of a small lower lip of 1, and an upper lip of 4 petals. Stigma undivided. Column elongated, springing back when touched. Ovary 2-celled.

Distribution: A large genus chiefly Australian but found also in tropical Asia. About 130 in Australia: 16 in Queensland; 8 in New South Wales; 5 in Victoria; 6 in South Australia; 108 in Western Australia; 13 in the Northern Territory.

(*stylos*, a column; referring to the united stamens and style.)

148

Leafy herb with scattered, crowded, narrow-linear mucronate leaves 1–3 cm long. Flowers pink or red in a long panicle. Fruit a small capsule.

S. laricifolium L. C. Rich.
(pl. 48)

(*laricifolium*, larch-leafed.)

Family SAPOTACEAE

Trees or shrubs, often with a milky juice, and with alternate, entire, coriaceous leaves without stipules.

Flowers perfect, regular. Calyx of 4–8 imbricate, free segments. Corolla of same number or twice number of petals as sepals. Stamens as many as corolla lobes and opposite them or twice as many; staminodes usually alternating with the petals, stamens hypogynous. Ovary superior, 2- or more celled, with 1 ovule in each cell. Style simple.

Fruit a berry or a drupe. A family distributed widely over the tropical and sub-tropical regions of the earth, in Australia confined to the brush areas.

PLANCHONELLA Pierre

Trees with latex and small greyish-white flowers in axillary inflorescences; 5 petals and 5 stamens alternating with 5 staminodes. Ovary 5-celled. Fruit a globular or ovoid berry with 3, rarely 4–5, seeds.

Distribution: A genus of wide distribution within the tropics, with a few in the sub-tropics. About 12 in Australia: 12 in Queensland; 5 in New South Wales; 1 in the Northern Territory.

Large glabrous tree, usually with shortly petiolate elliptical-oblong leaves. Flowers small, inconspicuous, in axillary clusters, or almost solitary on short pedicels. Fruit a fleshy globose berry of a deep-plum colour with few large compressed seeds.

P. australis (R. Br.) Pierre
(pl. 1)

(*australis*, southern.)

Family SOLANACEAE

Herbs, shrubs or small, soft-wooded trees with alternate leaves without stipules.

Flowers solitary or in inflorescences, at first terminal but

149

becoming lateral by the elongation of the shoot, without bracts. Flowers perfect, regular. Calyx free, of 5 sepals, corolla of 5 segments, induplicate-plicate. Stamens 5, hypogynous, alternating with the petals. Ovary superior, 2-celled or spuriously 4-celled. Style simple, terminal.

Fruit an indehiscent berry or a capsule with many seeds.

A common order in the tropical and warmer regions of the globe, particularly South America, containing several plants with poisonous properties and such economic plants as Potato, Tomato, Tobacco.

SOLANUM L.

Herbs, shrubs or soft-wooded trees, often armed with prickles, with alternate leaves. Flowers usually purple or white. Fruit a 2-celled berry.

Distribution: A very large genus of wide distribution in the warmer temperate regions, most abundant in tropical America. About 80 in Australia: 45 in Queensland; 27 in New South Wales; 8 in Victoria; 25 in South Australia; 11 in Western Australia; 23 in the Northern Territory; 3 in Tasmania.

(*solor*, to comfort; possibly in reference to the narcotic properties of some species.)

Plant without prickles. Erect, glabrous, vigorous undershrub. Leaves lanceolate, acute. Flowers purple, few, large, in short, loose, lateral racemes. Berries ovoid or globular, green or yellow, rather large. *S. aviculare* Ait. (pl. 8)

(*aviculare*, belonging to little birds.)

Prickles on the branches, leaves and flowers.

Diffuse glabrous undershrub. Leaves ovate or broadly oblong-lanceolate, acute, sinuate-lobed or divided with acute lobes. Flowers purple, 2–3 or rarely more, in lateral, loose racemes. Berry globular.

S. prinophyllum Dunal
(*S. xanthocarpum* Schrad. et Wendl.)
(pl. 3)

(*prinophyllum*, oak-leaved.)

Family MENYANTHACEAE

Aquatic or marsh-loving herbs of temperate regions, with alternate or trifoliate, entire leaves without stipules.

Flowers regular and perfect. Sepals, petals and stamens 5.

150

Stamens hypogynous. Ovary superior, usually 1-celled with 2 parietal placentas.

Fruit a capsule opening by 2 or 4 valves, rarely fleshy. Many have a bitter taste and some are used as narcotics or emetics.

VILLARSIA Vent.

Perennial water plants with alternate, almost all radical, broad, thickish leaves on long petioles dilated at the base. Flowers in loose cymose panicles with alternate bracts. Fruit a capsule.

Distribution: A genus found in Europe, North America, South Africa, tropical Asia, and Australia. About 14 in Australia: 1 in Queensland; 2 in New South Wales; 1 in Victoria; 2 in South Australia; 8 in Western Australia; 2 in Tasmania.

(Villars, French eighteenth-century botanist.)

    Erect marshy plant with radical petiolate leaves in a dense tuft, orbicular or reniform, more or less cordate at the base, entire or slightly toothed. Petals yellow, spreading.
                       V. exaltata (Soland. ex. Sims) F. Muell.
                                        (pl. 28)

(*exaltata*, raised.)

Family CONVOLVULACEAE

Herbs, often twining, or rarely shrubs, woody twiners, even trees, or leafless, twining parasites. Flowers often large and showy, usually in inflorescences though often 1-flowered.

Flowers regular, perfect. Calyx free, of 5 sepals, much imbricate. Corolla of 5 fused petals, disc or funnel-shaped, folded in the bud. Stamens 5, hypogynous, inserted in the corolla-tube, alternate with the petals, often of unequal length; anthers of 2 parallel cells, opening longitudinally. Ovary 2–3 or 4-celled, with 1 or 2 ovules in each cell, or 1-celled with 2 or 4 ovules; style single or divided into 2 branches.

Fruit a capsule opening in 2, 3 or more valves, transversely or irregularly, or succulent and indehiscent.

    Stigmatic lobes nearly globular.   *Ipomoea.*
    Stigmatic lobes elongated.   *Convolvulus.*

IPOMOEA L.

Mostly twining herbs with large axillary flowers on solitary peduncles. Corolla campanulate or tubular, the limbs spreading.

Distribution: A genus widely distributed in tropical and subtropical regions. About 40 in Australia: about 30 in Queensland;

8 in New South Wales; 5 in South Australia; 4 in Western Australia; 26 in the Northern Territory.

(*Ipo*, Bindweed (erroneous); *homoios*, like.)

Glabrous muricate twiner. Leaves digitately divided. Peduncles several-flowered. Flowers purple, pink, or white. *I. cairica* (L.) Sweet (*I. palmata* Forsk.)
(pl. 43)

(*cairica*, from Cairo, one of its habitats.)

CONVOLVULUS L.

Herbs with slender trailing or twining stems with petiolate, lobed leaves. Flowers axillary on solitary peduncles. Corolla campanulate.

Distribution: A large genus very widely distributed, mainly in temperate and colder regions. Only 1 in Australia, in all States.

(*Convolvulus*, old name.)

Prostrate, glabrous perennial with more or less sagittate-cordate leaves. Peduncles 1-flowered. Flowers white or pink. *C. erubescens* Sims
(pl. 34)

(*erubescens*, reddish.)

Family ACANTHACEAE

Herbs, shrubs or, rarely, trees, with opposite, entire or, rarely, lobed leaves. Flowers in axillary or terminal inflorescences, with conspicuous bracteoles.

Flowers perfect, irregular. Calyx of 5 sepals, divided. Corolla of 5 petals with a long tube, the limb 2-lipped or with short, spreading lobes, contorted or otherwise imbricate in bud, or expanded into a single lower lip. Stamens 4, in pairs, or 2 only, inserted in the corolla-tube, hypogynous. Ovary superior, 2-celled, with 2 or more ovules in each cell; style simple with an entire or 2-lobed stigma, the upper lobe often reduced to a small tooth.

Fruit a capsule opening loculicidally in 2 valves. A large family, chiefly within the tropics.

Corolla lobes 5, equal. Stamens 4. *Brunoniella.*
Corolla lobes 5, subequal. Stamens 2. *Pseuderanthemum.*

BRUNONIELLA Bremek.

Mostly perennial herbs with sessile, axillary blue flowers. Corolla lobes nearly equal, contorted in bud.

A small genus mainly restricted to warm climates though one species extends to Victoria. 4 in Australia: 1, possibly 3, in Queensland; 2 in New South Wales; 1 in Victoria; 2 in the Northern Territory.

(Robert Brown, eighteenth- and nineteenth-century botanist.)

Small perennial, sparsely hirsute, with obovate-oblong or oblong-lanceolate leaves. Flowers blue, axillary, sessile or shortly petiolate. *B. australis* (R. Br.) Hassk. (pl. 18)

(*australis*, southern.)

PSEUDERANTHEMUM Radl.

Herbs or shrubs with ovate or linear leaves. Flowers tubular, blue with spreading lobes, nearly equal and imbricate but not contorted in bud; stamens 2, partly exserted. Fruit a capsule.

Distribution: A considerable genus of tropical and sub-tropical. regions. 2 in Australia: 2 in Queensland; 1 in New South Wales.

(*eran*, lover; *anthemon*, flower.)

Erect perennial with a creeping underground stem, with ovate, linear leaves. Flowers blue or white in a narrow terminal raceme, rather short.

P. variabile (R. Br.) Radl. ex Lindau (pl. 30)

(*variabile*, changing.)

Family GERANIACEAE

Herbs or shrubs with opposite, alternate, toothed leaves, each usually with 2 stipules. Flowers in axillary inflorescences, 1–2 flowered or in umbels of several flowers.

Flowers perfect, regular or irregular. Sepals 5 or fewer. Petals as many as sepals or rarely wanting. Stamens twice as many as petals, some often without anthers; filaments free and filiform or dilated and connate at the base; anthers with 2 parallel cells. Disc often bearing 5 glands alternating with the petals, and protruding into a short axis in the centre of the ovary. Ovary superior, 3- to 5-lobed, with as many cells, hypogynous. Carpels adnate to the axis up to the insertion of the ovules and often produced above that into a beak bearing the style or stigmas; stigmas as many as ovary cells, raised on the style or sessile on the carpels. Ovules 1 or 2 in each cell.

Fruit a lobed capsule, the lobes 1-seeded, separating from the axis with the seed and elastically rolled upwards along the beak, or the lobes several-seeded, remaining attached to the axis but opening loculicidally. A common family of the temperate regions of the northern hemisphere.

PELARGONIUM L'Hér.

Herbs or shrubs with opposite, slightly lobed leaves on long petioles. Petals 5, unequal. Stamens 10, usually only 5–7 bearing anthers. Fruit separating into 5 1-seeded carpels.

Distribution: A large genus mainly confined to South Africa. 8 in Australia: 1 in Queensland; 4 in New South Wales; 3 in Victoria; 3 in South Australia; 5 in Western Australia; 2 in Tasmania.

(*pelargos*, a stork; on account of the long-beaked fruits.)

Pubescent herb, with reniform-cordate or broadly ovate-cordate leaves. Peduncles bearing umbel of many small, rosy-red flowers. *P. australe* Willd.

(pl. 52)

(*australe*, southern.)

Family ASCLEPIADACEAE

Herbs or shrubs, frequently twining, usually with milky juice. Leaves opposite, entire; stipules absent.

Flowers regular, perfect. Calyx of 5 sepals, imbricate in bud. Corolla of 5 petals, free, nearly rotate and contorted in bud. Stamens hypogynous; filaments short, usually connate and with dorsal appendages; anthers connate with stigma into a mass; pollen consolidated into 1 or 2 masses in each cell, attached in pairs or fours to the small processes of the stigma. Ovary of 2 distinct carpels, united by the style; stigma dilated. Ovules numerous.

Fruit of 2 follicles or rarely 1 only, owing to the abortion of the second carpel. A well-distributed family in the tropics and containing also a few temperate species.

MARSDENIA R. Br.

Twiners with flowers in axillary inflorescences. Flowers fragrant, light-coloured. Corolla with a corona of 5 segments. Pollen masses 2. Fruiting carpels turgid, usually only 1 developed.

Distribution: A fairly large genus in the tropical regions all over the world. 14 in Australia: 14 in Queensland; 7 in New South Wales; 2 in Victoria; 1 in Western Australia; 3 in the Northern

Territory.
(W. Marsden, eighteenth-century orientalist.)
Twining plant with lanceolate to almost ovate, dark-green leaves. Flowers greenish-white, very fragrant in simple axillary umbels. *M. suaveolens* R. Br.
(pl. 57)
(*suaveolens*, sweet-scented.)

Family EPACRIDACEAE

Shrubs or, rarely, trees with alternate or very rarely opposite leaves, without stipules, often crowded or imbricate, rigid, entire with several longitudinal, parallel veins. Flowers axillary or terminal, either solitary or in closely set leaves or in spikes or racemes, each flower subtended by a bract and enclosed within bracteoles.

Flowers perfect, regular. Calyx of 5, rarely 4, distinct sepals, much imbricate in bud. Corolla of 5, rarely 4, petals united to form a campanulate, urceolate or cylindrical tube with free, expanding tips, valvate in bud. Stamens as many as petals or, rarely, fewer, hypogynous, free or adnate to the corolla-tube; anthers versatile or, rarely, adnate, 1-celled, opening by a single longitudinal slit in 2 valves. Disc annular or cup-shaped, entire, 5-lobed or of 5 distinct scales. Ovary superior, of 5 or fewer, rarely 6-10 cells, ovules 1 or several in each cell. Style simple, and undivided, stigma small, terminal, capitate or peltate, sometimes slightly lobed.

Fruit an indehiscent drupe or a capsule splitting loculicidally.

The family is confined to Australia, New Zealand, New Caledonia and the Antarctic Islands. It is closely related to the family Ericaceae, which contains the true heaths of the northern and southern hemispheres, being separated from it mainly by the fact that the anthers in Ericaceae are 2-celled, open by pores and are usually twice as many as the petals.

1. Fruit succulent.
   Anthers wholly exserted. Corolla-tube long. *Styphelia.*
1. Fruit dry.
   2. Leaves with a sheathing base.
      3. Branches smooth, without scars.   *Sprengelia.*
      3. Branches with annular scars.   *Dracophyllum.*
   2. Leaves not sheathing, though frequently sessile.
      Corolla lobes not twisted in bud.   *Epacris.*

155

STYPHELIA Sm.

Shrubs with sessile or subsessile leaves and solitary flowers with several imbricate bracts and 2 bracteoles. Corolla cylindrical, hairy inside; stamens exserted. Ovary 5-celled. Fruit a drupe with a bony endocarp.

Distribution: The genus is confined to Australia. About 15 in Australia: 2 in Queensland; 6 in New South Wales; 1 in Victoria; 2 in South Australia; about 4 in Western Australia; 1 in Tasmania.

(*styphelos*, rough; in reference to stiff habit.)
1. Branches pubescent-hirsute.
  2. Corolla greenish. Leaves 2–5 cm long, lanceolate tapering very gradually to a short point.   *S. longifolia*
(pl. 29)
(*longus*, long; *folium*; a leaf.)
  2. Corolla yellow to red. Leaves less than 2 cm long, ovate or broadly oblong, shortly tapering to a fine point.
S. laeta
(pl. 56)
(*laeta*, pleasing.)
1. Branches glabrous or very finely pubescent.
  3. Corolla red or rarely pale. Leaves oblong-linear with recurved margins, abruptly mucronate about 1 cm long tapering abruptly into a long point.   *S. tubiflora*
(pl. 46)
(*tubus*, a pipe or trumpet; *flos, floris*, a flower.)
  3. Corolla pink and yellow. Leaves narrow to broad lanceolate, often ovate at base of the shoots. *S. triflora*
(pl. 29)
(*tri*, three; *flos, floris*, a flower.)

SPRENGELIA Sm.

Glabrous herbs with stem-clasping, shortly sheathing leaves completely concealing the branches, rigid and tapering to a point. Flowers terminal, surrounded by leafy bracts.

Distribution: The genus is confined to Australia. 4 in Australia: 1 in Queensland; 3 in New South Wales; 1 in Victoria; 1 in South Australia; 2 in Tasmania.

(Sprengel, German botanist.)
  1. Corolla purplish, the lobes narrow, almost valvate in bud.

156

Erect small shrub with leaves tapering from a broad
base. Flowers often few together.   *S. incarnata* Sm.
(pl. 29)

(*incarnata*, flesh-coloured.)

1. Corolla white, the lobes broad, much imbricate in bud.
Erect, somewhat spreading, small shrub with broad,
concave, spreading or incurved leaves, acuminate
and pungent-pointed.

S. monticola (A. Cunn. ex DC.) Druce
(pl. 56)

(*monticola*, mountain-dwelling.)

DRACOPHYLLUM Labill.

Shrubs or trees with crowded leaves completely sheathing the
branches and leaving annular scars on falling. Flowers in terminal
racemes or panicles with very deciduous bracts.

Distribution: The genus is found in all places where the family
is recorded. 3 in Australia: 1 in Queensland; 1 in New South
Wales; 2 in Tasmania.

(*Draco*, from *Dracaena draco*, the Dragon Plant; *phyllos*, a leaf.)

Rather small, weak, erect shrub with spreading, linear-
lanceolate, acuminate leaves completely sheathing
the branches. Flowers in terminal raceme-like one-
sided panicles, white or pinkish. Fruit a capsule,
splitting loculicidally.   *D. secundum* R. Br.
(pl. 29)

(*secundum*, following; as the flowers are all on one side of the
stem.)

EPACRIS Cav.

Shrubs or undershrubs with articulate leaves. Flowers axillary,
solitary on short peduncles, or almost solitary, glabrous; bracts
numerous, usually passing gradually into sepals. Stamens fused
to corolla-tube.

Distribution: The genus is confined to Australia and New
Zealand. About 33 in Australia: 4 in Queensland; about 20 in
New South Wales; 10 in Victoria; 1 in South Australia; 11 in
Tasmania.

(*epi*, upon; *acris*, a hilltop.)

1. Corolla-tube much longer than the sepals. Straggling shrub,
with sessile, cordate to ovate-lanceolate leaves closely
set. Corolla-tube red tipped with white or, rarely, the
whole corolla white.   *E. longiflora* Cav.
(pl. 1)

157

(*longus*, long; *flos, floris*, a flower.)
1. Corolla-tube shorter or not much longer than the sepals.
  2. Leaves, sepals and bracts obtuse, flowers white.
      Erect virgate shrub with oblong-elliptical, thick, obtuse
         slightly concave leaves. Corolla-tube slightly exceed-
         ing the sepals, cylindrical or slightly campanulate.
         Flowers white, numerous along the branches, almost
         or quite sessile.   *E. obtusifolia* Sm.
                                          (pl. 56)
(*obtusus*, blunt; *folium*, a leaf.)
   2. Leaves acute, acuminate or mucronate.
     3. Leaves narrow-lanceolate, not cordate.
        Small shrub with closely set leaves narrowed at the
         base. Flowers white in upper axils, forming leafy
         spikes. Corolla-tube narrow, as long or slightly longer
         than the sepals, the lobes broad and spreading.
                           E. paludosa R. Br.
                                          (pl. 56)
(*paludosa*, boggy.)
   3. Leaves cordate-ovate, short.
      Erect twiggy shrub with slender branches often bearing
         flowers for a considerable time. Flowers sessile or on
         very short peduncles in leaf axils, very numerous.
         Corolla-tube broad, shorter than the sepals, the lobes
         as long as the tube.   *E. microphylla* R. Br.
                                          (pl. 66)
(*micro*, small; *phyllos*, a leaf.)

Family MYOPORACEAE

Shrubs or small trees with simple, usually alternate leaves without stipules. Flowers axillary, solitary or clustered.

Flowers perfect, irregular or nearly regular. Calyx persistent, of 5 sepals. Corolla caducous, with 4 or 5 almost equal, imbricate lobes or 2-lipped, the upper lip outside the lower in bud. Stamens 4, hypogynous, inserted in the corolla-tube and alternate with the lower lobes, anther cells confluent at the summit. Ovary superior, of 2 carpels, 2-celled but becoming 4-celled by 2 intruding placentas with 2 or several ovules in each cell or sometimes the cells 2–5, distinct with 1 ovule in each cell. Style simple, stigma entire.

Fruit a drupe, sometimes almost dry.

EREMOPHILA R. Br.

Shrubs with alternate leaves and comparatively large flowers with 5 petals, the corolla 2-lipped. Stamens 4, one pair longer than the other. Ovary 2-celled. Fruit a drupe.

Distribution: An entirely Australian genus of shrubs, inhabiting dry country. About 70 in Australia: 8 in Queensland; 16 in New South Wales; 22 in South Australia; 7 in Victoria; 43 in Western Australia; 21 in the Northern Territory.

(*eremophilos*, desert-loving.)

> Hoary shrub with alternate, glabrous, lanceolate to ovate-lanceolate, acute leaves. Corolla red, usually spotted with yellow. Fruit globuar, acuminate.
>
> *E. maculata* F. Muell.
>
> (pl. 32)

(*maculatus*, spotted; in reference to the flowers.)

Family SCROPHULARIACEAE

Herbs or rarely shrubs, widely dispersed over every part of the globe, with alternate, opposite or whorled leaves without stipules. Flowers usually in racemes.

Flowers perfect, usually irregular. Calyx 4–5 lobed. Corolla 4–5 lobed, imbricate in bud, flat or 2-lipped when open. Stamens usually 4, in pairs (2 long, 2 short), inserted in the corolla-tube and alternate with the lower lobes, hypogynous. Ovary superior, 2-celled, with a few or many ovules. Style 1; stigma entire or 2-lobed.

> Fruit a 2-celled capsule, opening by valves.
>
> Upper lip of 2 lobes, covering lower lip in bud. Sepals or petals 5, stamens 4. *Mimulus*.
>
> Upper lip of 2 lobes covered by lower lip in bud. Sepals or petals 4, stamens 2. *Parahebe*.

PARAHEBE Oliver (VERONICA L.)

Herbs or shrubs, usually with opposite leaves. Flowers solitary or in racemes, usually without bracteoles.

Distribution: Several in Australia: several in New South Wales, Victoria, South Australia, and Tasmania; 1 in Queensland.

(*Parahebe*, resembling *Hebe*, a related plant.)

> Glabrous perennial, with ovate to ovate-lanceolate, opposite leaves, connate or stem-clasping at the base, occasionally in whorls of 3. Flowers perfect, in slender

racemes, blue or blue streaked with purple.
P. *perfoliata* B. Briggs & Ehrend. (*V. perfoliata* R. Br.)
(pl. 3)
(*perfoliata*, passing through; the stem passes through the leaf-base.)

MIMULUS L.

Herbs with opposite leaves. Flowers solitary on axillary peduncles, usually bluish or violet with a yellowish tube.

Distribution: 6 in Australia: 3 in Queensland; 3 in New South Wales; 3 in Victoria; 5 in South Australia; 2 in Western Australia; 4 in the Northern Territory; 2 in Tasmania.

(*mimulus*, a little actor; since the flowers are mask-like.)

Small glabrous creeping perennial, with thick sessile black-dotted leaves, ovate to oblong. Flowers solitary, tubular. Blue with a yellowish tube. *M. repens* R. Br.
(pl. 3)
(*repens*, creeping.)

Family BIGNONIACEAE

Shrubs or woody climbers with opposite, compound leaves without stipules. Flowers solitary in the axils or in panicles.

Flowers perfect, irregular. Calyx tubular or campanulate, of 5 sepals. Corolla tubular, usually elongated with 5 spreading lobes usually arranged in 2 lips. Stamens 2, or 4 in pairs, hypogynous, inserted in a tube, with a rudimentary fifth stamen in the form of a staminode in most cases. Anthers 2-celled. Ovary superior, 2-celled, with several ovules. Style filiform with 2 short stigmatic lobes.

Fruit a capsule, often elongated, opening loculicidally in 2 valves, seeds often winged. An order almost entirely confined to the tropics, mainly of South America. Many very showy climbers are cultivated in gardens.

PANDOREA Endl.

Tall woody climbers with opposite, pinnate leaves, and terminal flowers in panicles. Fruit a follicle with winged seeds.

Distribution: Mostly found in South America. 4 in Australia: 4 in Queensland; 4 in New South Wales; 1 in Victoria; 1 in South Australia; 1 in the Northern Territory.

(Pandorea, also Pandora, beautiful woman of Greek mythology.)

Woody climber. Leaflets ovate-oblong. Flowers creamy-

160

yellow, tinged inside with red, in loose terminal
panicles.   *P. pandorana* (Andr.) Steenis
                                                    (pl. 6)
(*pandorana*, gifted.)
    Shrub with twining branches. Leaflets linear. Flowers
    creamy with reddish-brown stripes, in loose terminal
    panicles. A variation of the normal species.
                    P. pandorana (A. Cunn. ex DC.) Steenis.
                                                    (pl. 39)

Family LAMIACEAE

Herbs and shrubs with 4-angled stems, and branches with opposite and whorled leaves, often toothed, without stipules. Flowers
usually in terminal or opposite cymes, rarely solitary. Leaves and
stems often containing glandular oil dots rendering the plant
highly aromatic.
    Flowers perfect, regular. Calyx persistent, of 5 sepals. Corolla
tubular, with 4–5 petals, often 2-lipped or nearly equal, imbricate
in bud, the upper lip outside. Stamens 2, or 4 in pairs, hypogynous, inserted in the corolla-tube and alternating with its lower
lobes. Anthers 2-celled, though one of these is sometimes aborted.
Ovary superior, of 4 lobes, with 1 ovule in each lobe, the 2 cells
being divided by false divisions to give the 4 lobes. Style single
with 2 stigmatic lobes.
    Fruit 4 seed-like nuts enclosed in the persistent calyx. A large
order widely distributed all over the world.
    Calyx nearly equally 5-lobed.
        Leaves whorled.   *Westringia.*
        Leaves opposite.   *Ajuga.*
    Calyx 2-lipped.
        Lower lip acutely 4-toothed.   *Plectranthus.*
        Calyx lips both entire.   *Prostanthera.*

PROSTANTHERA Labill.

Shrubs or undershrubs, usually strongly scented, with opposite
leaves. Flowers solitary and axillary or forming terminal racemes.
Corolla-tube dilated upwards. Nuts rugose.
    Distribution: The genus is confined to Australia. About 60 in
Australia: 13 in Queensland; about 40 in New South Wales; 17
in Victoria; 13 in South Australia; 13 in Western Australia; 2 in
the Northern Territory; 3 in Tasmania.

(*prostas*, a vestibule; *anthera*, an anther; alluding to the anther appendages.)

Leaves mostly entire, rarely slightly crenate.

Leaves ovate, rather thick, petiolate. Calyx lips nearly equal. Flowers purple, in loose, terminal racemes.

P. ovalifolia R. Br.
(pl. 21)

(*ovalis*, oval; *folium*, a leaf.)

Leaves more or less deeply incised.

Leaves rather thin, ovate-lanceolate. Lower calyx lips longer and narrower than the upper. Flowers pale-purple, axillary, in short inflorescences. *P. incisa* R. Br.
(pl. 34)

(*incisa*, cut.)

PLECTRANTHUS L'Hér.

Herbs or undershrubs with opposite leaves. Flowers in false whorls, the floral leaves reduced to minute deciduous bracts. Corolla-tube gibbous in the upper part.

Distribution: 4 in Australia: 4 in Queensland; 2 in New South Wales; 1 in Victoria, South Australia, the Northern Territory and Western Australia.

(*plectron*, cock's spur; *anthos*, a flower; in reference to the spurred corolla base.)

Erect pubescent shrub with rather fleshy stems. Leaves ovate to orbicular, coarsely crenate, rather thick, rugose. Flowers small, bluish-purple, in false whorls of about 10. *P. parviflorus* Willd.
(pl. 8)

(*parvus*, small; *flos, floris*, a flower.)

WESTRINGIA Sm.

Bushy shrubs with whorled, entire, mostly rigid leaves. Flowers axillary, sessile or nearly so, with a pair of small bracts under the calyx. Corolla usually hairy. Nuts rugose.

Distribution: About 26 in Australia: 11 in Queensland; 9 in New South Wales; 5 in Victoria; 3 in South Australia; 5 in Western Australia; 5 in Tasmania.

(J. P. Westring, eighteenth-century Swedish physician.)

Robust, bushy tomentose shrub. Leaves in whorls of 4, oblong-lanceolate, lanceolate or linear, coriaceous, glabrous and shining, recurved or revolute. Flowers almost sessile, white or pale-blue.

W. fruticosa (Willd.) Druce (*W. rosmariniformis* Sm.)

(pl. 58)

(*fruticosa*, bushy.)

AJUGA L.

Herbs with chiefly radical leaves. Flowers in false whorls in the axils of floral leaves, with linear bracts. Nuts rugose.

Distribution: A widely distributed genus in the extra-tropical regions of Asia and Europe. 2 in Australia : 1 in Queensland, New South Wales, Victoria, South Australia, Tasmania.

(*Ajuga*, old name, origin obscure.)

Pubescent perennial with leaves chiefly radical, ovate-oblong or obovate, coarsely toothed, contracted into a long petiole. Flowers blue, nearly sessile, in false whorls of 6 to over 20. *A. australis* R. Br.

(pl. 30)

(*australis*, southern.)

Family VERBENACEAE

Herbs, shrubs, or woody climbers with opposite or rarely alternate, whorled leaves without stipules. Flowers perfect, irregular or, rarely, regular. Calyx persistent, of 4 or 5 sepals. Corolla 4 or 5 petals, nearly always 2-lipped, imbricate in bud, the upper lip or the lateral petals on the outside. Stamens 4, in pairs or nearly equal, hypogynous, inserted in the corolla-tube ; anthers 2-celled. Ovary superior, not lobed but usually perfectly divided into 2 or 4 partitions with 1 ovule in each. Style terminal, simple, entire, or with 2 short stigmatic lobes. Fruit dehiscent, of 4 cells or separating into 4 nuts.

CHLOANTHES R. Br.

Perennial herbs or shrubs with opposite or whorled leaves. Corolla of 5 petals, 2-lipped. Stamens 4, scarcely exserted. Ovary imperfectly 2-celled. Fruit dry, 4-celled.

Distribution: The genus is limited to Australia. About 4 in Australia : 2 in Queensland ; 2 in New South Wales ; 1 in Victoria ; 1 in Western Australia.

(*chloa-*, yellowish-green; *anthos*, a flower.)

Erect perennial, with opposite, linear or lanceolate leaves, often appearing terete on account of the revolute margins, obtuse, bullate-rugose on the upper surface. Flowers green or yellowish-green, on very short axillary

pedicels, with a pair of linear, rugose bracteoles about the middle.   *C. stoechadis* R. Br.
(pl. 12)

(*stoechas*, a kind of plant, one of the lavenders.)

Family HYDROCHARITACEAE

Aquatic herbs, entirely submerged, or the leaf floating. Leaves simple. Flowers when young enclosed in a spathe, the staminate flowers 1 or more in a spathe, the pistillate always solitary.

Flowers regular, unisexual. Perianth of 3 or 6 segments, all petaloid or the 3 outer ones herbaceous and smaller, with the tube adherent to the ovary in the pistillate flowers and with no tube in the staminate. Stamens 3–12, epigynous. Anthers 2-celled. Ovary inferior, 1-celled with 3 parietal placentas or 3-, 6-, or 9-celled. Styles 3, 6, or 9 with entire or trifid stigmas. Ovules numerous.

Fruit indehiscent, ripening under water.

OTTELIA Pers.

Fresh-water plants with leaves in radical tufts. Flowers solitary and sessile within a 2-lobed spathe. Stamens 6 or more. Fruit more or less completely 2-celled.

Distribution: A genus widely spread over tropical Asia and Africa. 2 in Australia: 2 in Queensland; 1 in New South Wales, Victoria, South Australia, Western Australia; 2 in the Northern Territory.

(*Ottel-ambel*, an Indian name for some species.)

Submerged plant with leaves on long petioles, ovate or oblong, dilated and tufted, obtuse, rounded at the base. Outer perianth segments green.
O. ovalifolia (R. Br.) Rich.
(pl. 67)

(*ovalis*, oval; *folium*, a leaf.)

Family BURMANNIACEAE

Herbs with radical leaves or all the leaves reduced to scales. Flowers sessile or on pedicels along the branches of a forked cyme sometimes reduced to a single flower. Perianth tubular, 3-angled or winged, the 3 inner segments small or wanting. Anthers 3, usually sessile, epigynous, the anther-cells short, separated by a broad connective. Ovary 3-celled, inferior. Fruit a capsule, with numerous ovules. Style single with 3 short stigmatic branches opening loculicidally in 3 valves.

BURMANNIA L.

Herbs with sessile or shortly pedicellate flowers. Calyx tubular, 3-angled, petaloid. Corolla small or wanting. Stamens 3, with a crested appendage on each anther. Fruit a capsule.

Distribution: A small genus widely distributed in damp habitats all over the world. 2 in Australia: 2 in Queensland; 1 in New South Wales; 2 in the Northern Territory.

(J. Burmann, eighteenth-century botanist.)

Slender herb with leaves chiefly radical, sessile, sheathing at the base, lanceolate, acute, spreading. Flowers deep-blue or purple in a once-forked cyme, usually very compact. *B. disticha* L. (pl.42)

(*disticha*, in 2 rows.)

Family ORCHIDACEAE

Perennial or annual herbs, either terrestrial with underground stems or swollen, tubercular roots, or epiphytes with aerial roots which cling to trunks or branches of trees or to rocks. Leaves alternate and sheathing at the base in flowering stems which, in the case of many epiphytes, are swollen to form pseudo-bulbs, or are in radical tufts at the base of the flowering stems. Flowers in inflorescences or solitary.

Flowers perfect, irregular. Perianth of 6 segments, all petal-like and free or variously united, sepals all similar and erect and spreading, or the dorsal one often in a ventral position on account of the twisted ovary; 2 or 3 petals similar, one on each side of the dorsal sepals, the third petal different, called a labellum, inserted between the lateral sepals and very varied, frequently large and conspicuous, differently coloured from the rest of the perianth, bearded, fringed or with other appendages. It usually forms a landing-stage for a specific insect-pollinating agent. Stamens united with stigma and style into a column, often separated by a structure called a rostellum. The pollen grains are generally united to form larger masses called pollinia of 1–4 pairs. Ovary inferior, 1-celled, with 3 parietal placentas.

Fruit a capsule, opening in 3 valves or longitudinal slits.
1. Anthers lid-like, usually deciduous. Pollen waxy or granular.
2. Epiphytes with pseudo-bulbs.
3. Lateral sepals dilated at the base. Labellum not spurred. *Dendrobium*.

3. Lateral sepals not dilated. Labellum spurred.

Sarcochilus.

2. Terrestrial leafless herbs with creeping stems, sometimes saprophytic.
   4. Column elongated. Flowers spotted.   *Dipodium.*
   4. Column very short. Flowers white.   *Galeola.*
1. Anthers erect, persistent. Pollen mealy. Terrestrial herbs usually with tuberous roots.
   5. Column short.
      6. Dwarf herbs, with solitary flowers, almost sessile.   *Corybas.*
      6. Erect herbs with flowers in spikes or racemes.
         7. Flowers reversed by a twist of the ovary.

Cryptostylis.

         7. Flowers not reversed.
            8. Flowers very small, in dense spikes.

Spiranthes.

            8. Flowers large, in racemes.
               9. Labellum undivided.   *Thelymitra.*
               9. Labellum 3-lobed.   *Diuris.*
   5. Column elongated.
               10. Labellum peltate or produced beyond its insertion on the claw into an appendage.
                  11. Leaves several. Dorsal petals hood-shaped.   *Pterostylis.*
                  11. Leaves solitary.   *Caleana.*
               10. Labellum not produced beyond its insertion.
                  12. Labellum papillose or beset with raised linear calli.
                     13. Labellum beset with papillae. Leaf smooth. Floral bracts large.   *Lyperanthus.*
                     13. Labellum beset with linear calli. Leaf usually hairy. Floral bracts small.

Caladenia.

                  12. Labellum almost smooth.
                     14. Labellum with erect, long, basal appendages. *Glossodia.*
                     14. Labellum without appendages.   *Acianthus.*

DENDROBIUM Sw.

Epiphytes, very variable in habit. Flowers usually in racemes. Lateral sepals dilated at the base and forming a spur with the basal projection of the column.

Distribution: A genus widely distributed in the warmer parts of the Old World. 52 in Australia: about 50 in Queensland; 17 in New South Wales; 2 in Victoria; 6 in the Northern Territory; 1 in Tasmania.

(*dendron*, a tree; *bios*, life; in reference to the epiphytic habit.)
1. Stems erect.
    2. Stems pseudo-bulbous.
        Racemes 1–3 at the end between the leaves. Flowers white except for the labellum which is streaked with purplish-red.   *D. aemulum* R. Br.
        (pl. 64)

(*aemulum*, rivalling.)
    2. Stems slender and branching.
        Flowers solitary on a single, flexuose peduncle with a long, scarious bract at the base. Flowers equal, greenish-yellow, very narrow. Labellum about the length of the other petals, white, faintly lined on the back with purple.   *D. beckleri* F. Muell.
        (pl. 6)

(After Dr Beckler.)
1. Stems creeping and rooting at the nodes.
    3. Leaves tuberculate.
        Flowers in short racemes of about 4 flowers on slender pedicels about 1 cm long. Flowers yellow-white, streaked with reddish-purple. Labellum shorter than the other perianth segments, white spotted with reddish-purple.   *D. cucumerinum* M'Leay
        (pl. 47)

(*cucumerinum*, cucumber-like.)
    3. Leaves not tuberculate.
        Flowers in racemes, 5–10 cm long with 6–20 flowers on slender pedicels. Flowers white. Labellum short, the lateral lobes rather broad.   *D. linguiforme* Sw.
        (pl. 59)

(*linguiforme*, tongue-shaped; in reference to the leaves.)

SARCOCHILUS R. Br.

Epiphytes with flat leaves, the stems often covered with the persistent, sheathing bases of the leaves. Flowers in axillary racemes with small bracts.

Distribution: The genus is common in Asia and Australia. 15 in Australia: 2 in Queensland; 11 in New South Wales; 2 in Victoria; 1 in Tasmania.

(*sarx*, fleshy; *cheilos*, a lip; from the fleshy lobe of the labellum.)
   Lateral sepals adnate to the base only of the column projection. Peduncles with 2–4 distant white flowers. Labellum streaked red with a little orange inside the lateral lobes, the rest white. *S. falcatus* R. Br.
(pl. 58)

(*falcatus*, sickle-shaped.)
   Lateral sepals adnate to the whole of the column projection. Peduncles flexuose. Flowers 3–12. Perianth segments of a dull, pale-purple or greenish colour. Labellum whitish with red markings.
S. olivaceus Lindl.
(pl. 32)

(*olivaceus*, olive-green.)

DIPODIUM R. Br.

Smooth, terrestrial herbs.

Distribution: A small genus occurring in Asia, New Caledonia and Australia. 3 in Australia: 3 in Queensland; 2 in New South Wales; 1 in Victoria; 1 in South Australia; 2 in the Northern Territory; 1 in Tasmania.

(*di*, two; *podos*, a foot; probably referring to the lobed pollen masses.)
   Leafless herb, inflorescences in long, thick, fleshy racemes 30–90 cm high, with sheathing scales. Flowers large, red, usually spotted with purple or deep-carmine. Labellum sessile, erect, adnate to the column at its base and then gibbous. *D. punctatum* (Sm.) R. Br.
(pl. 13)

(*punctatum*, spotted.)

GALEOLA Lour.

Leafless climbers. Flowers in axillary, much-branched, bracteate panicles.

Distribution: A genus found in India, Java, New Caledonia, and Australia. 2 in Australia: 2 in Queensland and New South Wales.

(*galeola*, a small helmet-shaped vessel; in reference to the dorsal sepal.)

168

Leafless plants with chocolate-brown stems, climbing and adhering closely to the stems of trees. Flowers brownish- or golden-yellow, glabrous. Labellum white with transverse coloured bands.

G. cassythoides (A. Cunn.) Reichb.
(pl. 32)

(*Cassytha*, a semi-parasitic twiner; *oides*, like; in reference to the habit.)

CORYBAS Salisb.

Slender herbs, leaves cordate or orbicular, flat on ground. Flowers solitary, hooded, on short peduncles.

Distribution: A genus found in New Zealand and Asia, as well as in Australia. 7 in Australia: 4 in Queensland; 7 in New South Wales; 5 in Victoria; 3 in South Australia; 2 in Western Australia; 1 in Tasmania.

(Corybas, priest of Cybele; possibly in reference to the hooded perianth.)

Leaf orbicular-cordate. Flowers solitary. Dorsal sepal hooded. Labellum tubular, spurred at base.

C. aconitiflorus Salisb.
(pl. 51)

(*Aconitum*, a poisonous plant; *flos, floris*, a flower.)

ACIANTHUS R. Br.

Very slender terrestrial glabrous herbs with small tubers. Radical leaves solitary, often purplish on the underside. Stem without sheathing bracts. Flowers in a spike-like raceme.

Distribution: The genus is found in New Zealand, New Guinea, New Caledonia and Australia. 7 in Australia: 4 in Queensland; 4 in New South Wales; 3 in Victoria; 3 in South Australia; 3 in Western Australia; 3 in Tasmania.

(*acus*, a needle; *anthos*, a flower; in reference to the pointed flowers.)

Small, fragile, glabrous herb, with an orbicular-cordate, reniform, sessile, radical leaf. Flowers light-red. Labellum obtuse, emarginate or with a short point, clawed, flat, undivided.   *A. reniformis* (R. Br.) Schltr.
(pl. 32)

(*reniformis*, kidney-shaped.)

CRYPTOSTYLIS R. Br.

Terrestrial glabrous herbs with a short rhizome and thickened

roots. Radical leaves few, on long petioles, the flowering stem
with a few sheathing scales. Flowers distant in a terminal raceme
on very short pedicels.

Distribution: The genus is distributed in Asia and Australia.
5 in Australia: 2 in Queensland; 4 in New South Wales; 3 in
Victoria; 1 in South Australia, Western Australia and Tasmania.

(*cryptos*, hidden; *stylos*, a column.)

> Leaves oval or broadly-lanceolate. Flowers greenish,
> reversed. Labellum longer and thicker than the other
> perianth segments, forming a kind of broad hood, erect,
> brown, conspicuously striped with dark veins.

C. erecta R. Br.
(pl. 18)

(*erecta*, straight.)

SPIRANTHES Rich.

Terrestrial herbs with thick clustered roots. Flowers small,
spirally arranged in a terminal spike.

Distribution: A fairly large genus generally distributed over
temperate and tropical regions. 1 in Australia: in Queensland,
New South Wales, Victoria, South Australia and Tasmania.

(*speira*, a screw; *anthos*, a flower; in reference to the spiral
arrangement of the flowers.)

> Stems glabrous, with linear or linear-lanceolate leaves.
> Spiral spikes fairly dense, of pink flowers with a white
> labellum. Labellum sessile, as long as the sepals, em-
> bracing the column by its broad base, undivided.

S. sinensis (Pers.) Ames
(pl. 48)

(*sinensis*, Chinese.)

THELYMITRA Forst.

Glabrous terrestrial herbs with ovoid tubers. Leaves usually
solitary, long and narrow, passing into a few sheathing scales on
the stem. Flowers few, in a terminal raceme with few bracts, often
blue.

Distribution: The genus is distributed in New Zealand, New
Caledonia and Timor, but principally in Australia. 50 in Aus-
tralia: in Queensland, New South Wales, Victoria, South
Australia, Western Australia and Tasmania.

(*thelys*, a woman; *mitra*, a cap; in allusion to the hooded
column.)

> Slender herb with broad, linear leaves and blue flowers

with dark veins in slender racemes. Sepals and petals all nearly equal and spreading, with slightly crisped margins. *T. venosa* R. Br. (pl. 44)

(*venosa*, veined; in reference to the petals.)

DIURIS Sm.

Erect terrestrial herbs, usually slender, with thick tubers. Leaves few, near the base of the stem, usually long and narrow, passing into sheathing scales. Flowers in a terminal raceme.

Distribution: The genus is practically confined to Australia. About 40 in Australia: in Queensland, New South Wales, Victoria, South Australia, Western Australia and Tasmania.

(*di*, two; *oura*, a tail.)
> Flowers purple.
>> Leaves linear. Flowers 2–5, sometimes dotted. Labellum about as long as the dorsal sepal.
>> *D. punctata* Sm. (pl. 41)

(*punctata*, dotted.)
> Flowers yellow.
>> Small slender species with narrow leaves. Flowers, on long pedicels, spotted or blotched with brown or purple. Labellum, without a conspicuous centre line, shorter than the dorsal sepal, the lateral lobes nearly as long as the middle lobe. *D. maculata* Sm. (pl. 49)

(*maculata*, spotted.)
>> Flowers orange, not spotted. Dorsal sepal nearly as long as the labellum. Labellum with a smooth ridge down the centre. *D. aequalis* F. Muell. (pl. 15)

(*aequalis*, equal; perhaps because the floral segments are more nearly equal than in any other species.)

PTEROSTYLIS R. Br.

Terrestrial herbs with small tubers. Leaves radical or along the stem. Flowers solitary or several, usually green or brown.

Distribution: The genus occurs in Australia, New Guinea, New Caledonia, New Zealand and the New Hebrides. About 60 in Australia: in Queensland, New South Wales, Victoria, South Australia, Western Australia and Tasmania.

171

(*pteron*, a wing; *stylos*, a column.)
>Radical leaves always present at the time of flowering. Flowers solitary. Labellum oblong-linear, obtuse, the basal appendage narrow-linear, curved, penicillate.
>
>>*P. nutans* R. Br.
>>(pl. 17)

(*nutans*, nodding.)
>Radical leaves absent at the time of flowering. Stem leaves from linear- to narrow-lanceolate, very acute. Flowers solitary and terminal, light-crimson, sometimes greenish with darker stripes. Labellum tapering to a point.
>
>>*P. coccinea* R. D. Fitzg.
>>(pl. 39)

(*coccinea*, scarlet.)

CALEANA R. Br.

Glabrous, terrestrial, slender herbs with small tubers. Leaves solitary, radical, narrow, often reddish-brown. Flowers brown, few in a raceme or sometimes solitary.

Distribution: The genus is confined to Australia and New Zealand. 1 in Australia: found in Queensland, New South Wales, Victoria, South Australia, Western Australia and Tasmania.

(G. Caley, nineteenth-century botanist.)
>Solitary radical leaf, linear- or narrow-lanceolate. Flowers red, on very short pedicels, each with a subtending bract. Labellum articulate at the base of the column, and irritable with a linear, incurved claw, the blade broadly ovate, peltately attached, the upper surface smooth, the centre inflated and hollow.
>
>>*C. major* R. Br.
>>(pl. 5)

(*major*, greater.)

LYPERANTHUS R. Br.

Glabrous terrestrial herbs, often with a creeping rhizome or clustered roots. Leaves usually radical. Flowers usually dry black.

Distribution: A small genus in New Zealand, New Caledonia and Australia. 4 in Australia: 1 in Queensland; 2 in New South Wales; 2 in Victoria; 1 in South Australia; 3 in Western Australia; 2 in the Northern Territory; 2 in Tasmania.

(*lyperos*, sad; *anthos*, a flower.)
>Solitary basal leaf, thick and succulent, nearly ovate, flat.

172

Flowers 2–8, pink, translucent, with deep-purple or reddish stripes, each subtended by a bract. Labellum shorter than the petals, recurved towards the end, the middle lobe with fringed margins, the erect portion with 2 rows of calli.   *L. nigricans* R. Br.
                                                                    (pl. 46)
(*nigricans*, blackish.)

CALADENIA R. Br.

Slender hairy terrestrial herbs with small tubers. Stem with a solitary leaf near the base and a small sheathing bract about the middle. Flowers 1-several subtended by bracts.

Distribution: A large genus in New Zealand, New Caledonia, Java and Australia. About 70 in Australia: in Queensland, New South Wales, Victoria, South Australia, Western Australia and Tasmania.

(*calos*, beautiful; *aden*, a gland.)
> Flowers white, tinged with brown, 2–5 on the stem.
>> Basal leaf long, narrow. Labellum with a broad, flat blade between the upturned margins, smooth, recurved; disc with 4 rows, 7 calli, the tip purple, the sides spotted.   *C. cucullata* R. D. Fitzg.
                                                                    (pl. 66)

(*cucullata*, hooded; in reference to the upper sepal.)
> Flowers white or pink with no tinge of brown, 1–3 on the stem.
>> Basal leaf narrow-linear, long. Lateral lobes of labellum broad, obtuse and prominent, the middle lobe lanceolate, recurved, fringed with a few linear calli; calli on the disc, linear, in 2 rows.   *C. carnea* R. Br.
                                                                    (pl. 17)

(*carnea*, flesh-coloured.)

GLOSSODIA R. Br.

Slender hairy terrestrial herbs with small tubers. Leaves solitary. Stem with a sheathing bract at or below the middle. Flowers usually solitary, bluish inside, paler outside, rarely pink or white.

Distribution: The genus is limited to Australia. 5 in Australia: 2 in Queensland; 2 in New South Wales; 2 in Victoria; 1 in South Australia; 3 in Western Australia; 1 in Tasmania.

(*glossa*, a tongue; *odos*, tooth; labellum (tongue) is tooth-shaped.)

Leaf solitary, hirsute, oblong to lanceolate. Flowers purple or blue, 1 or rarely 2. Labellum sessile, undivided, ovate, broad, biconvex and pubescent, with white hairs in the lower half, lanceolate and glabrous in the upper half with 2 single, linear appendages erect against the column at the base, 2-lobed.   *G. major* R. Br.

(pl. 43)

(*major*, greater.)

Family IRIDACEAE

Herbs with perennial creeping stems with radical or alternate leaves sheathing at the base, linear. Flowers solitary and terminal or in spikes and clusters within 1 or 2 bracts, mostly blue, white, or yellow.

Flowers perfect, regular or irregular. Perianth with a short or distinct tube, 3 petaloid sepals, 3 petals, often small. Stamens 3, epigynous; anther-cells 2, parallel, erect. Ovary inferior, 3-celled with several ovules in each cell. Style more or less divided into 3 lobes or branches, sometimes broad and petal-like.

Fruit a capsule opening loculicidally in 3 valves.

Petals much shorter than the sepals.   *Patersonia.*
Petals and sepals nearly equal, spreading.   *Libertia.*

PATERSONIA R. Br.

Herbs with short rhizomes and narrow-linear leaves in radical tufts. Flowers usually in a terminal cluster enclosed by 2 bracts, blue or purple with a papery perianth.

Distribution: The genus is limited to extra-tropical Australia. About 20 in Australia: 2 in Queensland; 4 in New South Wales; 5 in Victoria; 2 in South Australia; 14 in Western Australia.

(W. Paterson, nineteenth-century botanist.)

Rather slender stem. The leaves tufted, long, narrow, glabrous except at the base. Peduncles rather slender, 1 or 2 on the stem. Flowers purple.   *P. glabrata* R. Br.

(pl. 44)

(*glabrata*, smooth.)

LIBERTIA Spreng.

Tufted herbs, usually glabrous with flat, grass-like, mostly radical leaves. Flowers in umbel-like paniculate clusters; bracts small, membranous.

Distribution: The genus is found in New Zealand, extra-tropical

South America and Australia. 2 in Australia: 1 in Queensland; 2 in New South Wales; 2 in Victoria; 1 in Tasmania.
(Mlle Libert, Belgian botanist.)

Leaves almost radical, grass-like, flaccid. Flowers white, in loose panicles. Capsule ovoid-globular.

L. paniculata (R. Br.) Spreng.
(pl. 58)

(*paniculata*, paniculate; flowers arranged in a loose inflorescence.)

Family AMARYLLIDACEAE

Herbs with a perennial underground stem and leaves radical or nearly so, usually narrow. Flowers in terminal heads, solitary or several, often within coloured or membranous spathes.

Flowers mostly white, yellow, or red, perfect. Perianth with 6 coloured, petal-like segments, mostly all equal. Stamens 6, epigynous, filaments free or united at the base into a corona or short tube; anthers usually versatile with 2 parallel cells. Ovary inferior, 3-celled usually with several ovules in each cell. Style single, with 3 adnate stigmas.

Fruit usually a capsule opening loculicidally at the free apex only or right to the base in 3 valves, rarely succulent and indehiscent.

CRINUM L.

Large bulbous herbs with linear, radical leaves. Flowers white in a long terminal umbel surrounded by a few large membranous bracts. Flowering stem usually leafless.

Distribution: A genus extending over tropical and southern Asia, Africa and Australia. About 12 in Australia: 10 in Queensland; 2 in New South Wales; 1 in Victoria; 1 in South Australia; 1 in Western Australia; 4 in the Northern Territory.

(*crinon*, a lily.)

Flowers in umbels of about 25. Leaves 80–100 cm long. Stems several to a plant, leafy in the upper part. Leaves glaucous, thick. Peduncles arising from the lower leaves. *C. pedunculatum* R. Br.
(pl. 63)

(*pedunculatum*, stalked; in reference to the long flower-head stalks.)

Flowers in umbels of about 6–8. Leaves 50–60 cm long. Base of stem ovoid. Leaves linear, the margins scabrous.

175

C. flaccidum Herb.
(pl. 60)
(*flaccidum*, drooping; in reference to the flower stems.)

Family HAEMODORACEAE

A family once included with Amaryllidaceae. Characteristics similar but spathes missing.

ANIGOZANTHOS Labill.

Herbs with a perennial thick rhizome and usually radical leaves with a sheathing blade. Stem erect, usually bearing 2 or 3 distant leaves. Flowers large, in close unilateral racemes. Perianth of 6 similar segments, split to the base; stamens 6.

Distribution: The genus is only recorded for Western Australia, which has about 10–11 species.

(*anigos*, unequal; *anthos*, a flower; referring to the oblique flowers.)

Flowers in a condensed raceme on short, thick pedicels covered with dense, plumose, green wool, except at the base where it is red.

A. manglesii D. Don
(pl. 35)

(Robert Mangles, of Berks, England, who cultivated and popularized the species.)

Family LILIACEAE

Perennial, rarely annual herbs, occasionally climbing, with a short underground stem. Leaves usually in radical tufts or crowded at the ends of the branches, sometimes spread along the branches, the bases often persistent after the leaves have fallen. Peduncles terminal or rarely axillary, leafless or with 1 or 2 leaves below the inflorescence, passing into bracts under the inflorescence or pedicels, here usually reduced to small scales. Perianth usually glabrous, mostly blue, yellow, white, purple, or red. Flowers perfect or dioecious, regular. Perianth of 6 coloured segments, imbricate in 2 series or the outer ones rarely valvate, all equal and similar or the 3 inner ones slightly different. Stamens almost or quite hypogynous, attached to the base of the segments, the 3 opposite the outer segments often smaller, filaments free or shortly united; anthers erect or versatile. Ovary superior, 3-celled, with several ovules in each cell; style single with a single,

176

terminal stigma or obscurely 3-lobed, rarely divided to the base. Fruit an indehiscent berry or a capsule opening loculicidally or in a few genera septicidally.

1. Fruit succulent.
    2. Stem climbing.   *Geitonoplesium.*
    2. Stem erect.   *Dianella.*
1. Fruit dry.
    3. Style deeply 3-lobed.
        4. Flowers axillary.   *Kreyssigia.*
        4. Flowers terminal.
            5. Flowers spicate, few.   *Anguillaria.*
            5. Flowers umbellate.
                6. Leaves broad.   *Schelhammera.*
                6. Leaves narrow.   *Burchardia.*
    3. Style unbranched.
            7. Sepals and petals united.   *Blandfordia.*
            7. Sepals and petals free.
                8. Anthers 3.   *Sowerbaea.*
                8. Anthers 6.
                    9. Petals fringed.   *Thysanotus.*
                    9. Petals not fringed.
                        10. Sepals and petals deciduous.
                        Bulbine.
                        10. Sepals and petals non-deciduous, anthers recurved after flowering.
                        Stypandra.

GEITONOPLESIUM A. Cunn.

Glabrous much-branched climbers, rather weak. Flowers in loose paniculate cymes, often terminal. Fruit succulent, nearly globular, with black seeds.

Distribution: The genus is limited to the single Australian species from Queensland, New South Wales and Victoria. It is also found in the South Pacific Islands.

(*geiton*, a neighbour; *plesion*, near; in reference to its similarity to the genus *Smilax*.)

Twining stem much branched with small, broad scales under each branch. Leaves linear or lanceolate-oblong. Flowers purplish-green, drooping, in loose terminal cymes. Fruit nearly globular, dark-blue, succulent, at length dry and opening in 3 valves; seeds few.

G. *cymosum* (R. Br.) A. Cunn. ex Hook.

(pl. 63)

(*cymosum*, bearing a cyme of flowers.)

SCHELHAMMERA R. Br.

Erect or spreading herbs with fibrous roots and leafy stems. Leaves sessile, broad. Flowers terminal without bracts.

Distribution: The genus is a small one, limited to Australia. 3 in Australia: 2 in Queensland; 1 in New South Wales; 1 in Victoria.

(G. C. Schelhammer, German systematic botanist.)

> Small branching herb with thin ovate-lanceolate leaves with undulate margins. Flowers pale-lilac, usually solitary, on slender peduncles. Fruit a rather succulent capsule. *S. undulata* R. Br.
> (pl. 11)

(*undulata*, wavy; referring to the leaf edges.)

BURCHARDIA R. Br.

Erect herbs with fibrous roots. Leaves narrow-linear, chiefly near the base at the stem. Flowers in a terminal umbel with small bracts.

Distribution: The genus is limited to Australia. 2–3 in Australia: 1 in Queensland; 1 in New South Wales; 1 in Victoria: 1 in South Australia; 2 in Western Australia; 1 in Tasmania.

(H. Burchard, systematic botanist.)

> Stem with 1–3 concave, narrow-linear leaves at the base. Flowers white, in a terminal umbel. Fruit a capsule, ovoid, deeply 3-furrowed and 3-angled.
> *Burchardia umbellata* R. Br.
> (pl. 57)

(*umbellata*, umbellate; alluding to the way in which the flowers are arranged.)

BLANDFORDIA Sm.

Erect shrubs with fibrous roots. Leaves long and narrow, chiefly radical with imbricate sheaths. Flowers large, in simple racemes.

Distribution: The genus is confined to eastern Australia. 4 in Australia: 1 in Queensland; 3 in New South Wales; 1 in Tasmania.

(George, Marquis of Blandford, nineteenth-century flower-lover.)

> 1. Flowers 7–18 in racemes.
> Peduncles as long as or slightly longer than bracts. Perianth tube broadening somewhat abruptly.
> *B. cunninghamii* Lindl.

(After A. Cunningham, botanist.)
    1. Flowers 3–10 in raceme. Peduncles longer than bracts.
       2. Perianth broadening abruptly. Flowers small.

B. nobilis Sm.

(*nobilis*, well-known.)
       2. Perianth much dilated from near the base, broadening gradually. Flowers large.

B. grandiflora R. Br.
(pl. 35)

(*grandiflora*, large flowered.)

THYSANOTUS R. Br.

Erect or, rarely, twining herbs with radical, very narrow leaves. Flowers blue or purple, in umbels or a few together; bracts short, scarious.

Distribution: This genus is practically confined to Australia. About 22 in Australia: 3 in Queensland; 4 in New South Wales; 4 in Victoria; 6 in South Australia; 14 in Western Australia; 2 in the Northern Territory; 1 in Tasmania. Genus under revision.

    (*thysanos*, a fringe.)
    Small perennial with a few narrow-linear radical leaves. Flowers purple, in a loose panicle, each branch terminating in an umbel of 1–4 flowers. Petals elegantly fringed. Fruit a globular capsule opening in 3 valves.

T. tuberosus R. Br.
(pl. 41)

(*tuberosus*, with tubers.)

BULBINE L.

Somewhat succulent, erect herbs with narrow-linear, radical leaves. Flowers yellow, in terminal bracteate racemes on leafless stems, pedicels articulate under the flowers. Fruit a slightly succulent capsule.

Distribution: This genus is found in South Africa as well as in Australia. 2 in Australia: 2 in Queensland, New South Wales, Victoria, South Australia and Tasmania; 1 in Western Australia.

    (*Bulbine*, ancient name for a species of bulb-bearing plants.)
    Small erect perennial with leaves all radical, linear-subulate, thick, grooved. Flowers yellow, filaments of stamens bearded above the middle. Ovary superior, 3-celled with several ovules in each cell; style filiform with a terminal stigma. Fruit a capsule, globular,

179

3-celled.   *B. bulbosa* (R. Br.) Haw.
                                                            (pl. 9)
(*bulbosus*, having bulbs.)

STYPANDRA R. Br.

Rather tall erect or ascending herbs with creeping rhizomes.
Flowers in loose terminal cymes, the pedicels slender, often 2 or
3 together. Fruit a capsule.

Distribution: The genus is limited to Australia. 6 in Australia:
1 in Queensland; 3 in New South Wales; 2 in Victoria; 1 in South
Australia; 2 in Western Australia; 1 in Tasmania.

(*stype*, tow; *andros*, a man; in reference to the woolly stamens.)
Erect herb with radical leaves shortly sheathing. Flowers
blue or purple. Fruit an oblong capsule.

                                                  S. caespitosa R. Br.
                                                            (pl. 42)
(*caespes*, turf; in reference to the habit.)

SOWERBAEA Sm.

Tufted herbs with fibrous roots. Leaves linear-filiform, basal,
rigid. Stem bractless, unbranched, rigid. Flowers pink or purple,
rather numerous, in a terminal, simple umbel; bracts scarious.
Fruit a short capsule.

Distribution: The genus is a small one, limited to Australia.
3 in Australia: 2 in Queensland; 1 in New South Wales; 1 in
Victoria; 2 in Western Australia; 1 in the Northern Territory.

(J. Sowerby, naturalist.)
Small plant with linear-filiform terete leaves, with
scarious, transparent, spreading margins. Flowers
purple, many, in umbels. Fruit a 3-celled capsule.

                                                    S. juncea Sm.
                                                            (pl. 51)
(*juncea*, rush-like.)

DIANELLA Lamk.

Glabrous, rather large perennials. Leaves 30–90 cm long with a
sheathing base. Flowers usually blue, often nodding, in a terminal
panicle. Fruit a berry, usually blue and nearly globular.

Distribution: The genus is a small one, chiefly Australian with
a few species in tropical Asia, the Pacific Islands, New Zealand
and South America. About 6 in Australia: about 2 in Queensland; 4 in New South Wales; 4 in Victoria; 2 in South Australia
and Western Australia; 3 in Tasmania. Genus under review.

(Dianella, diminutive of Diana.)

   Variable plant with a few leaves at the base, flat, with
   smooth edges. Flowers blue, in a loose panicle with
   small bracts at the base of the pedicels. Fruit a blue
   globular berry.   *D. laevis* R. Br.
                                                        (pl. 8)
(*levis*, smooth.)

KREYSSIGIA Reichb.

Distribution: There is only a single species and this is limited
to Australia, in Queensland and New South Wales.
(F. L. Kreysig, German botanist.)

   Small smooth plant with an underground stem, ovate
   leaves, stem-clasping with a cordate base, acute. Peduncles bearing 1, 2, or 3 pink flowers, on slender pedicels
   with 3 or 4 linear bracts at the base of the pedicels.
   Capsule nearly globular.   *K. multiflora* Reichb.
                                                        (pl. 12)
(*multus*, many; *flos, floris*, a flower.)

ANGUILLARIA R. Br.

Small erect bulbous herbs. Flowers solitary and terminal or few
in a flexuose spike without bracts.
Distribution: The genus is confined to Australia. 3 in Australia:
1 in Queensland, New South Wales, Victoria, South Australia,
the Northern Territory and Tasmania; 3 in Western Australia.
(L. Anguillaria, sixteenth-century Italian botanist.)

   Small herb with few linear leaves. Flowers white, often
   dioecious, solitary and terminal, or 1–2 or more, sessile
   along a flexuose peduncle. Fruit a 3-celled capsule, and
   3-angled.   *A. dioica* R. Br.
                                                        (pl. 4)
(*di*, away; *oicos*, a house; alluding to the fact that staminate and
   pistillate flowers are on separate plants.)

Family COMMELINACEAE

Herbs, sometimes erect, but more commonly prostrate, with
parallel-veined leaves with sheathing bases. Flowers usually blue,
purple, or rarely white or yellow in inflorescences.

   Flowers usually perfect, slightly irregular. Perianth of 6 segments, free or rarely united at the base, distinctly shown as calyx
and corolla, the sepals thin and membranous, the petals delicate,

coloured and spreading. Stamens 6 or fewer by abortion, hypogynous; anthers when perfect 2-celled. Ovary 3-celled or rarely 2-celled. Style simple with a terminal, entire or 3-lobed stigma. Fruit a capsule or rarely dry and indehiscent.

COMMELINA Plum.

Weak glabrous shrubs with the flowers enclosed in a large oblique spathe opposite the last leaves. Sepals 3, petals 3, coloured, stamens 6 with only 3 fertile. Fruit dry, dehiscent.

Distribution: A genus widely spread over the warmer regions of both hemispheres. 7 in Australia: 4 in Queensland; 3 in New South Wales; 1 in South Australia; 7 in the Northern Territory.

(J. and K. Commelin, eighteenth-century Dutch botanists.)
Spathe acute. Leaves ovate-lanceolate, 4–5 cm long. Petals blue, slightly over 1 cm long.   *C. cyanea* R. Br.
(pl. 8)

(*cyanea*, bluish.)

Family ARACEAE

Herbs with underground stems, leaves radical and entire or divided, often very large.

Flowers are unisexual in a dense spike called a spadix enclosed in a convolute or rarely flat, leaf-like bract, often coloured, called a spathe. Perianth absent or scale-like; stamens 6, hypogynous, anthers usually 2-celled on a thick filament, the cells opening in terminal pores or longitudinal slits. Ovary superior, 1–3 celled, with 1 or more ovules in each cell. Fruit a berry.

GYMNOSTACHYS R. Br.

Erect herb with long narrow radical leaves. Flowers small. Sepals 2, petals 2, scale-like; stamens 4. Fruit an ovoid berry.

Distribution: There is only 1 species found in Australia, in Queensland and New South Wales.

(*gymnos*, naked; *stachys*, spike; in reference to the naked heads.)
Leaves several feet long, very tough. Flowering stem usually taller than leaves, with acute edges. Flowers crowded in inflorescences 5–8 cm long in axils of leafy bracts.   *G. anceps* R. Br.
(pl. 44)

(*anceps*, 2-edged.)

182

Family XYRIDACEAE

Erect, tufted, rush-like herbs with short, simple stems and radical, elongate, narrow-linear, flat or terete, shortly sheathing leaves.

Flowers sessile in rigid dark-brown imbricating bracts of a terminal head or spike, perfect. Sepals 3, deciduous, scarious, embracing the claws of the petals, 2 lateral, 1 dorsal. Petals 3, clawed, erect, spreading, golden-yellow, papery. Stamens 3, hypogynous, anthers sagittate; staminodes 3, alternating with the inner segments, filiform, sometimes wanting. Ovary superior, imperfectly 3-celled, with many ovules. Style trifid, stigmas capitate or dilated. Fruit a capsule.

XYRIS L.

Tufted perennials with radical or basal leaves and with solitary flowers sessile within imbricate, rigid, glume-like scales, forming a terminal head or short spike, the outer bracts of the head usually empty.

Distribution: Widely spread over the warmer regions of both hemispheres. About 12–15 in Australia: 4 in Queensland; 6 in New South Wales; 2 in Victoria; 1 in South Australia; 4 in Western Australia; 2 in the Northern Territory; 2 in Tasmania.

(*Xyris*, old name for Iris.)

> Small perennial with persistent tufts of shining brown leaf-sheaths, some of them produced into very narrow leaves. Flowering stems slender, enclosed at the base in rather a long sheath. Flowers yellow. Fruit an obovoid capsule.
>
> <div align="right">X. <i>operculata</i> Labill.</div>
> (pl. 9)

(*operculata*, capped.)

Family PHILYDRACEAE

Erect herbs with linear or flag-like leaves and sessile solitary flowers within more or less sheathing bracts along the stem of a simple spike or a terminal panicle.

Flowers perfect, irregular. Perianth persistent, of 2 broad petal-like segments. One perfect stamen, usually hypogynous, filament flattened, anthers with 2 parallel cells opening in longitudinal slits; staminodes 2. Ovary superior, 3-celled, style terminal, simple with a terminal stigma.

Fruit a capsule opening loculicidally in 3 valves.

PHILYDRUM Banks

Tall perennial with flag-like leaves and sessile flowers along the stem of a long terminal spike.

Distribution: A single species found only in Australia: in Queensland, New South Wales, Victoria and the Northern Territory.

(*philos*, loving; *hyd-*, water.)

> Perennial covered with white wool, wearing away with age. Leaves 30–45 cm long, sheathing at the base of the stem. Inflorescence a long, terminal, interrupted spike with closely sessile, yellow flowers. Fruit a capsule.
>
> *P. lanuginosum* Gaertn.
>
> (pl. 28)

(*lanuginosus*, wool-bearing.)

GLOSSARY OF BOTANICAL TERMS

Achene, a dry, indehiscent fruit of one carpel and one seed in which the outer covering is not woody.

Acicular, needle-shaped.

Acuminate, tapering suddenly.

Acute, pointed.

Adnate, attached throughout the whole length.

Adventitious, applied to an organ arising in an abnormal position, such as roots rising from the base of the stem and not from the tap root.

Albumen, a food substance, usually starch or oil, in which the embryo of some seeds is embedded.

Alternate, placed alternately; not opposite, used of leaves and flowers or of stamens in relation to petals.

Annual, a plant completing its life in one year.

Annular, ring-shaped.

Anterior, applied to parts of a flower in relation to the axis. Anterior parts are those farthest from the axis.

Anther, the top of the stamen, holding the pollen.

Apiculate, ending in a sharp point.

Apocarpous, a pistil consisting of one carpel. Applied also to an ovary of several one-carpelled ovaries.

Appendage, a subordinate or subsidiary part.

Appressed, closely pressed against another organ, as leaves along a stem.

Aquatic, growing in water.

Aromatic, fragrant.

Aril (arillus), an expansion of the seed stalk of some seeds.

Articulate, jointed.

Ascending, spreading horizontally, and then becoming erect.

Astringent, contracting or binding.

Auricle, an ear-shaped appendage.

Awn, a stiff bristle-like appendage.

Axil, the angle formed by a leaf with the branch.

Axillary, arising from the axis.

Axis, a line passing through the centre of a body, e.g. the stem.

Barb, one of the hairs of a plumose bristle.

Barbellate, furnished with barbs too small for the bristle to be called plumose.

Basifixed, applied to anther attached to the filament by its base.

Berry, a succulent, usually indehiscent fruit of any number of carpels, and the seeds scattered about in a fleshy pulp.

Bi-, two.

Biennial, a plant completing its life in two years.

Bisexual, a flower containing both stamens and pistil.

Bract, a leaf often associated with a flower or inflorescence and differing in form from a foliage leaf.

Bracteate, having bracts.

Bracteole, a small bract immediately below the calyx of a flower.

Brush, dense forest as tropical or near-tropical jungle.

Bulb, a short, thickened, underground stem surrounded by fleshy leaves, outside of which are protective scale leaves.

Bullate, applied to leaves when the thin parts of the blade are covered with small depressions on one side.

Caducous, applied to parts of a flower falling off very early in comparison with other parts.

Callous, thickened.

Callus, a hard protuberance.

Calyx, the outer whorl of a flower, consisting of sepals.

Campanulate, bell-shaped.

Capitate, in the shape of a head.

Capitulum, a head of flowers as in members of Compositae.

Capsule, a dry, dehiscent fruit of two or more united carpels.

Carpel, a modified leaf forming the whole or portion of an ovary, and extended to form the style and stigma. The leaf is folded, or united with others to form an enclosure for the ovules.

Catkin, an inflorescence of sessile, unisexual flowers.

Cell, the cavity of the ovary or the anther. Properly meaning the individual unit of the plant body.

Ciliate, bordered by hairs.

Circumsciss, applied to capsules which split by a transverse, circular line.

Clavate, club-shaped.

Claw, the lower part of a petal or bract.

Coccus, the one-seeded carpels of a syncarpous fruit which split apart from one another when ripe.

Collateral, side by side.

Column, the combination of stamens and pistil into a solid body.

Comose, hairy, applied to seeds or fruits.

Compound, composed of several parts, as a leaf of several leaflets.

Cone, a woody, ovoid or globular collection of fruits consisting of scales surrounding a central axis.

Confluent, united at one part.

Connate, so closely united that separation can only be effected by tearing.

Connective, part of a two-celled anther connecting the cells.

Connivent, organs approaching one another at the summit.

186

Contorted, twisted.

Convolute, rolled or wound together, one part upon another.

Cordate, heart-shaped; often applied to leaves with a cordate base only.

Coriaceous, leathery.

Corolla, the whorl of the flower inside the calyx, consisting of petals.

Corona, an aggregation of appendages seated upon the inner surface of the corolla or perianth.

Corymb, an indefinite inflorescence in which the stalks are increasingly longer towards the outside, thus bringing the individual flowers to the same level. (See also Inflorescence.)

Cotyledons, seed-leaves of the embryo.

Crenate, bordered by blunt or rounded teeth.

Cuneate, wedge-shaped.

Cyme, a definite inflorescence, the central flower opening first, the branches usually opposite and divided again, each branch bearing a flower. (See also Inflorescence.)

Deciduous, falling off, or opposite to persistent—remaining beyond the period of maturity.

Declinate, inclined to one side.

Decumbent, ascending, applied to stems.

Decurrent, extending downwards from the point of insertion; applied to leaves when their blades are continued down the stem, forming raised lines.

Decussate, opposite; leaves crossing each other in pairs at right angles.

Definite, applied to parts of a flower when they are constant in number in the same species. (See also Inflorescence.)

Deflexed, bent downwards.

Dehiscent, opening at maturity; applied to fruits.

Dentate, toothed.

Denticulate, finely toothed.

Depressed, flattened vertically.

Diadelphous, applied to stamens united by their filaments into two clusters.

Dichotomous, divided into two branches.

Didynamous, having four stamens in two pairs, usually one pair shorter.

Diffuse, spreading over the ground; applied to stems.

Digitate, applied to a compound leaf whose leaflets spring from a common centre, like the palm of a hand.

Dioecious, plants with staminate and pistillate flowers on different plants.

Disc, an extension of the receptacle of a single flower; applied also to the inner florets of a composite flower.

Dissemination, scattering, applied to seeds, fruits and pollen.

Distinct, separate, free.

Divaricate, branching off horizontally, or nearly so, and spreading irregularly in various directions.

Dorsal, relating to the back.

Drupe, an indehiscent fruit of one carpel in which the protective covering is

divided into a central, hard stone, a fleshy central part and an outer skin.
Drupel, a small drupe.

Elliptical, like an ellipse in shape.
Emarginate, notched at the summit.
Embryo, the young plant still within the seed consisting of radicle or rudimentary root, plumule or rudimentary stem and cotyledons or leaves.
Endemic, peculiar to a particular region.
Endocarp, the inner portion of the wall of the fruit.
Entire, without any division.
Epigynous, applied to a flower when sepals, petals and stamens are attached above the ovary.
Epiphyte, a plant which grows upon another plant but which does not derive nourishment from it.
Ex-albuminous, without albumen, the fleshy substance round the embryo.
Exserted, projecting beyond the surrounding parts.

Falcate, scythe-shaped.
Family, a group of genera botanically related.
Fertile, producing fruit.
Filament, the stalk of a stamen.
Filiform, thread-like.
Flaccid, flabby.
Flexuose, bending.
Floral, belonging to the flower.
Floret, one of the small flowers in a compact head.
Floriferous, blooming freely.
Flower, the part of the plant which reproduces seed, when perfect containing 4 whorls, pistil, stamens, corolla and calyx.
Foliaceous, leaf-like.
Foliolate, applied to a leaf, according to the number of leaflets, thus uni-foliolate, trifoliolate, etc.
Follicle, a dry dehiscent fruit of one carpel and any number of seeds dehiscing along one side.
Free central, a term applied to a placenta in which the placenta arises as a column from the base of the ovary, and is unconnected with the walls.
Fruit, the matured ovary with fertilized seeds and any other parts of the flower which adhere to it.
Fungus (Fungi), a group of dependent plants, comprising mushrooms, toadstools, rusts, smuts, mildews and the like.

Genus, the smallest natural group of species having certain essential characters in common.
Gibbous, with a short spur or swelling.
Glabrous, devoid of hairs.
Gland, an excrescence usually secreting a fluid.

Glaucous, bluish-green.
Globular, globose, rounded, spherical.
Glume, dry, scaly bracts of grasses and grass-like plants.

Habit, the general external appearance of a plant.
Habitat, the natural home of a plant.
Hastate, spear-shaped.
Herb, a plant which does not develop a woody stem.
Herbaceous, green and more or less succulent, not woody.
Hispid, densely covered with short, stiff hairs.
Hirsute, covered with rather long, spreading hairs.
Hoary, covered with very short hairs giving a whitish or greyish appearance.
Hypogynous, applied to a flower when sepals, petals and stamens are attached
    below the ovary.

Imbricate, overlapping.
Imperfect, applied to flowers in which all whorls are not fully developed.
Incised, deeply cut.
Indigenous, native.
Indehiscent, not splitting when mature.
Induplicate, applied to sepals and petals which are folded inwards in bud but
    are not overlapping.
Indusium, a covering, as over the stigma in Goodeniaceae.
Inferior, applied to an organ below another; the ovary is inferior when the
    flower is epigynous.
Inflexed, bent or turned abruptly inwards or downwards or towards the axis.
Inflorescence, the general arrangement of flowers. An inflorescence is definite
    when there is a terminal flower bud, which thus prevents further elonga-
    tion of the flowering stem; indefinite when there is no terminal bud.
Interrupted inflorescence, applied to a head of flowers in clusters with bare spaces
    between them.
Involucre, a number of bracts surrounding the base of a head or umbel of
    flowers or leaves.
Involute, applied to floral organs whose edges are rolled inwards.
Irregular, applied to a flower in which the parts of any whorl are not all
    similar to each other.

Keel, applied to the two lowest petals of pea flowers.

Labellum, the lowest petal of orchids and of *Stylidium*.
Labiate, lipped.
Laciniate, irregularly cut.
Lanceolate, shaped like the head of a small lance.
Leaflet, a division of a compound leaf.
Legume, a dry dehiscent fruit of one carpel splitting along two sides; the
    characteristic fruit of families Papilionaceae, Mimosaceae, and Caesal-

piniaceae.

Limb, the upper spreading part of a calyx or corolla.

Linear, long and narrow, with parallel edges.

Lobe, a division of a leaf, petal or sepal.

Loculicidally, applied to fruits which split along the back between the placentas.

Membranous, thin, transparent and not stiff.

Mericarp, one of the half fruits of family Umbelliferae.

Mesophyte, a plant adapted to living under normal conditions of moisture.

Monadelphous, applied to stamens united by their filaments into a cluster.

Monoecious, a plant with staminate and pistillate flowers on the one plant.

Mucronate, terminating abruptly in a sharp point.

Muricate, covered with short, hard points.

Naked, devoid of any hairs or other covering.

Nectary, glands at the base of a flower which secrete nectar.

Node, point where buds arise.

Nut, a dry indehiscent fruit of one carpel with a woody covering.

Oblong, much longer than broad.

Obovate, ovate with the broadest part above the middle.

Obovoid, egg-shaped with the broad end towards the apex.

Opposite, applied to branches, leaves, flowers when two proceed from the same level.

Orbicular, perfectly or nearly circular.

Ovary, the lowest part of the pistil containing the ovules and, on fertilization, becoming the fruit.

Ovate, egg-shaped and broader below the middle.

Ovoid, egg-shaped; applied to solid organs such as fruits.

Ovule, the unfertilized seed.

Palmate, used for a compound leaf in which the leaflets diverge from the same point.

Panicle, an inflorescence in which the axis is divided into branches.

Papilla, a small elongated protuberance.

Pappus, the persistent limb of the calyx of some members of family Compositae often used in fruit dispersal.

Parasite, a plant deriving its nourishment from another plant or animal.

Parietal, attached to the sides, applied to the attachment of ovules to placenta.

Pedicel, the stalk of the individual flower of an inflorescence.

Peduncle, the stalk of an individual flower or the main-stalk of an inflorescence.

Pellucid, transparent.

Peltate, arrangement in which the leaf stem or style is attached to the under-surface of the leaf or stigma instead of to its edge.

Pendulous, hanging.

Penicillate, arranged like a tuft of hairs.

Penniveined, feather-veined.

Perennial, a plant which lives for several years.

Perfect, applied to a flower containing both stamens and pistil.

Perfoliate, applied to a sessile leaf whose base entirely surrounds the stem or to two united, sessile, opposite leaves.

Perianth, single term for calyx and corolla: used especially in flowers in which the two whorls are very similar.

Perigynous, applied to sepals, petals and stamens when they are inserted on a cup-like or tubular receptacle round the ovary.

Persistent, lasting: applied to calyx or corolla which surrounds the fruit and to non-deciduous leaves.

Petal, one of the segments of the corolla.

Petaloid, resembling a petal, applied to coloured sepals and to winged stamens.

Petiole, the leaf-stalk.

Phyllodes (*phyllodia*), flattened leaf-stalks resembling and functioning as leaves. Found in the Acacias particularly.

Pinna, a primary division of a compound leaf.

Pinnate, a compound leaf whose pinnae are arranged on opposite sides of a common petiole.

Pinnatifid, a leaf cut into lobes about halfway to the midrib.

Pinnule, the second or third division of a compound leaf.

Pistil, the innermost part of the flower consisting of one or more carpels which contain the ovules.

Pistillate, applied to a flower which contains pistil but no stamens.

Placenta, the part of the ovary to which the seeds are attached.

Plicate, folded together longitudinally.

Plumose, covered with long, branching hairs.

Pod (legume), the dry, single-carpelled fruit of Fabaceae (Leguminosae), Mimosaceae and Caesalpiniaceae.

Pollen, powdery substance in the anthers by means of which the ovules are fertilized.

Pollination, the transference of pollen from stamens to stigma.

Pollinia, pollen masses cohering into a single body as in orchids.

Pome, a false fruit in which the fleshy receptacle surrounds five dry carpels as in the Apple.

Procumbent, trailing along the ground but not actually prostrate.

Prostrate, lying flat on the ground.

Pseudo-bulbs, the swollen bulb-like portions of the stems of many epiphytic orchids.

Pubescent, covered with short, soft hair.

Pulvinate, cushion-shaped.

Pungent, penetrating.

Pyriform, pear-shaped.

Raceme, an indefinite inflorescence with an undivided axis and equally pedicellate flowers. (See also Inflorescence.)

Radical, springing from the root.

Radicle, the embryonic root.

Ray, the outer part of a composite flower-head which has disc florets and outer florets.

Receptacle, the summit of the pedicel or peduncle on which the parts of the single flower are arranged. It is sometimes quite inconspicuous, at other times enlarged to form a disc, cup, or tube. Also applied to the common support for the inflorescence of composite flowers.

Recurved, bent backwards.

Regular, applied to flowers in which the segments of each whorl are all similar, and they are all arranged regularly round the axis.

Reniform, kidney-shaped.

Revolute, applied to the margins of leaves when they are rolled back towards the midrib.

Rhizome, a prostrate or subterranean stem.

Rhomboid (rhomboidal), approximating to the geometrical form of a rhomboid.

Root, the descending axis of the plant, developed from the radicle.

Rosaceous, applied to petals which are similar in shape to those of the rose.

Rostellum, an extension of the upper edge of the stigma in orchids.

Rotate, wheel-shaped: applied to a corolla with a short tube and regular, spreading limb.

Rotundate, rounded.

Rugose, covered with wrinkles.

Saccate, like a pouch.

Sagittate, arrow-shaped.

Saprophyte, an organism living on dead organic matter.

Samara, a one-seeded, winged fruit.

Scabrous, rough to the touch.

Scarious, membranous.

Scattered, applied to leaves irregularly arranged on a stem.

Seed, a ripened ovule containing the embryo.

Segment, each division of a divided leaf or an individual perianth division.

Sensitive, applied to parts of plants such as leaves or columns which show movement under the influence of external stimuli such as touch.

Sepal, an individual calyx segment.

Septate, divided.

Septicidal, applied to a fruit which splits open through the partitions and the carpels fall away separately.

Serrate, toothed like a saw.

Sessile, without a stalk.

Setaceous, bristle-like.

Shrubs, woody plants not attaining the size of trees and having several branches arising from the roots.

Simple, applied to an undivided leaf: opposed to compound.

Sinuate, applied to a leaf whose edge consists of alternate irregular lobes and hollows.

Spadix, an indefinite inflorescence of sessile, crowded flowers on a fleshy axis surrounded by a special bract.

Spathe, large bract enclosing a special inflorescence, the spadix of the arum, the inflorescence of the palm, or two or more united bracts surrounding the inflorescence in the families Iridaceae and Amaryllidaceae.

Spathulate, spoon-shaped.

Species, a division of a genus; each species possessing characters distinguishing it from other species of the same genus.

Spike, an indefinite inflorescence of sessile flowers. (See also Inflorescence.)

Stamen, individual parts, the second whorl of the flower, consisting of a stalk or filament to which is attached the anther, containing the pollen.

Staminate, applied to flowers which have stamens but no pistil.

Staminode, an aborted or sterile stamen.

Standard, the large posterior petal of the pea flowers.

Stellate, star-shaped; used for hairs with radiating branches.

Stem, the ascending axis of a plant.

Sterile, non-productive, applied to anthers without pollen or ovaries without seeds.

Stigma, the top of the pistil which acts as the receiving surface for the pollen.

Stipe, small stalk, usually applied to that of the ovary.

Stipitate, stalked, applied to the ovary.

Stipule, appendage at the base of the petiole.

Stolon, a trailing branch just above or just below the ground, taking root at intervals.

Striate, marked with parallel, longitudinal lines.

Style, the stalk joining the ovary to the stigma of the pistil.

Subulate, narrow and gradually tapering to a fine point.

Succulent, juicy.

Superior, applied to the ovary of a flower in which sepals, petals and stamens are inserted below it. Thus in all hypogynous and some perigynous flowers.

Symmetrical, applied to a flower in which each whorl has the same number of parts or multiples of the number.

Tendril, clasping organ of a climbing plant.

Terete, nearly cylindrical, not angular.

Terminal, at the extremity.

Ternate, arranged in threes as the leaflets of some compound leaves.

Terrestrial, growing in the earth.

Testa, the outer coat of seeds.

Throat, the opening in the upper part of the tube of a flower.

Tomentose, covered with closely matted, short hairs.

Tree, a large woody plant usually with a single stem rising from the ground.

Trifid, cut about halfway into three parts.

Trifoliolate, a leaf of three leaflets.

Truncate, terminating abruptly.
Tuber, a swollen underground stem.
Tuberculate, with warty protuberances.
Tufted, applied to stems or leaves when many grow close together.
Turgid, swollen.

Umbel, an indefinite inflorescence in which the divergent rays or branches all start from the one point. (See also Inflorescence.)
Uncinate, hooked.
Undershrub, a small shrub in which the flowering branches die off in winter.
Undulate, wavy on the edges.
Unisexual, a flower containing stamens or pistil only.
Urceolate, urn-shaped.

Valvate, sepals or petals whose edges meet but do not overlap in bud.
Valves, distinct portions of certain parts such as fruits or anthers which become detached on splitting.
Variety, sub-division of a species.
Vascular bundle, conducting elements of a plant.
Versatile, applied to an anther attached so slightly to the middle of the filament as to swing freely.
Verticillate, in whorls or rings.
Villous, covered with long, weak hairs.
Virgate, twiggy.
Viscid, sticky.
Vitta, linear oil-vessel in the fruits of some of family Umbelliferae.

Whorl, a set of organs proceeding from the same node and arranged in a circle round the axis.
Wing, the membranous margin of a seed or fruit or other organ, applied also to the two lateral petals of pea flowers of family Fabaceae (**Leguminosae**).

Xerophyte, a plant adapted to live under conditions of limited water-supply.

BOOKS OF REFERENCE

ANDERSON, R. H., *Trees of New South Wales*, Sydney, 1956.

AUDAS, J. W. C., *The Australian Bushland*, Melbourne, 1947.

BATLEY, F. MANSON, *The Queensland Flora*, Brisbane, 1905.

BEADLE, N. C. W., EVANS, O. D., CAROLIN, R. C., *Handbook of the Vascular Plants of the Sydney District and Blue Mountains*, Sydney, 1976.

BENTHAM, GEORGE, *Flora Australiensis*, London, 1863.

BLACK, J. M., *Flora of South Australia* (2nd Edition), Pts. I–III, Adelaide, 1948–65.

BLACKALL, W. E. (Edited by B. J. Grieve), *Western Australian Wild Flowers*, Pts. I, II, III and IV, Perth 1954–75.

COCHRANE, G. R., FURHER, B. A., ROTHERHAM, E. B. WILLIS, J. H., *Flowers and Plants of Victoria*, A. H. & A. W. Reed, Sydney 1968.

CURTIS, W. M., *The Student's Flora of Tasmania*, Pts. I, II and III, Hobart, 1956–75.

CURTIS, W. M. and STONES, MARGARET, *The Endemic Flora of Tasmania*, Pts. I, II, III, IV and V, London 1967–75.

ERICSON, RICE, GEORGE, A. S., MARCHANT, N. G., MORCOMBE, M. K., *Flowers and Plants of Western Australia*, A. H. & A. W. Reed, Sydney, 1973.

EWART, A. J., *Flora of Victoria*, Melbourne, 1930.

FRANCIS, W. D., *Australian Rain-forest Trees* (3rd Edition), Canberra, 1970.

FITZGERALD, R. D., *Australian Orchids*, Sydney, 1892.

GARDNER, C. A., *Flora of Western Australia*, Pts. I, II and III, Perth, 1952.

LORD, E. E., *Shrubs and Trees for Australian Gardens*, Melbourne, 1976.

McARTHUR, KATHEEN, *Queensland Wildflowers*, Brisbane, 1958.

MAIDEN, J. H., *Illustrations of New South Wales Plants*, Sydney, 1907–11.

MOORE, C. and BETCHE, E., *Handbook of the Flora of New South Wales*, Sydney, 1893.

NICHOLLS, W. H., *Orchids of Australia*, Complete Edition, Melbourne, 1969.

ROTHERHAM, E. R., BRIGGS, BARBARA G., BLAXELL, D. F., CAROLIN, R. C., *Flowers and Plants of New South Wales and Southern Queensland*, A. H. & A. W. Reed, 1975.

RUPP, H. M. R., *Guide to Orchids of New South Wales*, Sydney, 1943, 1969.

SULMAN, FLORENCE, *A Popular Guide to Wild Flowers of New South Wales*, Vols. I and II, Sydney 1914, 1926.

WILLIS, J. H., *A Handbook to Plants in Victoria*, Vols 1 and II, Melbourne, 1962, 1972.

NAMES OF AUTHORS
AND THEIR ABBREVIATIONS

ADANSON, M. (Adans.).
AITON, W. (Ait.).
AMES, O. (Ames).
ANDREWS, H. C. (Andr.).
ASCHERSON, P. (Aschers.).

BACKHOUSE, J. (Backh.).
BAEKER, C. H. (Baeker).
BANKS, SIR JOSEPH (Banks).
BARTLING, F. G. (Bartl.).
BAUER, F. (F. Bauer).
BENTHAM, G. (Benth.).
BETCHE, E. (Betche).
BLACK, J. M. (Black).
BLAXELL, D. F. (Blaxell).
BLUME, K. L. (Blume).
BREMEKAMP, C. E. B. (Bremek.).
BRIGGS, BARBARA (B. Briggs).
BROWN, ROBERT (R. Br.).
BURMANN, J. (Burm.).

CANDOLLE, A. P. DE (DC.).
CASSINI, A. H. G. (Cass.).
CAVANILLES, A. J. (Cav.).
CHEEL, E. (Cheel).
COURT, A. (Court).
CUNNINGHAM, A. (A. Cunn.).
CURTIS, W. (Curt.).

DANSER, B. H. (Dans.).
DESFONTAINES, R. L. (Desf.).
DESROUSSEAUX, M. (Desr.).
DOMIN, K. (Domin).
DON, D. (D. Don).
DON, G. (G. Don).
DONN, J. (Donn).
DRUCE, G. C. (Druce).
DUNAL, M. F. (Dunal).

EHRENDORFER, F. (Ehrend.).
ENDLICHER, S. L. (Endl.).

FITZGERALD, R. D. (R. D. Fitzg.).
FORD, N. (Ford).
FORSKAL, P. (Forsk.).
FORSTER, G. (Forst. f.).
FORSTER, J. R. (Forst.).

GAERTNER, J. (Gaertn.).
GAY, J. (Gay).
GILG, E. (Gilg).
GIORDANO, F. (Giord.).

HASSKARL, J. K. (Hassk.).
HAWORTH, A. H. (Haw.).
HENCKEL, VON DONNERSMARCK L.
  (Henck.).
HERBERT, W. (Herb.).
HOCHREUTINER, C. F. (Hochr.).
HOOKER, SIR J. D. (Hook. f.).
HOOKER, SIR W. J. (Hook.).

JACQUIN, N. J. BARON VON (Jacq.).
JOHNSON, L. A. S. (L. Johnson).
JUSSIEU, A. L. DE (Juss.).

KENNEDY, EDMUND B. (Kennedy).
KNIGHT, (Knight).
KUNTZE, O. (O. Kuntze).

LABILLARDIÈRE, J. J. H. DE (Labill.).
LAMARCK, J. B. DE (Lamk.).
LANDER, N. S. (N. S. Lander).
LEHMANN, J. G. C. (Lehm.).
LESSING, C. F. (Less.).
L'HÉRITER, C. L. (L'Hér.).
LINDAU, G. (Lindau).
LINDLEY, J. (Lindl.).
LINK, H. F. (Link.)
LINNÉ, C. VON (C. Linnaeus), (L.).
LINNÉ, C. VON (Linnaeus) the
  younger (L. f.).
LOUDON, J. C. (Loud.).

LOUREIRO, J. (Lour.).

M'LEAY, W. S. (M'Leay).
MAIDEN, J. H. (Maiden).
McGILLIVRAY, D. J.
  (D. J. McGillivray).
MARTIUS, K. F. P. VON (Mart.).
MEISSNER, K. F. (Meissn.).
MERRILL, E. D. (Merrill).
MILL, O. (Mill).
MOENCH, K. (Moench).
MOORE, C. (Moore).
MUELLER, F. BARON VON (F. Muell.).

NECKER, M. J. VON (Neck.).
NEES, VON ESENBECK, C. G. (Nees).

OLIVER, W. R. B. (Oliver).
OTTO, F. (Otto).

PERRY, L. M. (Perry).
PERSOON, C. H. (Pers.).
PIERRE, JEAN-BAPTISTE (Pierre).
PLUMIER, C. (Plum.).
PLUNKENET, L. (Plunk.).
POIRET, J. L. M. (Poir.).

RADLKOFER, L. (Radlkf.).
REICHENBACH, H. G. L. (Reichb.).
RENEAULME, P. DE (Ren.).
RICHARD, A. (A. Rich.).
RICHARD, L. C. (Rich.).
ROEMER, J. J. (Roem.).
ROGERS, R. S. (Rogers).
RUDGE, E. (Rudge).

SALISBURY, R. A. (Salisb.).
SCHAUER, J. C. (Schau.).
SCHLECHTENDAL, D. F. L. VON
  (Schlecht.).
SCHLECHTER, R. (Schltr.).
SCHOTT, H. W. (Schott).
SCHRADER, H. A. (Schrad.).
SCHULTES, J. A. (Schult.).
SCHULTES, J. H. (Schult. f.).
SCHWEINFURTH (Schweinf.).
SIEBER, F. W. (Sieber).
SIMS, J. (Sims).
SKEELS, H. C. (Skeels).
SMITH, SIR J. E. (Sm.).
SOLANDER, D. C. (Soland.).
SPRENGEL, K. P. J. (Spreng.).
STAPF, O. (Stapf).
STEENIS, C. G. G. J. VAN (Steenis).
SWARTZ, O. (Sw.).
SWEET, R. (Sweet).

THUNBERG, C. P. (Thunb.).
TIEGHEM, P. VAN (Tiegh.).
TOURNEFORT, J. P. DE (Tournef.).

VAILLANT, S. (Vaill.).
VENTENAT, E. P. (Vent.).
VICKERY, J. (Vickery).

WENDLAND, H. L. (Wendl.).
WILLDENOW, C. L. (Willd.).
WILLIS, J. H. (J. H. Willis).
WIMMER, C. F. H. (Wimm.).

INDEX

(**Numbers in bold type indicate a page and plate reference.**)

204